Index to Afro-American
Reference Resources

Recent Titles in
Bibliographies and Indexes in Afro-American and African Studies

A Bibliographical Guide to Black Studies Programs in the United States:
An Annotated Bibliography
Lenwood G. Davis and George Hill, compilers

Wole Soyinka: A Bibliography of Primary and Secondary Sources
James Gibbs, Ketu H. Katrak, and Henry Louis Gates, Jr., compilers

Afro-American Demography and Urban Issues: A Bibliography ·
R. A. Obudho and Jeannine B. Scott, compilers

Afro-American Reference: An Annotated Bibliography of Selected Resources
Nathaniel Davis, compiler and editor

The Afro-American Short Story: A Comprehensive, Annotated Index with
Selected Commentaries
Preston M. Yancy, compiler

Black Labor in America, 1865-1983: A Selected Annotated Bibliography
Joseph Wilson, compiler and editor

Martin Luther King, Jr.: An Annotated Bibliography
Sherman E. Pyatt, compiler

Blacks in the Humanities, 1750-1984: A Selected Annotated Bibliography
Donald Franklin Joyce, compiler

The Black Family in the United States: A Revised, Updated, Selectively
Annotated Bibliography
Lenwood G. Davis, compiler

Black American Families, 1965-1984: A Classified, Selectively Annotated
Bibliography . .
Walter R. Allen, editor

Index to Poetry by Black American Women
Dorothy Hilton Chapman, compiler

Black American Health: An Annotated Bibliography
Mitchell F. Rice and Woodrow Jones, Jr., compilers

Ann Allen Shockley: An Annotated Primary and Secondary Bibliography
Rita B. Dandridge, compiler

Index to Afro-American Reference Resources

Compiled by
Rosemary M. Stevenson

Bibliographies and Indexes in Afro-American and African Studies, Number 20

Greenwood Press
New York • Westport, Connecticut • London

Library of Congress Cataloging-in-Publication Data

Stevenson, Rosemary M.
  Index to Afro-American reference resources.

  (Bibliographies and indexes in Afro-American and
African studies, ISSN 0742-6925 ; no. 20)
  Bibliography: p.
  Includes index.
  1. Afro-Americans—Indexes. 2. Reference books—
Afro-Americans—Indexes. 3. Blacks—Indexes.
4. Reference books—Blacks—Indexes. I. Title.
II. Series.
Z1361.N39S77 1988 [E185]   973'.0496073   87-28028
ISBN 0-313-24580-0 (lib. bdg. : alk. paper)

British Library Cataloguing in Publication Data is available.

Library of Congress Catalog Card Number: 87-28028
ISBN: 0-313-24580-0
ISSN: 0742-6925

First published in 1988

Greenwood Press, Inc.
88 Post Road West, Westport, Connecticut 06881

Printed in the United States of America

The paper used in this book complies with the
Permanent Paper Standard issued by the National
Information Standards Organization (Z39.48-1984).

10 9 8 7 6 5 4 3 2 1

Contents

Acknowledgments

I would like to express my gratitude to several groups and individuals in the University of Illinois at Urbana-Champaign Library for their support of this project. They include the staffs of the Afro-Americana and Africana Units, the Research and Publication Committee, and typists Jytte Millan, Sonya Davidson and Kay Bainter. Special thanks go to Linda Wicklund, who prepared the final manuscript. In addition, the encouragement of Michael Gorman and Danuta Gorecki helped considerably.

I thank God for giving me the strength and perseverance to complete this project.

Introduction

Information on Black people is available in a vast quantity of books, periodicals and documents. This index illustrates the great wealth of resources on the many aspects of the Afro-American experience in dictionaries, encyclopedias, catalogs, indexes, abstracts, bibliographies, social commentaries and history texts. Consequently, works indexed in this book represent titles generally considered to be reference tools, in addition to selected resources that fall outside the traditional reference area. Bibliographies, biographical dictionaries and almanacs are core resources of a reference library. Nevertheless, since several history texts, sociological works and general anthologies contain valuable information on Afro-Americans, this index cites such works as Before the Mayflower, The Negro Impact on Western Civilization and Philosophy Born of Struggle.

Index to Afro-American Reference Resources is an analysis by subject of books that contain information on the Black experience throughout America. Although the emphasis is on the United States, citations on Canada, the Caribbean and South America comprise a significant portion of this book. Sources on the Black experience in Africa, Asia and Europe have been incorporated selectively, particularly if they are relevant to such issues as African cultural survivals in the Americas. For example, African art, music and religion are significant for an understanding of their Afro-American counterparts.

This index identifies complete works as well as parts of works which include helpful information on the Black experience. Most of the citations are to books, chapter titles or essay titles. In a few instances references are made to a source's index, as in the case of In Black and White. This analytical approach makes available materials that are not always identified by a work's general title and highlights a wealth of information that has been offered by writers on various aspects of the experiences of Black people in the Americas and in other places where the African impact has been significant.

A considerable amount of writing on the Afro-American experience has been produced since the arrival of Blacks in this hemisphere several centuries ago. Unfortunately, much of this material has not been as accessible as it should be, due to historical difficulties in getting

Black related resources published, exclusionary book reviewing practices, and insufficient bibliographic control of Afro-American publications. Since the 1960's, this has been gradually changing, and one area showing dramatic improvement is bibliographic access. During these past two decades, bibliographies, directories, and other reference works on the Afro-American experience have proliferated.

Several decades before this period of heightened Black awareness and increased publishing interest in Afro-American themes, pioneering scholars such as Monroe Work labored meticulously to bring order out of bibliographic chaos. Work's groundbreaking compilation, A Bibliography of the Negro in Africa and America, published in 1928, contains comprehensive listings on Africa, the United States, the Caribbean and Latin America. In 1950, the Index to Selected Periodicals was initiated by the staff of the Hallie Q. Brown Library of Central State University to provide a subject and author guide to articles in Black journals. This continued an earlier effort by A. P. Marshall, who compiled a Guide to Negro Periodical Literature in the early 1940's. The Index to Selected Periodicals eventually became an annual cumulation compiled in conjunction with the staff of the Schomburg Collection of the New York Public Library. Currently entitled Index to Periodical Articles by and About Blacks, it now cites articles in almost forty journals.

The Black power movement of the 1960's brought about a proliferation of Black published materials. This explosion of books, journals and other printed items included many works of fiction, poetry, history, music, politics, biography and social commentary. Reference works on Afro-American topics were comparatively fewer in number. Nevertheless, this relatively small quantity of handbooks, encyclopedias, guides, bibliographies and directories were much-needed contributions to the emerging field of Black Studies.

One of the primary works to initiate this pioneering decade of Black reference books was The Negro Almanac, first published in 1967. This comprehensive volume includes information on such topics as history, economics, civil rights, sports, the media, and religion. In 1970 Dorothy Porter, then curator of Howard University's Moorland-Spingarn Collection, compiled The Negro in the United States: A Bibliography, a listing by subject of books on the Afro-American experience. Another useful tool is Blacks in America: Bibliographical Essays, published in 1971. These essays combine historical background with bibliographical citations on a variety of historical, literary, social and cultural topics. During the same year, Mary Mace Spradling produced her first edition of In Black and White, a guide to biographical information on a large number of Afro-Americans. Fisk librarians Ann Shockley and Sue Chandler collaborated on the 1974 publication, Living Black American Authors: A Biographical Directory, which provides data on writers in a variety of fields. Guy Westmoreland's Annotated Guide to Basic Reference Books on the Black American Experience, produced in 1974, filled a need for information on the gradually but steadily increasing group of Afro-American reference materials.

In addition, 1974 was the publication date of Afro-American History: A Bibliography, which cites and abstracts almost three thousand articles on Black people in North America. During the following year Geraldine Matthews and the Afro-American Materials Project Staff compiled Black American Writers, 1773-1949: A Bibliography and Union List, which lists by subject books by Black authors and indicates which of the participating Southeastern U.S. libraries carries each title. Also taking place in 1975 was the publication of Black American Writers Past and Present: A Biographical and Bibliographical Dictionary. This comprehensive two-volume work provides personal and bibliographical data on novelists, poets, playwrights and literary critics. Another valuable tool is the 1976 publication, The Black American Reference Book, which provides comprehensive essays on such subjects as history, the economy, the family, religion, politics, foreign relations, literature, theatre, art, and the media. As this ground-breaking decade came to a close, these were among the titles that set a firm foundation for an upcoming surge in Black reference books.

During the last decade an unprecedented quantity of reference books on the Afro-American experience have been produced. In addition to general comprehensive tools, works on specific topics such as literature, slavery, art, music and women have been published. In 1978 John Zwed and Roger Abrahams compiled Afro-American Folk Culture: An Annotated Bibliography of Materials from North, Central and South America and the West Indies. This two-volume work contains thousands of citations on Black folklore and customs. Mary Mace Spradling revised In Black and White in 1980, and this third edition has information on more than 6,700 Black individuals and groups. A supplement was published in 1985. Another much-needed work published in 1980 was The Progress of Afro-American Women: A Selected Bibliography and Resource Guide by Janet Sims. Arranged by subject into more than thirty chapters, this bibliography cites books, articles and disertations on issues concerning Black women. Lynn Moody Igoe in 1981 compiled 250 Years of Afro-American Art: An Annotated Bibliography. This thorough research guide cites books, articles and catalogs on hundreds of artists as well as on illustration, ironwork, quiltmaking and other facets of art. Published during the same year was the Encyclopedia of Black America, edited by W. Augustus Low and Virgil Clift. This compilation contains biographies and articles on subjects concerning Afro-Americans, including, for example, "Benjamin Quarles," "Arthur Schomburg," "Xavier University," "Scientists" and "Social Classes." At the same time, Volume Two of Afro-American History: A Bibliography provided new citations and a more detailed index. The Education of Poor and Minority Children by Meyer Weinberg is an extensive bibliography including citations on Black education in all parts of the World. Bibliographic access to books, articles and theses on music increased dramatically in Bibliography of Black Music, a four volume set by renown musicologist, Dominique-Rene De Lerma. The first volume, Reference Works, published in 1981, cites encyclopedias, discographies, periodicals and other resources. The second volume, Afro-American Idioms provides bibliographic information on ragtime, concert music, blues, gospel, jazz and other types of music. Volume three, Geographical Studies, provides access to resources on Black music of countries in Africa, the Caribbean, South America, Canada and the United States. Volume four, published in 1984, is Theory, Education and Related Studies.

Another significant work on Black music is Eileen Southern's Biographical Dictionary of Afro-American and African Musicians, published in 1982. An additional publication of that year was The Harlem Renaissance: An Annotated Bibliography and Commentary by Margaret Perry. This resource includes bibliographies on individual authors of the

Harlem Renaissance. A Paul Robeson Research Guide: A Selected Annotated Bibliography is the magnum opus of Lenwood G. Davis, the prolific compiler of bibliographies on art, athletes, women, Black Studies, the elderly and other subjects. Black Slavery in the Americas: An Interdisciplinary Bibliography, 1865-1980 by John David Smith, provides geographical and subject access to literature on slavery. The Dictionary of American Negro Biography, edited by Rayford Logan and Michael Winston, is a compilation of scholarly essays on historical Afro-Americans.

Among the 1983 publications were The Afro-American Cinematic Experience: An Annotated Bibliography and Filmography by Marshall Hyatt and the extremely useful fourth edition of The Negro Almanac, edited by Harry Ploski and James Williams. Bruce Keller authored The Harlem Renaissance: A Historical Dictionary for the Era in 1984. This year was also the date of publication of the Dictionary of Literary Biography's first volume of the Afro-American series, edited by Trudier Harris and Thadious Davis. Each volume is composed of biographical articles which contain critical information and bibliographical citations on each author. The articles are scholarly essays contributed by knowledgeable writers. The Afro-American titles in this series include: Afro-American Fiction Writers After 1955 (V. 33), 1984; Afro-American Writers After 1955 (V. 38), 1955; Afro-American Poets Since 1955 (V. 41), 1985; and Afro-American Writers Before the Harlem Renaissance (V. 50), 1986.

Selected Black American, African and Caribbean Authors: A Bio-Bibliography by James Page was published in 1985. This updated his Selected Black American Authors: An Illustrated Bio-Bibliography. Nathaniel Davis' Afro-American Reference: An Annotated Bibliography of Selected Resources, is a useful guide to information on many topics, including history, economics, music, Los Angeles and California, Latin America, miscegenation and biography. Donald F. Joyce's 1986 publication, Blacks in the Humanities, 1750-1984: A Selected Annotated Bibliography, contains descriptive citations on the Black experience in philosophy, music, art, literature, journalism, library science and other areas of culture. The 1986 edition of Black Resource Guide, published by R. Benjamin Johnson and Jacqueline L. Johnson, is a directory of organizations, periodicals, television stations, museums, government officials, educational facilities and other resources.

These titles, mainly focusing on Blacks in the United States, are just a few of the many reference books which provide a new depth of information and access. Reference material on the Afro-American experience outside the United States has been a more gradual phenomenon. In addition to information included in works primarily concerning the United States, several bibliographies, biographical dictionaries and guides published during the last decade have contributed to the scholarship on Black people in the Caribbean and Central and South America. These include: The Complete Caribbeana, 1900-1975: A Bibliographic Guide to the Scholarly Literature (1977) by Lambros Comitas, Afro-Braziliana: A Working Bibliography (1978), by Dorothy Porter, Historical Dictionary of the French and Netherlands Antilles (1978), by Albert Gastmann, The Afro-Spanish Author: An Annotated Bibliography of Criticism (1980), by Richard Jackson, Belize (1980) by Ralph Woodward, Race and Ethnic Relations in Latin America and the Caribbean (1980), Robert Levine, The Complete Haitiana: A Bibliographical Guide to the Scholarly Literature (1982), Michel

Laguerre, and <u>Fifty Caribbean Writers: A Bio-Bibliographical Critical Sourcebook</u> (1986), edited by Daryl Dance.

Several non-reference titles were included in this index because they provide background, expanded explanation, analysis or, in some cases, information which is difficult to find, such as in the chapter "Pirates and Privateers" in <u>Black Men of the Sea</u>, by Michael Cohn and Michael Platzer. These texts, anthologies and social commentaries cover such diverse topics as history, literary criticism, politics, religion, women, men, art, music, education, philosophy, the experience of slavery, and the Black Power revolution. A few of the titles cited in this category include: <u>Sex and Race</u> (J. A. Rogers), <u>The Negro Impact on Western Civilization</u> (Joseph Slaby), <u>The Slave Community</u> (John Blassingame), <u>The Other Slaves</u> (James Newton and Ronald Lewis <u>From Columbus to Castro</u> (Eric Williams), <u>Philosophy Born of Struggle</u> (Leonard Harris), and <u>We Are Your Sisters</u> (Dorothy Sterling).

In addition to the works cited in this index, many new works useful for Afro-American reference are being published and several older titles are being updated. A convincing argument could be made that reference is currently the most rapidly expanding area of Afro-American scholarship.

Cited Works

The African Background Outlined; or Handbook for the Study of the Negro, Carter G. Woodson. New York: Negro Universities Press, 1971, C 1936. 478 p.

The Afro-American Cinematic Experience: An Annotated Bibliography and Filmography, compiled and edited by Marshall Hyatt. Wilmington, Delaware: Scholarly Resources, 1983. 260 p.

Afro-American Education, 1907-1932: A Bibliographic Index. New York: Lambeth Press, 1984. 178 p.

Afro-American Fiction Writers After 1955, edited by Thadious M. Davis and Trudier Harris. Detroit: Gale Research, 1984. (Dictionary of Literary Biography, Volume 33). 350 p.

Afro-American Folk Culture: An Annotated Bibliography of Materials from North, Central and South America and the West Indies, John F. Szwed and Roger Abrahams. Philadelphia: Institute for the Study of Human Issues, 1978. 2 V.

Afro-American History; A Bibliography, edited by Dwight L. Smith. Santa Barbara, California: ABC-Clio, 1974. 856 p.

Afro-American History II; A Bibliography, edited by Dwight L. Smith. Santa Barbara, California: ABC-Clio, 1981. 394 p.

Afro-American History; Sources for Research, edited by Robert L. Clarke. Washington: Howard University Press, 1981. 236 p.

The Afro-American Novel, 1965-1975: A Descriptive Bibliography of Primary and Secondary Material, Helen Ruth Houston. Troy, New York: Whitson, 1977. 214 p.

Afro-American Poetry and Drama, 1760-1975: A Guide to Information Sources. "Afro-American Poetry, 1760-1975", William P. French, Michel J. Fabre, Amritjit Singh. "Afro-American Drama, 1850-1975," Genevieve E. Fabre. Detroit: Gale Research, 1979. 493 p.

Afro-American Poets Since 1955, edited by Trudier Harris and Thadious M. Davis. Detroit: Gale Research, 1985. (Dictionary of Literary

Biography, volume 41). 401 p.

Afro-American Reference: An Annotated Bibliography of Selected
    Resources, Nathaniel Davis. Westport, Connecticut: Greenwood Press,
    1985. 288 p.

Afro-American Writers After 1955: Dramatists and Prose Writers, Thadious
    M. Davis and Trudier Harris. Detroit: Gale Research, 1985.
    (Dictionary of Literary Biography, volume 38). 390 p.

Afro-American Writers Before the Harlem Renaissance, edited by Trudier
    Harris and Thadious Davis. Detroit: Gale, 1986. (Dictionary of
    Literary Biography, volume 50). 369 p.

Afro-Braziliana: A Working Bibliography, Dorothy B. Porter. Boston: G.
    K. Hall, 1978. 294 p.

The Afro-Spanish Author: An Annotated Bibliography of Criticism, Richard
    L. Jackson. New York: Garland, 1980. 129 p.

American Negro Slave Revolts. Herbert Aptheker. New York: International
    Publishers, 1983. 411 p.

The American South: A Historical Bibliography, edited by Jessica S.
    Brown. Santa Barbara, California: ABC Clio, 1986.

An Annotated Guide to Basic Reference Books on the Black American
    Experience, Guy T. Westmoreland. Wilmington, Delaware: Scholarly
    Resources, 1974. 98 p.

Anthology: Quotations and Sayings of People of Color, Walter B. Hoard.
    San Francisco: R. & E. Research Associates, 1973. 137 p.

Beautiful Also Are the Souls of My Black Sisters: A History of the Black
    Woman in America, Jeanne Noble. Englewood Cliffs, New Jersey:
    Prentice-Hall, 1978. 353 p.

Before the Mayflower: A History of Black America, Lerone Bennett. 5th
    edition. New York: Penguin Books. 1982. 681 p.

Belize, Ralph Lee Woodward. Santa Barbara, California: Clio Press, 1980.
    229 p.

Beyond Identity: Education and the Future Role of Black Americans: A
    Book of Readings, edited by Samuel A. Robinson and Roy A Weaver.
    Ann Arbor, Michigan: University Microfilms, 1978. 156 p.

Bibliographical Guide to Black Studies Programs in the United States: An
    Annotated Bibliography, Lenwood G. Davis and George Hill. Westport,
    Connecticut: Greenwood Press, 1985. 130 p.

A Bibliography of Black Music, Dominique-Rene de Lerma. Westport,
    Connecticut: Greenwood Press, 1981-1984.
    V. 1: Reference Materials. 1981. 124 p.
    V. 2: Afro-American Idioms. 1981. 220 p.
    V. 3: Geographical Studies. 1982. 284 p.
    V. 4: Theory, Education and Related Studies. 1984. 254 p.

A Bibliography of Pidgin and Creole Languages, John E. Reinecke.
Honolulu: University Press of Hawaii, 1975.

Bibliography of the Negro in Africa and America, Monroe N. Work. New
York: Octagon Books, 1970, c 1928. 698 p.

Biographical Sketches of Our Pulpit, Edward Randolph Carter. Chicago:
Afro-Am Press, 1969. c 1888. 216 p.

Black Access: A Bibliography of Afro-American Bibliographies, Richard
Newman. Westport, Connecticut: Greenwood Press, 1984. 249 p.

The Black Aged in the United States: An Annotated Bibliography, Lenwood
G. Davis. Westport, Connecticut: Greenwood Press, 1980. 200 p.

Black American Fiction: A Bibliography, Carol Fairbanks. Metuchen, New
Jersey: Scarecrow Press, 1978. 351 p.

Black American Playwrights, 1800 to the Present: A Bibliography, Esther
Spring Arata. Metuchen, New Jersey: Scarecrow Press, 1976. 295 p.

The Black American Reference Book, edited by Mabel M. Smythe. Englewood
Cliffs, New Jersey: Prentice-Hall, 1976. 1026 p.

Black Americans in Autobiography: An Annotated Bibliography of
Autobiographies and Autobiographical Books Written Since the Civil
War, Russell C. Brignano. Revised and expanded edition. Durham,
North Carolina: Duke University Press, 1984. 193 p.

Black Apostles at Home and Abroad: Afro-Ameicans and the Christian
Mission from the Revolution to Reconstruction, edited by David W.
Willis and Richard Newman. Boston: G. K. Hall, 1982. 321 p.

Black Artists in the United States in the United States: An Annotated
Bibliography of Books, Articles, and Dissertations on Black
Artists, 179-1979. Lenwood G. Davis and Janet Sims. Westport,
Connecticut: Greenwood Press, 1980. 138 p.

Black Athletes in the United States: A Bibliography of Books, Articles,
and Biographies on Black Professional Athletes in the United
States, 1800-1981, Lenwood G. Davis and Belinda S. Daniels.
Westport, Connecticut: Greenwood Press, 1981. 265 p.

Black Authors and Education: An Annotated Bibliography of Books, James
Edward Newby. Washington: University Press of America, 1980. 103 p.

Black Child Development in America, 1927-1977: An Annotated
Bibliography, Hector F. Myers, Phyllis G. Rana and Marcia Harris.
Westport, Connecticut: Greenwood Press, 1979. 470 p.

Black Children and Their Families: A Bibliography, Charlotte J. Dunmore.
San Francisco: R and E Research Associates, 1976. 103 p.

Black Chronology from 4000 B.C. to the Abolition of the Slave Trade,
Ellen Irene Diggs. Boston: G. K. Hall, 1983. 312 p.

Black Demography in the United States: An Annotated Bibliography With a

Review Essay, Jamshid Momeni. Westport, Connecticut: Greenwood
     Press, 1983. 354 p.

The Black Family in the United States: A Revised, Updated, Selectively
     Annotated Bibliography, Lenwood Davis. Westport, Connecticut:
     Greenwood Press, 1986. 234 p.

Black Genesis, James Rose and Alice Eichholz, Detroit: Gale Research,
     1978. 326 p.

Black Higher Education in the United States: A Selected Bibliography on
     Negro Higher Education and Historically Black Colleges and
     Universities, Frederick Chambers. Westport, Connecticut: Greenwood
     Press, 1978. 268 p.

Black History: A Guide to Civilian Records in the National Archives,
     Debra L. Newman. Washington: National Archives Trust Fund Board
     General Services Administration, 1984. 379 p.

Black-Jewish Relations in the United States, 1752-1984: A Selected
     Bibliography, Lenwood G. Davis. Westport, Connecticut: Greenwood
     Press, 1984. 130 p.

Black Journals of the United States, Walter C. Daniel. Westport,
     Connecticut: Greenwood Press, 1982. 432 p.

The Black Librarian in the Southeast: Reminiscences, Activities,
     Challenges, edited by Annette L. Phinazee. Durham: Alumni
     Association Office, North Carolina Central University, 1980. 281 p.

Black Masculinity: the Black Male's Role in American Society, Robert
     Staples. San Francisco: Black Scholar Press, 1982. 181 p.

Black Media in America: A Resource Guide, George H. Hill. Boston: G. K.
     Hall, 1984. 333 p.

Black Men, edited by Lawrence Gary. Beverly Hills: Sage, 1981. 295 p.

Black Men of the Sea, Michael Cohn and Michael Platzer. New York: Dodd,
     Mead, 1978. 158 p.

Black Music, Dean Tudor and Nancy Tudor. Littleton, Colorado: Libraries
     Unlimited, 1979. 262 p.

Black Music in America: A Bibliography, JoAnn Skowronski. Metuchen, New
     Jersey: Scarecrow Press, 1981. 723 p.

Black Photographers, 1840-1940: A Bio-Bibliography, Deborah Willis-
     Thomas. New York: Garland, 1985. 141 p.

Black Playwrights, 1823-1977: An Annotated Bibliography of Plays, James
     V. Hatch and Omanii Abdullah. New York: Bowker, 1977.

Black Resource Guide, Washington: R. Benjamin Johnson and Jacqueline L.
     Johnson, 1986. 245 p.

Black Rhetoric: A Guide to Afro-American Communciation, Robert W. Glenn.

Metuchen, New Jersey: Scarecrow Press, 1976. 376 p.

Black Scholars on Higher Education in the 70's, edited by Roosevelt
    Johnson. Columbus, Ohio: ECCA Publications, 1974. 368 p.

Black Separatism: A Bibliography, Betty Lanier Jenkins and Susan
    Phillis. Westport, Connecticutt: Greenwood Press, 1976. 163 p.

Black Slavery in the Americas: An Interdisciplinary Bibliography, 1865-
    1980, John David Smith. Westport, Connecticut. Greenwood Press,
    1982. 2 V., 1847 p.

Black Women and Religion: A Bibliography, Marilyn Richardson. Boston: G.
    K. Hall, 1980. 139 p.

Black Women in Antiquity, edited by Ivan Van Sertina. New Brunswick, New
    Jersey: Transaction Books, 1984. 159 p.

Black Writers in New England: A Bibliography, With Bibliographical
    Notes, of Books by and about Afro-American Writers Associated with
    New England in the Collection of Afro-American Literature, Suffolk
    University, Museum of Afro-American History, Boston Afro-American
    National Historic Site, Edward Clark. Boston: U. S. Department of
    the Interior, National Park Service, 1985. 76 p.

Blacks in America; Bibliographical Essays, James M. McPherson and
    Others. Garden City, New York: Doubleday, 1971. 430 p.

Blacks in Hispanic Literature: Critical Essays, edited by Miriam
    DeCosta. Port Washington, New York: Kennikat Press, 1977. 157 p.

Blacks in the Humanities, 1750-1984: A Selected Annotated Bibliography,
    Donald F. Joyce. Westport, Connecticut: Greenwood Press, 1986. 209
    p.

Blacks in the Year 2000, edited by Joseph R. Washington, Jr.
    Philadelphia: University of Pennsylvania, 1981. 70 p.

Blood and Flesh: Black American and African Identifications, Josephine
    Moraa Moikobu. Westport, Connecticut: Greenwood Press, 1981. 226 p.

Blues Who's Who: A Biographical Dictionary of Blues Singers, Sheldon
    Harris. New Rochelle, New York: Arlington House, 1979. 775 p.

Burelle's Black Media Directory, 1983-1984. Livingston, New Jersey:
    Burrelle's Media Directories, 1983. 154 p.

Carindex: Social Sciences, ACURIL Indexing Committee. St. Augustine,
    Trinidad: Association of Caribbean University Research and
    Institutional Libraries, biannual.

Catalog of the E. Azalia Hackley Collection of Negro Music, Dance and
    Drama. Boston: G. K. Hall, 1979. 510 p.

Catalog of the Old Slave Mart Museum and Library, Charleston, South
    Carolina. Boston: G. K. Hall, 1978. 2 V.

Central American Writers of West Indian Origin: A New Hispanic
    Literature, Ian Smart. Washington: Three Continents Press, 1984.
    149 p.

Chicago Afro-American Union Analytic Catalog; An Index to Materials on
    the Afro-American in the Principal Libraries of Chicago. Boston: G.
    K. Hall, 1972. 5 V.

Child Development in the Caribbean: An Annotated Bibliography - 1962 to
    1982, Leachim Semaj. Mona, Jamaica: Regional Preschool Child
    Development Centre; 1984. 184 p.

Choral Music by Afro-American Composers: A Selected Annotated
    Bibliography, Evelyn Davidson White. Metuchen, New Jersey:
    Scarecrow, 1981. 167 p.

The Complete Annotated Resource Guide to Black American Art, Oakley N.
    Holmes. Spring Valley, New York: Black Artists in America, 1978.

The Complete Caribbeana, 1900-1975: A Bibliographic Guide to the
    Scholarly Literature, Lambros Comitas. Millwood, New York: KTO
    Press, 1977. 4 V. 2193 p.

The Complete Haitiana: A Bibliographic Guide to the Scholarly
    Literature, 1900-1980, Michel Laguerre. Millwood, New York Kraus
    International, 1982. 2 V.

A Comprehensive Bibliography for the study of American Minorities, V. 1.
    New York: New York University, 1976. "Black Americans," p. 3-262.

Contemporary Black Thought: Alternative Analyses in Social and
    Behavioral Science, edited by Molefi K. Asante and Abdulai S.
    Vandi. Beverly Hills: Sage, 1980. 302 p.

Contributions of Black Women to America, edited by Marianna W. Davis.
    Columbia, South Carolina: Kenday Press, 1982. 2

A Critical Introduction to Twentieth Century American Drama, C. W. E.
    Bigsby. New York: Cambridge University Press, 1982. Volume 1.

Demography of the Black Population in the United States: An Annotated
    Bibliography with a Review Essay, Jamshid A. Momeni. Westport,
    Connecicut: Greenwood Press, 1983. 354 p.

Dictionary Catalog of the Arthur B. Spingarn Collection of Negro
    Authors, Howard University Library, Washington D.C. Boston: G. K.
    Hall, 1970, 2

Dictionary Catalog of the Jesse E. Moorland Collection of Negro Authors,
    Howard University Library, Washington, D.C. Boston: G. K. Hall,
    1970, 9 V.

Dictionary Catalog of the Negro Collection of the Fisk University
    Library, Nashville, Tennessee. Boston: G. K. Hall, 1974, 6 V.

Dictionary Catalog of the Schomburg Collection of Negro Literature and
    History, New York Public Library. Boston: G. K. Hall, 1962. 9 V.

First Supplement, 1967. 2 V. Second Supplement, 1972, 4 V. 1974 -
Supplement, 580 p. Updated annually by the Bibliographic Guide to
Black Studies, 1975 -

Dictionary Catalog of the Vivian G. Harsh Collection of Afro-American
    Literature and History, Chicago Public Library. Boston: G. K. Hall,
    1978. 4 V.

A Dictionary of Africanisms: Contributions of Sub-Saharan Africa to the
    English Language, Gerard M. Dalgish. Westport, Connecticut:
    Greenwood Press, 1982. 203 p.

Dictionary of Afro-Latin American Civilization, Benjamin Nunez.
    Westport, Connecticut: Greenwood Press, 1980. 515 p.

Dictionary of American Negro Biography, edited by Rayford W. Logan and
    Michael Winston. New York: Norton, 1982. 680 p.

Dictionary of Black Culture, Wade Baskin and Richard Runes. New York:
    Philosophical Library, 1973. 493 p.

Directory of Blacks in the Performing Arts, Edward Mapp. Metuchen, New
    Jersey: Scarecrow Press, 1978. 428 p.

Directory of Career Resources for Minorities: A Guide to Career
    Resources and Opportunities for Minorities, edited by Alvin
    Renetzby. Santa Monica: Ready Reference Press, 1980. 335 p.

Directory of Special Programs for Minority Group Members. Willis L.
    Johnson, Third edition. Garrett Park, Maryland: Garrett Park Press,
    1980.

The Ebony Handbook, edited by Doris Saunders. Chicago: Johnson
    Publishing, 1974. 553 p.

The Economics of Minorities: A Guide to Information Sources, edited by
    Kenneth L. Gagala. Detroit: Gale, 1976. 212 p.

The Education of Poor and Minority Children: A World Bibliography, Meyer
    Weinberg. Westport, Connecticut: Greenwood Press, 1981. 2 V. 1563
    p.

Encyclopedia of Black America, W. Augustus Low and Virgil A. Clift. New
    York: McGraw-Hill, 1981. 921 p.

Ethnic Collections in Libraries, edited by E. J. Josey and Marva L.
    DeLoach. New York: Neal-Schuman, 1983. 361 p.

Ethnic Genealogy: A Research Guide, edited by Jessie Carney Smith.
    Westport, Connecticut: Greenwood Press, 1983. 440 p.

Facts About Blacks, 1984-1985. Los Angeles: Jeffries and Associates,
    1986. 48 p.

Famous First Facts About Negroes, Romeo B. Garrett. New York: Arno
    Press, 1972. 212 p.

Fifty Caribbean Writers: A Bio-Bibliographical Critical Sourcebook,
    edited by Daryl Cumber Dance. Westport, Connecticut: Greenwood
    Press, 1986. 530 p.

Folk Festivals: A Handbook for Organization and Management, Joseph T.
    Wilson and Lee Udall. Knoxville: University of Tennessee Press,
    1982. 278 p.

Free at Last: A Bibliography of Martin Luther King, Jr., William H.
    Fisher. Metuchen, New Sersey: Scarecrow, 1977. 169 p.

Free Heads of Household in the New York State Federal Census, 1790-1830,
    Alice Eickholz and James M. Rose. Detroit: Gale Research, 1981. 301
    p.

From Columbus to Castro: The History of the Caribbean, 1492-1969, Eric
    Williams. New York: Vintage Books, 1984, C 1970. 576 p.

From DuBois to Van Vechten: The Early New Negro Literature, 1903-1926,
    Chidi Ikonne. Westport, Connecticut: Greenwood Press, 1981. 218 p.

From Slavery to Freedom: A History of Negro Americans, John Hope
    Franklin. 5th edition. New York: Knopf, 1980. 554 p.

Gatekeepers of Black Culture: Black-Owned Book Publishing in the United
    States, 1817-1981, Donald Franklin Joyce. Westport, Connecticut.
    Greenwood Press, 1983. 249 p.

Guide to the Heartman Manuscripts on Slavery. Boston: G. K. Hall, 1982.
    221 p.

Handbook of Intercultural Communication, edited by Molefi K. Asante,
    Eileen Newmark, Cecil A. Blake. Beverly Hills: Sage, 1979. 479 p.

The Harlem Renaissance: An Annotated Bibliography and Commentary,
    Margaret Perry. New York: Garland, 1982. 272 p.

Historical Dictionary of Haiti, Roland I. Perusse. Metuchen, New Jersey:
    Scarecrow Press, 1977. 124 p.

Historical Dictionary of the British Caribbean, William Lux. Metuchen,
    New Jersey: Scarecrow Press, 1975. 266 p.

Historical Dictionary of the French and Netherlands Antilles, Albert
    Gastmann. Metuchen, New Jersey: Scarecrow Press, 1978. 162 p.

How Capitalism Underdeveloped Black America: Problems in Race, Political
    Economy and Society, Manning Marable. Boston: South End Press,
    1983. 343 p.

Howard University Bibliography of African and Afro-American Religious
    Studies: With Locations in American Libraries, Ethel L. Williams
    and Clifton F. Brown. Wilmington, Delaware: Scholarly Resources,
    1977. 525 p.

In Black and White: A Guide to Magazine Articles, Newspaper Articles,
    and Books Concerning More Than 15,000 Black Individuals and Groups,

Mary Mace Spradling. Detroit: Gale, 1980. 2 V, 1282 p.

Index to Black American Writers in Collective Biographies, Dorothy W.
    Campbell. Littleton, Colorado: Libraries Unlimited, 1983. 162 p.

Index to Black American Literary Anthologies, Jessamine S. Kallenbach.
    Boston: G. K. Hall, 1979. 219 p.

Index to Black Poetry, Dorothy H. Chapman. Boston: G. K. Hall, 1974. 541
    p.

Index to the American Slave, edited by Donald M. Jacobs. Westport,
    Connecticut: Greenwood Press, 1981. 274 p.

Interviews With Black Writers, John O'Brien. New York: Liveright, 1973.
    274 p.

Ishmael Reed: A Primary and Secondary Bibliography, Elizabeth A. Settle.
    Boston: G. K. Hall, 1982. 155 p.

Jamaica, K. E. Ingram. Santa Barbara: Clio Press, 1984. 369 p.

James Baldwin, A Reference Guide, Fred L. Standley. Boston: G. K. Hall,
    1980. 310 p.

Jazz-Bibliography: International Literature on Jazz, Blues, Spirituals,
    Gospel and Ragtime Music with a Selected List of Works on the
    Social and Cultural Background from the Beginning to the Present,
    Bernahard Hefele. New York: K. G. Saur, 1981. 368 p.

Jazz Reference and Research Materials: A Bibliography, Eddie S.
    Meadows. New York: Garland, 1981. 300 p.

Latin America and Caribbean Contemporary Record. New York: Holmes and
    Meier, 1983-. Annual.

Lemuel Haynes: A Bio-Bibliography, Richard Newman. New York: Lambeth
    Press, 1984. 138 p.

Long Memory: The Black Experience in America, Mary F. Berry and John W.
    Blassingame. New York: Oxford University Press, 1982. 486 p.

Martin Luther King, Jr.: An Annotated Bibliography, Sherman Pyatt.
    Westport, Connecticut: Greenwood Press, 1986. 154 p.

Men of Mark; Eminent, Progressive and Rising, William J. Simmons. New
    York: Arno Press, 1986 (Reprint of the 1887 edition). 1141 p.

Modern Diasporas in International Politics, edited by Gabriel Sheffer.
    London: Croom Helm, 1986. 349 p.

More Black American Playwrights, 1800 to the Present: A Bibliography,
    Esther Spring Arata and Nicholas John Rotoli. Metuchen, New Jersey:
    Scarecrow Press, 1976.

The National Civil Rights Directory: An Organizations Directory, edited
    by Mary Lee Bundy and Irvin Gilchrist. College Park, Maryland:

Urban Information Interpreters, 1979. 183 p.

The Negro Almanac: A Reference Work on the Afro-American, Harry A.
    Ploski and James Williams, 4th edition. New York: Wiley, 1983. 1550
    p.

The Negro Impact on Western Civilization, Joseph Roucek and Thomas
    Kiernan. New York: Philosophical Library, 1970. 506 p.

The Other Slaves: Mechanics, Artisans and Craftsmen, edited by James E.
    Newton and Ronald L. Lewis. Boston: G. K. Hall, 1978. 245 p.

A Paul Robeson Research Guide: A Selected Annotated Bibliography,
    Lenwood G. Davis. Westport, Connecticut: Greenwood Press, 1982. 879
    p.

Personalities Caribbean: The International Who's Who in the West
    Indies-Bahamas-Bermuda. 7th edition. Kingston, Jamaica:
    Personalities Ltd., 1983. 1027 p.

Phillis Wheatley: A Bio-Bibliography, William H. Robinson Boston: G. K.
    Hall, 1981. 166 p.

Philosophy Born of Struggle: Anthology of Afro-American Philosophy from
    1917, edited by Leonard Harris. Dubuque, Iowa: Kendall/Hunt, 1983.
    316 p.

The Popular Image of the Black Man in English Drama, 1550-1688, Elliot
    H. Tokson. Boston: G. K. Hall, 1982. 178 p.

The Progress of Afro-American Women: A Selected Bibliography and
    Resource Guide, Janet L. Sims. Westport, Connecticut: Greenwood
    Press, 1980. 378 p.

The Psychology and Mental Health of Afro-American Women: A Selected
    Bibliography, Glenell S. Young and Janet Sims-Wood. Temple Hills,
    Maryland: Afro Resources 1984. 102 p.

Publishing in the Third World: Trend Report and Bibliography, Philip G.
    Altbach and Eva Maria Rathgeber. New York: Praeger, 1980. 186 p.

Quotations in Black, edited by Anita King. Westport, Connecticut:
    Greenwood Press, 1981. 344 p.

Race and Ethnic Relations in Latin America and the Caribbean: An
    Historical Dictionary and Bibliography, Robert M. Levine. Metuchen,
    New Jersey: Scarecrow Press, 1980. 252 p.

Rare Afro-Americana: A Reconstruction of the Adger Library, Wendy Ball
    and Tony Martin. Boston: G. K. Hall, 1981. 235 p.

Reluctant Reformers: Racism and Social Reform Movements in the United
    States, Robert L. Allen. Washington: Howard University Press, 1974.
    324 p.

Research in Black Child Development: Doctoral Dissertation Abstracts,
    1927-1979, Hector F. Meyers. Westport, Connecticut: Greenwood

Press, 1982. 737 p.

Reshaping America: Society and Institutions, 1945-1960, Robert H.
    Bremner and Gary W. Reichard. Columbus: Ohio State University
    Press, 1982. 403 p.

Richard Wright: A Primary Bibliography, Charles T. Davis and Michel
    Fabre. Boston: G. K. Hall, 1982. 232 p.

The Rise of Industrial America: A People's History of the Post-
    Reconstruction Era, Page Smith. New York: McGraw-Hill, 1984. 965 p.

Roots and Branches: Current Directions in Slave Studies, edited by
    Michael Craton. New York: Pergamon Press, 1979. 292 p.

Roots of Black Music: The Vocal, Instrumental and Dance Heritage of
    Africa and Black America, Ashenafi Kebede. Englewood Cliffs, New
    Jersey: Prentice-Hall, 1982. 162 p.

Scandalize My Name: Black Imagery in American Popular Music, Sam
    Dennison. New York: Garland, 1982. 594 p.

Selected Black American, African and Caribbean Authors: A Bio-
    Bibliography, James A. Page and Jae Min Roh. Littleton, Colorado:
    Libraries Unlimited, 1985. 388 p.

Sex and Race, J. A. Rogers. New York: Helga M. Rogers, 1942-1944.
    V. 1, The Old World. 303 p.
    V. 2, The New World. 411 p.
    V. 3, "Why White and Black Mix in Spite of Opposition." 359 p.

The Slave Community: Plantation Life in the Antebellum South, John W.
    Blassingame. Revised and enlarged edition. New York: Oxford
    University Press, 1979. 414 p.

Slavery: A Comparative Teaching Bibliography, Joseph Calder Miller.
    Waltham, Massachusetts: Crossroads Press, 1977. 123 p.

Slavery: A Worldwide Bibliography, 1900-1982, Joseph C. Miller. White
    Plains, New York: Kraus International, 1985. 451 p.

Slavery and Abolition: A Journal of Comparative Studies, 2(2):1981.

Slavery and Race Relations in Latin America, Robert Brent Toplin.
    Westport, Connecticut: Greenwood Press, 1974. 450 p.

The State of Black America, 1984. New York: National Urbana League,
    1984.

The State of Black America, 1985. New York: National Urban League, 1985.
    231 p.

The State of Black America, 1986. New York: National Urban League,
    1986. 220 p.

250 Years of Afro-American Art: An Annotated Bibliography, Lynn Moody
    Igoe. New York: Bowker, 1981. 1266 p.

We are Your Sisters: Black Women in the 19th Century, edited by Dorothy
    Sterling. New York: Norton, 1984. 535 p.

Who's Who Among Black Americans, edited by William Matney. 4th edition.
    Lake Forest, Illinois: Educational Communications, 1985. 1043 p.

Women of Color: A Filmography of Minority and Third World Women, Maryann
    Oshana. New York: Garland, 1985. 338 p.

Writings by W. E. B. DuBois in Non-Periodical Literature, edited by
    Herbert Aptheker. White Plains, New York: Kraus International,
    1982.

Writings by W.E.B. DuBois in Periodicals Edited by Athers, edited by
    Herbert Aptheker. White Plains, New York: Kraus International,
    1982.

Index to Afro-American Reference Resources

ABOLITION MOVEMENT

"Black Militancy Confronts Militant Abolitionism" in <u>Reluctant Reformers</u>. 1975. pp. 9-49.

"The Generation of Crisis" in <u>Before the Mayflower</u>. 1982. pp. 140-186.

"The Movement to Manumit Negroes" in <u>From Slavery to Freedom</u>. 1980. pp. 92-94.

ABOLITION MOVEMENT - BIBLIOGRAPHY

"The Abolition Movement" in <u>A Bibliography of the Negro</u>. 1928. pp. 296-306.

"The Abolitionist Movement, 1830-1865" in <u>Blacks in America; Bibliographical Essays</u>. 1971. pp. 89-92.

"Antislavery Movement" in <u>Black Rhetoric</u>. 1976. pp. 68-74.

"The Antislavery Movement before Garrison" in <u>Blacks in America; Bibliographical Essays</u>. 1971. pp. 86-88.

"Slavery and Abolition as Public and Cultural Issues" in <u>Afro-American History, 1</u>. 1974. pp. 153-248.

"Slavery and Abolition as Public and Cultural Issues" in <u>Afro-American History, 2</u>. 1981. pp. 87-107.

"Slavery and Intersectional Strife" in <u>From Slavery to Freedom</u>. 1981. pp. 525-527.

"That All Men May Be Free" in <u>From Slavery to Freedom</u>. 1981. p. 518.

ABOLITION MOVEMENT - BRAZIL - BIBLIOGRAPHY

"The African Slave Trade, Slavery and Abolition" in <u>Afro-Braziliana</u>. 1978. pp. 21-37.

ABOLITION MOVEMENT - VENEZUELA

"The Abolition of Slavery in Venezuela: A Non-Event," John V. Lombardi
    in Slavery and Race Relations in Latin America. 1974. pp. 228-252.

ABOLITIONISTS - BIBLIOGRAPHY

"Biographies, Individuals Connected with the Antislavery Movement" in A
    Bibliography of the Negro. 1928. pp. 306-308.

ABOLITIONISTS - BIOGRAPHY - INDEX

"Abolitionists" in In Black and White. 1980. See index, V. 2, p. 1103.

ABOLITIONISTS, BLACK - BIBLIOGRAPHY

"Black Abolitionists" in Black Rhetoric. 1976. pp. 74-78.

"Black Abolitionists" in Blacks in America; Bibliographical Essays.
    1971. pp. 92-94.

ABOLITIONISTS, JEWISH - BIBLIOGRAPHY

"Jews in the Antislavery Movement" in Black-Jewish Relations. 1984. p.
    91.

ABOLITIONISTS, WHITE - BIBLIOGRAPHY

"White Abolitionist Writers" in Blacks in America; Bibliographical
    Essays. 1971. pp. 96-98.

ACCORDIANISTS - BIOGRAPHY - INDEX

"Musicians: Instrumental: Accordian" in In Black and White. 1980. See
    index, V. 2, p. 1103.

ACCOUNTANTS - BIBLIOGRAPHY

"Accounting" in The Progress of Afro-American Women. 1980. p. 76.

ACCOUNTANTS - BIOGRAPHY - INDEX

"Accountants" in In Black and White. 1980. See index, p. 1103.

ACCOUNTING - BIBLIOGRAPHY

"Accounting" in The Progress of Afro-American Women. 1980. p. 76.

ACCOUNTING FIRMS - DIRECTORY

"Accounting Firms" in Black Resource Guide. 1986. pp. 1-6.

ACCULTURATION - SLAVERY

"The Americanization of the Slave, and the Africanization of the South"
    in The Slave Community. 1979. pp. 49-104.

"Enslavement, Acculturation, and African Survivals" in The Slave
    Community. 1979. pp. 3-48.

ACROBATS - BIOGRAPHY - INDEX

"Acrobats" in In Black and White. 1980. See index, V. 2, p. 1003.

ACTIVISTS - BIOGRAPHY - INDEX

"Activists" in In Black and White. 1980. See index, V. 2, pp. 1103-1106.

ACTORS AND ACTRESSES

"The Black Entertainer in the Performing Arts" in The Negro Almanac.
    1983. pp. 1077-1126.

ACTORS AND ACTRESSES - BIOGRAPHY - INDEX

"Actors" in In Black and White. 1980. See index, V. 2, pp. 1106-1110.

ACTORS AND ACTRESSES - DIRECTORIES

Directory of Blacks in the Performing Arts. 1978. 428 p.

ACTORS AND ACTRESSES - FILMOGRAPHY

"Black Athletes in Films" in Black Athletes in the United States. 1981.
    pp. 247-253.

"Blacks in Major Roles" in The Afro-American Cinematic Experience. 1983.
    pp. 241-244.

"Blacks in Supporting Roles" in The Afro-American Cinematic Experience.
    1983. pp. 211-220.

ADGER, ROBERT M.

"Introduction. Race Men, Bibliophiles, and Historians: The World of
    Robert M. Adger and the Negro Historical Society of Philadelphia"
    in Rare Afro-Americana. 1982. pp. 1-55.

ADMINISTRATION, PUBLIC - ECONOMIC ASPECTS - BIBLIOGRAPHY

"Blacks and Governmental Law and Policy" in The Economics of Minorities.
    1976. pp. 145-163.

ADMINISTRATORS - EDUCATION

"The Despicable Caricature: Black Administrators in White Schools,"
    Roosevelt Johnson in Black Scholars on Higher Education. 1974. pp.
    19-34.

ADMINISTRATORS - EDUCATION - BIBLIOGRAPHY

"Administrators" in The Education of Poor and Minority Children. 1981.
    pp. 684-689.

ADOPTION AGENCIES - DIRECTORY

"Adoption Agencies and Services" in Black Resource Guide. 1986. pp. 7-

10.

ADOPTION - BIBLIOGRAPHY

"Black Family and Adoption" in The Black Family in the United States. 1986. pp. 102-103 and 175-177.

ADVERTISING - BIBLIOGRAPHY

"Advertising (Newspaper and Magazine Articles)" in Black Media in America. 1984. pp. 88-99.

ADVERTISING AGENCIES - DIRECTORY

"Advertising Agencies and Marketing Research Companies" in Black Resource Guide. 1986. pp. 11-13.

AESTHETICS - BIBLIOGRAPHY

"Aesthetics" in 250 Years of Afro-American Art. 1981. pp. 233-237.

AFFIRMATIVE ACTION - BIBLIOGRAPHY

"Jews and Affirmative Action" in Black-Jewish Relations. 1984. p. 23.

"Jews' Opinion on Affirmative Action" in Black-Jewish Relations. 1984. pp. 91-92.

AFRICA

"Sub-Saharan Africa: The Emerging Nations" in The Negro Almanac. 1983. pp. 1383-1464.

AFRICA - BIBLIOGRAPHIES - BIBLIOGRAPHY

"A Bibliography of Bibliographies on Africa" in A Bibliography of the Negro. 1928. pp. 242-247.

AFRICA - BIBLIOGRAPHY

"The Negro in Africa" in A Bibliography of the Negro. 1928. pp. 1-241.

"A Selected Bibliography: Africa" in The Negro Almanac. 1983. p. 1497.

AFRICA - DISCOVERY AND EXPLORATION - BIBLIOGRAPHY

"Discovery and Exploration in Africa from Ancient Times to 1800" in A Bibliography of the Negro. 1928. pp. 1-17.

"Discovery and Exploration in Africa since 1800" in A Bibliography of the Negro. 1928. pp. 18-27.

AFRICA - MUSIC - BIBLIOGRAPHY

"Africa" in A Bibliography of Black Music. 1981. V. 3, pp. 9-40.

AFRICA - RELIGION - BIBLIOGRAPHY

"African Heritage" in <u>Howard University Bibliography of African and Afro-American Religious Studies</u>. 1977. pp. 1-115.

AFRICA - SLAVERY - BIBLIOGRAPHY

"Africa" in <u>Slavery: A Worldwide Bibliography</u>. 1985. pp. 211-233.

"Africa (Non-Islamic)" in <u>Slavery</u>. 1977. pp. 62-69.

"Indigenous African Slavery," Paul Lovejoy in <u>Roots and Branches</u>. 1979. pp. 19-61.

"Indigenous African Slavery: Commentary One," Igor Kopytoff in <u>Roots and Branches</u>. 1979. pp. 62-77.

"Indigenous African Slavery: Commentary Two," Frederick Cooper in <u>Roots and Branches</u>. 1979. pp. 77-83.

"Modern Slavery in Africa" in <u>A Bibliography of the Negro</u>. 1928. pp. 180-184.

"Slavery and the Slave Trade Within Africa" in <u>A Bibliography of the Negro</u>. 1928. pp. 111-116.

AFRICAN CULTURAL SURVIVALS

"Africa, Slavery, and the Shaping of Black Culture" in <u>Long Memory</u>. 1982. pp. 3-32.

"African Music and the Western Hemisphere" in <u>The Roots of Black Music</u>. 1980. pp. 125-155.

"The Transplantation of African Culture" in <u>From Slavery to Freedom</u>. 1980. pp. 28-29.

AFRICAN CULTURAL SURVIVALS - BIBLIOGRAPHY

"African Cultural Survivals Among Black Americans" in <u>Blacks in America</u>; <u>Bibliographical Essays</u>. 1971. pp. 32-39.

"African Influence and Survivals" in <u>250 Years of Afro-American Art</u>. 1981. pp. 237-239.

"Bibliography: Africa, Slavery, and the Shaping of Black Culture" in <u>Long Memory</u>. 1982. pp. 425-427.

"Cultural Continuities" in <u>The Complete Caribbeana</u>. 1977. V. 2, pp. 651-670.

"Cultural Continuity" in <u>The Complete Haitiana</u>. 1982. V. 1, pp. 627-643.

AFRICAN CULTURAL SURVIVALS - BRAZIL - BIBLIOGRAPHY

"African Influence on Brazilian Cooking" in <u>Afro-Braziliana</u> . 1978. p. 79.

"Africanisms in the Brazilian Portuguese Language" in <u>Afro-Braziliana</u>.

1978. pp. 75-78.

AFRICAN CULTURAL SURVIVALS - DICTIONARY

A Dictionary of Africanisms. 1982. 203 p.

AFRICAN EMBASSIES - DIRECTORY

"Embassies and Consulates - African" in Black Resource Guide. 1986. pp.
    75-77.

AFRICAN METHODIST EPISCOPAL CHURCH - BIBLIOGRAPHY

"African Methodist Episcopal" in Howard University Bibliography of
    African and Afro-American Religious Studies. 1977. pp. 183-190.

AFRICAN METHODIST EPISCOPAL ZION CHURCH - BIBLIOGRAPHY

"African Methodist Episcopal Zion" in Howard University Bibliography of
    African and Afro-American Religious Studies. 1977. pp. 190-192.

AFRICAN STUDIES - LIBRARY COLLECTIONS

"Africana Library Collections," Beverly Gray in Ethnic Collections.
    1983. pp. 246-269.

AFRICAN SUPPORT ORGANIZATIONS - DIRECTORY

"Support Organizations" in Black Resource Guide. 1986. p. 79.

AFRICANS IN LITERATURE - BIBLIOGRAPHY

"The Native African in Literature" in A Bibliography of the Negro. 1928.
    pp. 238-241.

AFRIKAANS - BIBLIOGRAPHY

"Afrikaans" in A Bibliography of Pidgin and Creole Languages. 1975. pp.
    322-337.

AFRO-AMERICAN/AFRICAN RELATIONS

"Africa in the Development of Black-American Nationalism," Emmanuel
    Akpan in Contemporary Black Thought. 1980. pp. 225-231.

"Black Americans and Africa," Inez Smith Reid in The Black American
    Reference Book. 1976. pp. 648-683.

Blood and Flesh: Black Americans and African Identification. 1981. 226
    p.

AFRO-AMERICAN/NATIVE AMERICAN RELATIONS

"Red, White and Black: Race and Sex" in Before the Mayflower. 1982. pp.
    297-325.

AFRO-AMERICAN/NATIVE AMERICAN RELATIONS - BIBLIOGRAPHY

"Black Slavery Among the Indians" in Black Slavery in the Americas. 1982. pp. 1031-1042.

AGED

"Aged Black Americans: Double Jeopardy Revisited," Jacqueline Johnson Jackson in The State of Black America, 1985. pp. 143-183.

AGED - BIBLIOGRAPHY

The Black Aged in the United States: An Annotated Bibliography. 1980. 200 p.

"Black Family and Aging" in The Black Family in the United States. 1986. pp. 81-82.

"Black Family and the Black Aged" in The Black Family in the United States. 1986. pp. 126-129.

AGRARIAN REFORM - HAITI - BIBLIOGRAPHY

"Agrarian Reforms" in The Complete Haitiana. 1982. pp. 1443-1445.

AGRICULTURAL ECONOMICS - CARIBBEAN - BIBLIOGRAPHY

"Agricultural Economics" in The Complete Caribbeana. 1977. V. 3, pp. 1439-1496.

AGRICULTURAL ECONOMICS - HAITI - BIBLIOGRAPHY

"Agricultural Economics" in The Complete Haitiana. 1982. V. 2, pp. 1297-1314.

AGRICULTURE

"The Black American in Agriculture," Calvin L. Beale in The Black American Reference Book. 1976. pp. 284-315.

"Blacks in Agriculture" in The Negro Almanac. 1983. pp. 555-557.

"Farms and Farming" in The Ebony Handbook. 1974. pp. 331-341.

AGRICULTURE - BIBLIOGRAPHY

"Black Farmers in the New South" in Blacks in America; Bibliographical Essays. 1971. pp. 166-167.

"The Negro in Agriculture" in A Bibliography of the Negro. 1928. pp. 493-497.

AGRICULTURE - CARIBBEAN - BIBLIOGRAPHY

"Soils, Crops and Livestock" in The Complete Caribbeana. 1977. V. 3, pp. 1913-2027.

AGRICULTURE - HAITI - BIBLIOGRAPHY

"Fruits, Vegetables and Other Crops" in The Complete Haitiana. 1982. V. 1, pp. 159-167.

AIDES - BIOGRAPHY - INDEX

"Aides" in In Black and White. 1980. See index, V. 2, pp. 1110-1111.

AIRLINE INDUSTRY - BIBLIOGRAPHY

"Airlines and Aviation" in The Progress of Afro-American Women. 1980. pp. 76-77.

ALABAMA - EDUCATION - BIBLIOGRAPHY

"Alabama" in The Education of Poor and Minority Children. 1981. pp. 194-202.

ALABAMA - EDUCATION, HIGHER - BIBLIOGRAPHY

"Higher Education by State: Alabama" in The Education of Poor and Minority Children. 1981. pp. 862-864.

ALABAMA - GENEALOGY - BIBLIOGRAPHY

"Alabama" in Black Genesis. 1978. pp. 117-121.

ALABAMA - LIBRARIANS

"Library Service and the Black Librarian in Alabama," Annie Greene King in The Black Librarian in the Southeast. 1976. pp. 21-24.

ALABAMA - SLAVERY - BIBLIOGRAPHY

"Alabama" in Black Slavery in the Americas. 1982. pp. 867-876.

ALASKA - EDUCATION - BIBLIOGRAPHY

"Alaska" in The Education of Poor and Minority Children. 1981. pp. 202-205.

ALBA, NANINA

"Nanina Alba," Enid Bogle in Afro-American Poets Since 1955. 1985. pp. 3-8.

ALCOHOLISM - MEN

"Alcohol Use and Abuse," Frederick D. Harper in Black Men. 1981. pp. 169-177.

ALGERIA - MUSIC - BIBLIOGRAPHY

"Algeria" in Bibliography of Black Music. 1981. V. 3, p. 52.

ALLEN, BETTY - BIBLIOGRAPHY

"Allen, Betty" in Black Music in America. 1981. pp. 1-11.

ALLEN, SAMUEL W.

"Samuel W. Allen," Ruth L. Britton in <u>Afro-American Poets Since 1955</u>.
    1985. pp. 8-17.

ALLFREY, PHYLLIS SHAND

"Phyllis Shand Allfrey," Elaine Campbell in <u>50 Caribbean Writers</u>. 1986.
    pp. 9-18.

ALPHA KAPPA ALPHA SORORITY - BIBLIOGRAPHY

"Alpha Kappa Alpha Sorority" in <u>The Progress of Afro-American Women</u>.
    1980. pp. 244-248.

AMBASSADORS - BIOGRAPHY - INDEX

"Ambassadors, Diplomats" in <u>In Black and White</u>. 1980. See index, V. 2,
    pp. 1111-1112.

AMERICA

"Blacks in the Western Hemisphere" in <u>The Negro Almanac</u>. 1983. pp.
    1465-1488.

"Race and the New World" in <u>Sex and Race</u>. 1944. pp. 1-13.

AMERICA - DISCOVERY AND EXPLORATION - BIBLIOGRAPHY

"The Negro and the Discovery of America" in <u>A Bibliography of the Negro</u>.
    1928. pp. 251-253.

AMERICAN ANTI-SLAVERY SOCIETY

"The American Anti-Slavery Society" in <u>The Negro Almanac</u>. 1983. p. 258.

AMERICAN MISSIONARY ASSOCIATION - BIBLIOGRAPHY

"American Missionary Association" in <u>Howard University Bibliography of
    Afro-American and African Studies</u>. 1977. p. 293.

AMINI, JOHARI M.

"Johari M. Amini (Jewel Christine McLawler Latimore/Johari M. Kunjufu),"
    Fahamisha Patricia Brown in <u>Afro-American Poets Since 1955</u>. 1985.
    pp. 17-23.

AMISTAD CASE - BIBLIOGRAPHY

"Noted Law Suits Relating to the Status of Slaves: Amistad Case" in <u>A
    Bibliography of the Negro</u>. 1928. p. 344.

ANATOMISTS - BIOGRAPHY - INDEX

"Anatomists" in <u>In Black and White</u>. 1980. See index, V. 2, p. 1112.

ANATOMY - BIBLIOGRAPHY

"Anatomical and Anthropological Studies" in A Bibliography of the Negro. 1928. pp. 612-614.

ANDERSON CASE - BIBLIOGRAPHY

"Noted Law Suits Relating to the Status of Slaves: Anderson Case" in A Bibliography of the Negro. 1928. p. 344.

ANGELOU, MAYA

"Maya Angelou," Lynn Z. Bloom in Afro-American Writers After 1955: Dramatists and Prose Writers. 1985. pp. 3-12.

ANGOLA - MUSIC - BIBLIOGRAPHY

"Angola" in Bibliography of Black Music. 1981. V. 3, p. 53.

ANGUILLA - BIBLIOGRAPHY

"Anguilla" in The Complete Caribbeana. 1977. See index, V. 4, p. 2151.

ANIMAL BREEDERS - BIOGRAPHY - INDEX

"Animal Breeders, Trainers" in In Black and White. 1980. See index, V. 2, p. 1112.

ANIMAL HUSBANDRY - CARIBBEAN - BIBLIOGRAPHY

"Soils, Crops and Livestock" in The Complete Caribbeana. V. 3, pp. 1913-2027.

ANIMAL TRAINERS - BIOGRAPHY - INDEX

"Animal Breeders, Trainers" in In Black and White. 1980. See index, V. 2, p. 1112.

ANIMALS - CARIBBEAN - BIBLIOGRAPHY

"Plant and Animal Life" in The Complete Caribbeana. V. 3, pp. 1735-1839.

ANIMALS - HAITI - BIBLIOGRAPHY

"Plant and Animal Life" in The Complete Haitiana. 1982. V. 2, pp. 127-157.

ANTHOLOGIES - BIBLIOGRAPHY

"Anthologies" in Black Rhetoric. 1976. pp. 6-26.

ANTHONY, MICHAEL

"Michael Anthony," Daryl Cumber Dance in 50 Caribbean Writers. 1986. pp. 19-25.

ANTHROPOLOGISTS - BIOGRAPHY - INDEX

"Anthropologists" in In Black and White. 1980. See index, V. 2, p. 1112.

ANTHROPOLOGY - BIBLIOGRAPHY

"Anatomical and Anthropological Studies" in A Bibliography of the Negro.
    1928. pp. 612-614.

"Anthropology" in Afro-American Reference. 1955. pp. 59-61.

ANTHROPOLOGY - HAITI - BIBLIOGRAPHY

"Human Biology and Anthropology" in The Complete Haitiana. 1982. V. 2,
    pp. 899-904.

ANTIGUA - BIBLIOGRAPHY

"Antigua" in The Complete Caribbeana. 1977. See index, V. 4, p. 2151.

ANTI-SEMITISM, BLACK - BIBLIOGRAPHY

"Black Anti-Semitism" in Black-Jewish Relations. 1984. pp. 10-17; 56-62.

ARABIA

"The Mixing of Black and White in Syria, Palestine, Arabia, Persia" in
    Sex and Race. 1944. V. 3, pp. 58-61.

ARCHAEOLOGISTS - BIOGRAPHY - INDEX

"Archeologists" in In Black and White. 1980. See index, V. 2, p. 1112.

ARCHAEOLOGY - CARIBBEAN - BIBLIOGRAPHY

"Archaeology and Ethnohistory" in The Complete Caribbeana. 1977. V. 1,
    pp. 135-168.

ARCHAEOLOGY - HAITI - BIBLIOGRAPHY

"Archaeology and Pre-Columbian History" in The Complete Haitiana. 1982.
    V. 1, pp. 177-184.

ARCHITECTS - BIBLIOGRAPHY

"Architects" in The Progress of Afro-American Women. 1980. p. 77.

ARCHITECTS - BIOGRAPHY - INDEX

"Architects" in In Black and White. 1980. See index, V. 2, pp. 1112-
    1113.

ARCHITECTS - DIRECTORY

"Architects" in Black Resource Guide. 1986. p. 14.

ARCHITECTURE - BIBLIOGRAPHY

"Architecture" in 250 Years of Afro-American Art. 1981. pp. 247-248.

"Architecture and Housing" in Afro-American Folk Culture. 1978. See index, p. 756.

ARCHITECTURE - CARIBBEAN - BIBLIOGRAPHY

"Housing and Architecture" in The Complete Caribbeana. V. 2, pp. 1157-1167.

ARCHITECTURE - HAITI - BIBLIOGRAPHY

"Housing and Architecture" in The Complete Haitiana. 1982. V. 2, pp. 1437-1441.

ARCHIVES

Black History: A Guide to Civilian Records in the National Archives. 1984. 379 p.

"Developing Ethnic Archives," Stanton Biddle and Verdia Jenkins in Ethnic Collections. 1983. pp. 273-292.

"Federal Archives: Their Nature and Use" in Afro-American History; Sources for Research. 1981. pp. 7-32.

"The Multipurpose Use of Federal Archives" in Afro-American History; Sources for Research. 1981. pp. 57-97.

"National Archives and Federal Records" in Black Genesis. 1978. pp. 24-28.

"Using Archives as Sources for Afro-American Research: Some Personal Experiences" in Afro-American History; Sources for Research. 1981. pp. 33-55.

"Using Federal Archives for Research; an Archivists Experience," Roland C. McConnell in Afro-American History; Sources for Research. 1981. pp. 41-46.

"Using Federal Archives" Some Problems in Doing Research," Okon Edet Uya in Afro-American History; Sources for Research. 1981. pp. 19-29.

ARGENTINA

"Uruguay, Argentina, Paraguay, Chile" in Sex and Race. 1942. V. 2. pp. 57-65.

ARGENTINA - BIBLIOGRAPHY

"Argentina" in The Education of Poor and Minority Children. 1981. pp. 1074-1075.

ARGENTINA - MUSIC - BIBLIOGRAPHY

"Argentina" in Bibliography of Black Music. 1981. V. 3, pp. 169-170.

ARGENTINA - SLAVERY - BIBLIOGRAPHY

"Argentina" in Slavery: A Worldwide Bibliography. 1985. pp. 139-141.

ARIZONA - EDUCATION - BIBLIOGRAPHY

"Arizona" in The Education of Poor and Minority Children. 1981. pp.
    205-206.

ARIZONA - EDUCATION, HIGHER - BIBLIOGRAPHY

"Higher Education by State: Arkansas" in The Education of Poor and
    Minority Children. 1981. pp. 865-866.

ARKANSAS - GENEALOGY - BIBLIOGRAPHY

"Arkansas" in Black Genesis. 1978. pp. 122-124.

ARKANSAS - SLAVERY - BIBLIOGRAPHY

"Arkansas" in Black Slavery in the Americas. 1982. pp. 876-880.

ARMSTRONG, LOUIS - BIBLIOGRAPHY

"Armstrong, Daniel Louis (Satchmo)" in Black Music in America. 1981. pp.
    11-53.

ARMY - BIOGRAPHY - INDEX

"Military Service: Army" in In Black and White. 1980. See index, V. 2,
    pp. 1174-1175.

ART

"Afro-American Art," Edmund B. Gaither in The Black American Reference
    Book. 1976. pp. 827-845.

"Contemporary Black American Art," James A. Porter in The Negro Impact
    on Western Civilization. 1970. pp. 489-506.

ART - AUDIO TAPES - BIBLIOGRAPHY

"Audio Tapes" in The Complete Annotated Resource Guide to Afro-American
    Art. 1978. pp. 212-215.

ART - BIBLIOGRAPHY

"Afro-American Art" in 250 Years of Afro-American Art. 1981. pp. 239-
    245.

"Art" in Afro-American Reference. 1985. pp. 98-99.

"Art" in The Progress of Afro-American Women. 1980. pp. 16-18.

"Art" in Black Women and Religion. 1980. pp. 95-106.

"Basic Bibliography" in 250 Years of Afro-American Art. 1981. pp. 1-232.

Black Artists in the United States. 1980. 138 p.

"Books and Doctoral Dissertations" in The Complete Annotated Resource

Guide to Afro-American Art. 1978. pp. 1-25.

"Ebony Visions in Color, Stone, Wood and Cloth: Afro-American Art" in
     Blacks in the Humanities. 1986. pp. 85-96.

"The Negro and Modern Art (Painting and Sculpture)" in A Bibliography of
     the Negro. 1928. pp. 452-453.

"The Plastic Arts" in A Comprehensive Bibliography. 1976. pp. 261-262.

"Slave Culture: Slave Art" in Black Slavery in the Americas. 1982. pp.
     1382-1389.

ART - BRAZIL - BIBLIOGRAPHY

"Art and Artisans" in Afro-Braziliana; a Working Bibliography. pp. 81-
     90.

ART - CARVING - BIBLIOGRAPHY

"Carving" in 250 Years of Afro-American Art. 1981. pp. 328-329.

ART - COLLEGES AND UNIVERSITIES - BIBLIOGRAPHY

"Colleges and Universities" in 250 Years of Afro-American Art. 1981. pp.
     330-354.

ART - DIRECTORIES

"Black Art Works at the National Archives" in Black Artists in the
     United States. 1980. pp. 123-127.

ART - EXHIBITS - BIBLIOGRAPHY

"Art Galleries and Museums" in 250 Years of Afro-American Art. 1981. pp.
     254-322.

"Brochures of Exhibition Catalogs of Art Shows" in The Complete
     Annotated Resource Guide to Afro-American Art. 1978. pp. 26-117.

ART - FILMS - BIBLIOGRAPHY

"Motion Pictures and Video Tapes" in The Complete Annotated Resource
     Guide to Afro-American Art. 1975. pp. 193-211.

ART - FILMSTRIPS - BIBLIOGRAPHY

"Large Prints, Slides and Filmstrips" in The Complete Annotated Resource
     Guide to Black American Art. 1978. pp. 175-191.

ART - HARLEM - BIBLIOGRAPHY

"Harlem" in 250 Years of Afro-American Art. 1981. pp. 369-379.

ART - MURALS - BIBLIOGRAPHY

"Murals" in 250 Years of Afro American Art. 1981. pp. 388-389.

ART - PERIODICALS - BIBLIOGRAPHY

"Periodicals" in The Complete Annotated Resource Guide to Black American
    Art. 1978. pp. 118-174.

ART - REFERENCE WORKS

The Complete Annotated Resource Guide to Black American Art. 1978. 275
    p.

ART - RESOURCES

"Chronological Listing of Group, Survey or Historical Exhibitions, Books
    and Films" in The Complete Annotated Resource Guide to Black
    American Art. 1978. pp. 261-275.

ART - SLIDES - BIBLIOGRAPHY

"Audio-Visual Materials: Slides" in Black Women and Religion. 1980. p.
    102.

"Large Prints, Slides and Filmstrips" in The Complete Annotated Resource
    Guide to Black American Art. 1978. pp. 175-191.

ART - VIDEO TAPES - BIBLIOGRAPHY

"Motion Pictures and Video Tapes" in The Complete Annotated Resource
    Guide to Black American Art. 1978. pp. 193-211.

ART, AFRICAN

"African Art from Prehistory to the Present," James A. Porter in The
    Negro Impact on Western Civilization. 1970. pp. 467-488.

ART, AFRICAN - BIBLIOGRAPHY

"African Art" in A Bibliography of the Negro. 1928. pp. 93-97.

ART, CHILDREN'S - BIBLIOGRAPHY

"Children's Art" in 250 Years of Afro-American Art. 1981. pp. 329-330.

ART, FOLK - BIBLIOGRAPHY

"Folk Art" in 250 Years of Afro-American Art. 1981. pp. 367-369.

ART, VISUAL - BIBLIOGRAPHY

"Material Culture" in Afro-American Folk Culture. 1978. See index, p.
    780.

"Visual Arts" in Afro-American Folk Culture. 1983. See index, p. 804.

ART CRITICS - BIOGRAPHY - INDEX

"Critics: Literary, Art, Music" in In Black and White. 1980. See index,
    V. 2, pp. 1134-1135.

ART EDUCATION

"The Black Arts in Perspective," Shirley Miles, Carol Morton in Beyond
    Identity. 1978. pp. 101-153.

ART EDUCATION - BIBLIOGRAPHY

"Art Education" in 250 Years of Afro-American Art. 1981. pp. 250-254.

ART GALLERIES

"Black Museums and Galleries" in The Negro Almanac. 1983. pp. 1011-1016.

ART GALLERIES - BIBLIOGRAPHY

"Art Galleries and Museums" in 250 Years of Afro-American Art. 1981. pp.
    254-322.

ART GALLERIES - DIRECTORIES

"Afro-American Art Organizations, Art Museums and Art Galleries" in The
    Complete Annotated Resource Guide to Black American Art. 1978. pp.
    216-239.

ART PROGRAMS - FEDERAL

"Federal Art Programs" in 250 Years of Afro-American Art. 1981. pp.
    364-367.

ART TEACHERS - BIOGRAPHY - INDEX

"Artists: Teachers" in In Black and White. 1980. See index, V. 2, pp.
    1117-1118.

ARTISANS - HISTORY

"The Antebellum Negro Artisan," W.E.B. DuBois in The Other Slaves. 1978.
    pp. 175-182.

ARTISANS, AFRICAN

"The African Artisan," W.E.B. DuBois in The Other Slaves. 1978. pp.
    171-174.

ARTISTS

"The Black Artist" in The Negro Almanac. 1983. pp. 1007-1051.

"Black Artists" in The Ebony Handbook. 1974. p. 437.

"The Negro as Artist," Alain Locke in The Other Slaves. 1978. pp. 205-
    207.

ARTISTS - BIBLIOGRAPHY

"Art" in Black Women and Religion: A Bibliography. 1980. pp. 95-98.

"Art" in The Progress of Afro-American Women. 1980. pp. 16-18.

"Artist Bibliography" in 250 Years of Afro-American Art. 1981. pp. 301-1261.

Black Artists in the United States. 1980. 138 p.

"Black Painters and Sculptors" in Blacks in America; Bibliographical Essays. 1971. pp. 269-273.

ARTISTS - BIOGRAPHY - INDEX

"Artists" in In Black and White. 1980. See index, V. 2, pp. 1113-1114.

ARTISTS - DIRECTORY

"Artist Bibliography" in 250 Years of Afro-American Art. pp. 301-1261.

ARTISTS - HISTORY

"Negro Craftsmen and Artists of Pre-Civil War Days," James A. Porter in The Other Slaves. 1978. pp. 209-220.

ARTISTS, COMMERCIAL - BIOGRAPHY - INDEX

"Artists: Commercial" in In Black and White. 1980. See index, p. 1114.

ARTS

"The Black Arts Movement," Larry Neal in Afro-American Writers After 1955: Dramatists and Prose Writers. 1985. pp. 293-300.

ARTS - CARIBBEAN - BIBLIOGRAPHY

"Creative Arts and Recreation" in The Complete Caribbeana. 1977. V. 2, pp. 713-746.

ARTS - HAITI - BIBLIOGRAPHY

"Creative Arts and Recreation" in The Complete Haitiana. 1982. V. 1, pp. 657-668.

ARUBA - BIBLIOGRAPHY

"Aruba" in The Complete Caribbeana. 1977. See index, V. 4, pp. 2151-2152.

ARUBA - MUSIC - BIBLIOGRAPHY

"Curacao and Aruba" in Bibliography of Black Music. 1981. V. 3, p. 143.

ASIA

"Race-Mixing in Africa and Asia Today" in Sex and Race. 1944. V. 1, pp. 130-141.

ASIAN AMERICAN STUDIES - LIBRARY COLLECTIONS

"Asian American Collections," Wei Chi Poon in <u>Ethnic Collections</u>. 1983.
     pp. 180-201.

ASIAN AMERICANS - EDUCATION, HIGHER - BIBLIOGRAPHY

"Higher Education: Asian-American Students" in <u>The Education of Poor and
     Minority Children</u>. 1981. pp. 934-936.

ASSOCIATION OF SOUTHERN WOMEN FOR THE PREVENTION OF LYNCHING -
BIBLIOGRAPHY

"Association of Southern Women for the Prevention of Lynching" in <u>The
     Progress of Afro-American Women</u>. 1980. p. 248.

ASTROLOGERS - BIOGRAPHY - INDEX

"Astrologers" in <u>In Black and White</u>. 1980. See index, V. 2, p. 1118.

ASTRONOMERS - BIOGRAPHY - INDEX

"Astronomers" in <u>In Black and White</u>. 1980. See index, V. 2, p. 1118.

ATHLETES

"The Black Amateur and Professional Athlete" in <u>The Negro Almanac</u>. 1983.
     pp. 905-963.

"The Black American in Sports," Edwin B. Henderson in <u>The Black American
     Reference Book</u>. 1976. pp. 927-963.

ATHLETES - AUTOBIOGRAPHY - BIBLIOGRAPHY

"Books by Black Athletes" in <u>Black Athletes</u>. 1981. pp. 13-19.

ATHLETES - BIBLIOGRAPHY

<u>Black Athletes in the U.S</u>. 1981. 265 p.

ATHLETES - BIOGRAPHY - BIBLIOGRAPHY

"Books about Black Athletes" in <u>Black Athletes</u>. 1981. pp. 20-64.

ATHLETES - DIRECTORY

"Athletes" in <u>Black Resource Guide</u>. 1986. pp. 44-47.

ATHLETES - REFERENCE WORKS - BIBLIOGRAPHY

"Major Reference Books" in <u>Black Athletes</u>. 1981. pp. 9-11.

ATKINS, RUSSELL

"Russell Atkins," Ronald Henry High in <u>Afro-American Poets Since 1955</u>.
     1985. pp. 24-32.

ATTITUDES, RACIAL - BIBLIOGRAPHY

"Racial Attitudes and Segregation" in <u>Afro-American History, 1</u>. 1974.
    pp. 421-460.

"Racial Attitudes and the Pattern of Discrimination (The Contemporary
    Scene)" in <u>Afro-American History, 1</u>. 1974. pp. 560-628.

ATTORNEYS - BIOGRAPHY - INDEX

"Lawyers, Barristers" in <u>In Black and White</u>. 1980. See index, V. 2, pp.
    1166-1169.

AUBERT, ALVIN

"Alvin Aubert," Norman Harris in <u>Afro-American Poets Since 1955</u>. 1985.
    pp. 32-36.

AUDIOLOGISTS - BIOGRAPHY - INDEX

"Audiologists" in <u>In Black and White</u>. 1980. See index, V. 2, p. 1118.

AUSTRALIA - BIBLIOGRAPHY

"Australia" in <u>The Education of Poor and Minority Children</u>. 1981. pp.
    1075-1085.

AUSTRIA

"Miscegenation in Holland, Belgium, Austria, Poland and Russia" in <u>Sex
    and Race</u>. 1944. V. 1. pp. 169-175.

AUTHORS

"Black Writers, Scholars and Poets" in <u>The Negro Almanac</u>. 1983. pp.
    965-1006.

<u>Interviews with Black Writers</u>. 1973. 274 p.

AUTHORS - BIBLIOGRAPHY

<u>Black Writers in New England</u>. 1985. 76 p.

<u>Index to Black American Writers</u>. 1983. 162 p.

"Literature" in <u>The Progress of Afro-American Women</u>. 1980. pp. 206-212.

<u>Selected Black American, African and Caribbean Authors</u>. 1985. 388 p.

AUTHORS - BIOGRAPHY - INDEX

"Authors, Compilers" in <u>In Black and White</u>. 1980. See index. V. 2, pp.
    1118-1120.

AUTHORS - DIRECTORIES

<u>Selected Black American, African, and Caribbean Authors</u>. 1985. 388 p.

AUTHORS, AFRICAN-DIRECTORIES

Selected Black American, African, and Caribbean Authors, 1985. 388 p.

AUTHORS, BRAZILIAN-BIBLIOGRAPHY

"Writings of Selected Authors, with Critical and Biographical
    References" in Afro-Braziliana. 1978. pp. 173-276.

AUTHORS, CARIBBEAN-DIRECTORIES

Fifty Caribbean Writers: A Bio-Bibliographical Critical Sourcebook.
    1986. 530 p.

Selected Black American, African and Caribbean Authors. 1985. 388 p.

AUTOBIOGRAPHICAL ESSAYS - BIBLIOGRAPHY

"Autobiographically-Based Essays" in A Comprehensive Bibliography. 1976.
    pp. 204-206.

AUTOBIOGRAPHY - BIBLIOGRAPHY

"Biographies and Autobiographies" in The Progress of Afro-American
    Women. 1980. pp. 33-51.

"Biographies and Autobiographies of Negroes" in A Bibliography of the
    Negro. 1928. pp. 473-476.

Black Americans in Autobiography. 1984. 192 p.

AUTOBIOGRAPHY - INDEX

"Autobiographies" in In Black and White. 1980. See index, V. 2, p. 1120.

AUTOBIOGRAPHY, SLAVE - BIBLIOGRAPHY

"Mind of the Slave: Autobiographical Writings" in Black Slavery in the
    Americas. 1982. pp. 1397-1414.

AUTOMOBILE INDUSTRY EMPLOYEES AND OFFICIALS - BIOGRAPHY - INDEX

"Automobile Industry" in In Black and White. 1980. See index. V. 2, p.
    1120.

AVIATION EMPLOYEES AND OFFICIALS - BIOGRAPHY - INDEX

"Aviation Industry" in In Black and White. 1980. See index. V. 2, p.
    1120.

AVIATORS - BIBLIOGRAPHY

"Airlines and Aviation" in The Progress of Afro-American Women. 1980. p.
    76.

AWARDS

"Awards and Prizes" in Before the Mayflower. 1982. pp. 639-640.

"Spingarn Medalists" in The Negro Almanac. 1983. pp. 1526-1528.

AWARDS, ART - BIBLIOGRAPHY

"Art Awards" in 250 Years of Afro-American Art. 1981. pp. 248-250.

AZANIA - MUSIC - BIBLIOGRAPHY

"Azania" in Bibliography of Black Music. 1981. V. 3, pp. 54-59.

BACTERIOLOGISTS - BIOGRAPHY - INDEX

"Bacteriologists" in In Black and White. 1980. See index. V. 2, p. 1120.

BAHAMAS

"Blacks in the Western Hemisphere: Bahama Islands" in The Negro Almanac.
    1983. p. 1484.

BAHAMAS - BIBLIOGRAPHY

"Bahamas" in The Complete Caribbeana. 1977. See index, V. 4, p. 2152.

BAHAMAS - MUSIC - BIBLIOGRAPHY

"Bahamas" in Bibliography of Black Music. 1981. V. 3, p. 135.

BAKER, DAVE - BIBLIOGRAPHY

"Baker, Dave" in Black Music in America. 1981. pp. 54-56.

BALDWIN, JAMES

"James Baldwin," John R. Roberts in Afro-American Fiction Writers After
    1955. 1984. pp. 3-16.

BALDWIN, JAMES - BIBLIOGRAPHY

"After Protest: Black Writers in the 1950s and 1960s - James Baldwin" in
    Blacks in America; Bibliographical Essays. 1971. pp. 258-259.

"Black Dramatists: James Baldwin" in Blacks in America; Bibliographical
    Essays. 1971. pp. 281-282.

James Baldwin, A Reference Guide. 1980. 310 p.

"James Baldwin's Opinion of Jews" in Black-Jewish Relationships. 1984.
    pp. 89-90.

BAMBARA, TONI CADE

"Toni Cade Bambara," Alice A. Deck in Afro-American Writers After 1955:
    Dramatists and Prose Writers. 1985. pp. 12-22.

BAND LEADERS - BIOGRAPHY - INDEX

"Musicians: Band, Orchestra Leaders" in In Black and White. 1980. See index, V. 2, pp. 1180-1181.

BANDS, MUSICAL - BIBLIOGRAPHY

"Band Music" in Bibliography of Black Music. 1981. V. 2, p. 87.

"Bands and Orchestras: in Afro-American Folk Culture. 1978. See index, p. 757.

BANJO PLAYERS - BIOGRAPHY - INDEX

"Musicians: Instrumental: Banjo" in In Black and White. 1980. See index, V. 2, p. 1184.

BANKERS - BIBLIOGRAPHY

"Banking" in The Progress of Afro-American Women. 1980. pp. 77-78.

BANKING - HAITI - BIBLIOGRAPHY

"Banking and Monetary Issues" in The Complete Haitiana. 1982. V. 2, pp. 1395-1420.

BANKING OFFICIALS AND EMPLOYEES - BIOGRAPHY - INDEX

"Banking Officials" in In Black and White. 1980. See index, V. 2, pp. 1120-1121.

BANKS

"The Potential and Problems of Black Financial Institutions," William D. Bradford in The State of Black America, 1985. pp. 127-142.

BANKS - DIRECTORY

"Banks" in Black Resource Guide. 1986. pp. 81-84.

BAPTIST CHURCH - BIBLIOGRAPHY

"National Baptist Convention, U.S.A.- Negro Baptist in General" in Howard University Bibliography of African and Afro-American Religious Studies. 1977. pp. 193-199.

BAPTIST CHURCH - CIVIL RIGHTS MOVEMENT - BIBLIOGRAPHY

"The Church, Synagogue and Integration: Baptist" in Howard University Bibliography of African and Afro-American Religious Studies. 1977. p. 315.

BAPTIST CHURCH - RACE RELATIONS - BIBLIOGRAPHY

"Baptist" in Howard University Bibliography of African and Afro-American Religious Studies. 1977. pp. 268-271.

BAPTIST CHURCH - SLAVERY - BIBLIOGRAPHY

"Slavery, Negroes and the Church: Baptist" in Howard University

<u>Bibliography of African and Afro-American Religious Studies</u>. 1977. pp. 128-129.

BAR ASSOCIATIONS - DIRECTORY

"Bar Associations" in <u>Black Resource Guide</u>. 1986. pp. 15-21.

BAR MAIDS - BIBLIOGRAPHY

"Bar Maids" in <u>The Progress of Afro-American Women</u>. 1980. p. 78.

BARAKA, IMAMU AMIRI

"Amiri Baraka (Leroy Jones)," Floyd Gaffney in <u>Afro-American Writers After 1955: Dramatists and Prose Writers</u>. 1985. p. 22-42.

BARAKA, IMAMU AMIRI - BIBLIOGRAPHY

"After Protest: Black Writers in the 1950s and 1960s - Leroi Jones" in <u>Blacks in America; Bibliographical Essays</u>. 1971. pp. 260-261.

"Black Dramatists: Leroi Jones" in <u>Blacks in America; Bibliographical Essays</u>. 1971. pp. 249-250.

"Leroi Jones' (Imamu Amiri Baraka) Opinion of Jews" in <u>Black-Jewish Relations</u>. 1984. p. 93.

BARBADOS

"Blacks in the Western Hemisphere: Barbados" in <u>The Negro Almanac</u>. 1983. pp. 1470-1471.

BARBADOS - BIBLIOGRAPHY

"Barbados" in <u>The Complete Caribbeana</u>. 1977. See index, V. 4, pp. 2153-2154.

BARBUDA - BIBLIOGRAPHY

"Barbuda" in <u>The Complete Caribbeana</u>. 1977. See index, V. 4, p. 2154.

BARRAX, GERALD WILLIAM

"Gerald William Barrax," Lucy K. Hayden in <u>Afro-American Poets Since 1955</u>. 1985. pp. 36-41.

BARRETT, LINDSAY

"Lindsay Barrett," Norval "Nadi" Edwards in <u>50 Caribbean Writers</u>. 1986. pp. 26-34.

BASEBALL - BIBLIOGRAPHY

"Articles: Baseball" in <u>Black Athletes</u>. 1981. pp. 68-119.

BASIE, COUNT - BIBLIOGRAPHY

"Basie, Count (William James)" in <u>Black Music in America</u>. 1981. pp. 56-76.

BASKETMAKING

"Basketmaking" in <u>250 Years of Afro-American Art</u>. pp. 324-326.

BASS PLAYERS - BIOGRAPHY - INDEX

"Bass Players" in <u>In Black and White</u>. 1980. See index, V. 2, pp. 1184-1185.

BEAUTICIANS - BIBLIOGRAPHY

"Beauty Culture" in <u>The Progress of Afro-American Women</u>. 1980. pp. 78-81.

BEAUTICIANS - BIOGRAPHY - INDEX

"Hair Stylists, Cosmeticians" in <u>In Black and White</u>. 1980. See index, V. 2, p. 1159.

BEAUTY - BIBLIOGRAPHY

"Beauty" in <u>The Progress of Afro-American Women</u>. 1980. pp. 168-171.

BEAUTY PAGEANTS - BIBLIOGRAPHY

"Beauty Pageants and Queens" in <u>The Progress of Afro-American Women</u>. 1980. pp. 171-174.

BECHET, SIDNEY - BIBLIOGRAPHY

"Bechet, Sidney" in <u>Black Music in America</u>. 1981. pp. 76-84.

BECKHAM, BARRY

"Barry Beckham," Joe Weixlmann in <u>Afro-American Fiction Writers After 1955</u>. 1984. pp. 17-20.

BELAFONTE, HARRY - BIBLIOGRAPHY

"Belafonte, Harry" in <u>Black Music in America</u>. 1981. pp. 84-91.

BELGIUM

"Miscegenation in Holland, Belgium, Austria, Poland, Russia" in <u>Sex and Race</u>. 1944. V. 1, pp. 169-175.

BELIZE - BIBLIOGRAPHY

"Belize" in <u>The Complete Caribbeana</u>. 1977. See index, V. 4, pp. 2154-2155.

"Belize" in <u>The Education of Poor and Minority Children</u>. 1981. p. 1087.

<u>Belize</u>. 1980. 229 p.

BELIZE - MUSIC - BIBLIOGRAPHY

"Belize" in Bibliography of Black Music. 1981. V. 3, p. 171.

"Performing Arts" in Belize. 1980. pp. 174-175.

BELL, JAMES MADISON

"James Madison Bell," Keith E. Byerman in Afro-American Writers Before
    the Harlem Renaissance. 1986. pp. 3-6.

BENIN - MUSIC - BIBLIOGRAPHY

"Benin" in Bibliography of Black Music. 1981. V. 3, p. 60.

BENNETT, HAL

"Hal Bennett," Ronald Walcott in Afro-American Fiction Writers After
    1955. 1984. pp. 20-28.

BENNETT, LOUISE

"Louise Bennett," Mervyn Morris in 50 Caribbean Writers. 1986. pp. 35-
    45.

BENNETT COLLEGE - BIBLIOGRAPHY

"Bennett College" in The Progress of Afro-American Women. 1980. pp.
    248-250.

BENSON, GEORGE - BIBLIOGRAPHY

"Benson, George" in Black Music in America. 1981. pp. 91-95.

BENTON, BROOK - BIBLIOGRAPHY

"Benton, Brook" in Black Music in America. 1981. pp. 95-96.

BEQUIA - BIBLIOGRAPHY

"Bequia" in The Complete Caribbeana. 1977. See index, V. 4, p. 2155.

BERMUDA

"Blacks in the Western Hemisphere: Bermuda" in The Negro Almanac. 1983.
    p. 1483.

BERMUDA - BIBLIOGRAPHY

"Bermuda" in The Complete Caribbeana. 1977. See index, V. 4, pp. 2155-
    2156.

BERRY, CHUCK - BIBLIOGRAPHY

"Berry, Chuck" in Black Music in America. 1981. pp. 96-99.

BETHUNE, MARY MCLEOD - DOCUMENTS

"Federal Archives as a Source for Determining the Role of Mary McLeod
     Bethune in the National Youth Administration," Elaine M. Smith in
     Afro-American history; Sources for Research. 1981. pp. 47-52.

BIBLIOGRAPHERS - BIOGRAPHY - INDEX

"Bibliographers" in In Black and White. 1980. See index, V. 2, p. 1121.

BIBLIOGRAPHICAL ESSAYS

Blacks in America; Bibliographical Essays. 1971. 430 p.

"A Guide to the Black-American Experience" in A Comprehensive
     Bibliography. 1976. pp. 3-30.

BIBLIOGRAPHIES - BIBLIOGRAPHY

"Bibliographies" in Black Rhetoric. 1976. pp. 1-5.

"Bibliographies" in A Comprehensive Bibliography. 1981. pp. 31-41.

"A Bibliography of Bibliographies on the Negro in the United States" in
     A Bibliography of the Negro. 1928. pp. 630-636.

Black Access: A Bibliography of Afro-American Bibliographies. 1984. 249
     p.

"General Bibliographies" in Afro-American Reference. 1985. pp. 4-9.

BIBLIOPHILES - BIOGRAPHY - INDEX

"Bibliophiles" in In Black and White. 1980. See index, V. 2, p. 1121.

BIG SISTERS - BIBLIOGRAPHY

"Big Sisters" in The Progress of Afro-American Women. 1980. p. 250.

BIOGRAPHERS - BIOGRAPHY - INDEX

"Biographers" in In Black and White. 1980. See index, V. 2, p. 1121.

BIOGRAPHICAL NOVELS - BIBLIOGRAPHY

"Biographies - Fiction" in The Progress of Afro-American Women. 1980. p.
     32.

BIOGRAPHY - BIBLIOGRAPHY

"Autobiographies and Biographies" in Black Women and Religion. 1980. pp.
     113-120.

"Autobiography and Biography" in Afro-American Folk Culture. 1978. See
     index, pp. 756-757.

"Biographies and Autobiographies" in The Progress of Afro-American
     Women. 1980. pp. 33-51.

"Biographies and Autobiographies of Negroes" in A Bibliography of the
    Negro. 1928. pp. 473-476.

"Biography" in Black Media in America. 1984. pp. 53-62.

"Biography and Autobiography" in Black Rhetoric. 1976. pp. 27-48.

"General Biographical Sources" in Afro-American Reference. 1986. pp.
    3-18.

"Individual Biographies and Autobiographies" in A Comprehensive
    Bibliography. 1976. pp. 196-203.

"A Selected Bibliography: Biography" in The Negro Almanac. 1983. pp.
    1514-1519.

BIOGRAPHY - CARRIBEAN - BIBLIOGRAPHY

"General History and Biography" in The Complete Caribbeana. 1977. V. 1,
    pp. 169-306.

BIOGRAPHY - DIRECTORY

Who's Who Among Black Americans. 1985. 1043 p.

BIOGRAPHY - HAITI - BIBLIOGRAPHY

"Biography" in The Complete Haitiana. 1982. V. 2, pp. 499-550.

BIOGRAPHY - INDEX

"Autobiographical and Biographical Index" in Howard University
    Bibliography of African and Afro-American Religious Studies. 1977.
    pp. 385-471.

In Black and White. 1980. 2 V., 1282 p.

BIOGRAPHY, COLLECTED

"Civil Rights and Black Power Leaders of the Past" in The Negro Almanac.
    1983. pp. 281-294.

"Current Civil Rights Leaders" in The Negro Alamanac. 1983. pp. 261-281.

Dictionary of American Negro Biography.

Men of Mark. 1887. 829 p.

"Prominent Black Americans: Biographies of Notable Men and Women" in The
    Negro Alamanac. 1983. pp. 1333-1356.

BIOGRAPHY, COLLECTED - BIBLIOGRAPHY

"Collected Biographies" in The Progress of Afro-American Women. 1980.
    pp. 52-54.

"Collective Biographies and Autobiographies" in A Comprehensive

Bibliography. 1976. pp. 193-196.

BIOGRAPHY, COLLECTED - INDEX

Index to Black American Writers. 1983. 162 p.

BIOLOGISTS - BIOGRAPHY - INDEX

"Biologists" in In Black and White. 1980. See index, V. 2, pp. 1121-
1122.

BIOLOGY - CARIBBEAN - BIBLIOGRAPHY

"Human Biology" in The Complete Caribbeana. 1977. V. 2, p. 847-864.

BIRD FANCIERS - BIOGRAPHY - INDEX

"Bird Fanciers" in In Black and White. 1980. See index, V. 2, p. 1122.

BIRTH CONTROL - BIBLIOGRAPHY

"Birth Control and Family Planning" in The Progress of Afro-American
Women. 1980. pp. 132-138.

"Black Fertility Regulation" in Black Demography in the United States.
1983. pp. 109-202.

BLACK AND TAN REPUBLICANS - BIBLIOGRAPHY

"Black and Tan Republicans" in The Study and Analysis of Black Politics.
1973. pp. 132-145.

BLACK/ARAB RELATIONS - BIBLIOGRAPHY

"Blacks and the PLO, Arabs, and Israel" in Black-Jewish Relations. 1984.
pp. 81-87.

BLACK CAUCUSES - RELIGION - BIBLIOGRAPHY

"Black Caucuses" in Howard University Bibliography of African and Afro-
American Religious Studies. 1977. pp. 363-364.

BLACK COLLEGES AND UNIVERSITIES

"Development of Urban-Related Programs in Black Colleges," Nebraska Mays
in Black Scholars on Higher Education. 1974. pp. 215-220.

"Educating Blacks for the 1970's: The Role of Black Colleges," Laurence
E. Gary and Lee P. Brown in Black Scholars on Higher Education.
1974. pp. 371-390.

"Educational Research and Development: A Training Model Proposed for
Predominantly Black Institutions," James B. Gunnell and Carol A.
Shepard in Black Scholars on Higher Education. 1974. pp. 159-173.

"Political Science Education in the Black College," Hanes Walton, Jr.
and Brenda D. Mobley in The Study and Analysis of Black Politics.

1973. pp. 146-153.

BLACK COLLEGES AND UNIVERSITIES - BIBLIOGRAPHY

Black Higher Education in the United States. 1978. 268 p.

"Historically Black Colleges" in The Education of Poor and Minority
    Children. 1981. pp. 918-930.

BLACK COLLEGES AND UNIVERSITIES - DIRECTORY

"Black Colleges and Universities" in Black Resource Guide. 1986. pp.
    68-74.

BLACK CONSCIOUSNESS - BIBLIOGRAPHY

"Race Consciousness" in A Bibliography of the Negro. 1982. pp. 585-587.

BLACK ENGLISH - BIBLIOGRAPHY

"Dialect" in Afro-American Folk Culture. 1978. See index, pp. 767-769.

"Jist Sayin' It: Blacks in Linguistics" in Blacks in the Humanities.
    1986. pp. 85-96.

"Language and Speech" in Black Rhetoric. 1976. pp. 54-57.

BLACK ENGLISH - DICTIONARIES - BIBLIOGRAPHY

"Dictionaries, Vocabulary Lists and Glossaries" in Afro-American Folk
    Culture. 1978. See index, p. 769.

BLACK ENGLISH - ETYMOLOGY

"Etymology" in Afro-American Folk Culture. 1978. See index, p. 772.

BLACK IDENTITY - BIBLIOGRAPHY

"Identity: Individual and Collective" in Black Separatism; a
    Bibliography. 1976. pp. 42-58.

BLACK IDENTITY - CARIBBEAN - BIBLIOGRAPHY

"Ethnic and National Identity" in The Complete Caribbeana. 1977. V. 2,
    pp. 693-711.

BLACK IMAGE - BIBLIOGRAPHY

"Black and Negro as Image, Category and Stereotype" in Blacks in
    America; Bibliographical Essays. 1971. pp. 19-22.

"The Black Image in the White Mind" in Black Rhetoric. 1976. pp. 48-52.

"Stereotypes" in Afro-American Folk Culture. 1978. See index, p. 799.

BLACK IMAGE IN ART - BIBLIOGRAPHY

"Blacks in Art" in <u>250 Years of Afro-American Art</u>. 1981. pp. 326-327.

"The Portrayal of Blacks in Paintings by Whites: Winslow Homer and Thomas Eakins" in <u>Blacks in America; Bibliographical Essays</u>. 1971. pp. 180-182.

BLACK IMAGE IN DRAMA

<u>The Popular Image of the Black Man in English Drama</u>. 1982. 178 p.

BLACK IMAGE IN DRAMA - BIBLIOGRAPHY

"The Figure of the Black in English Renaissance Drama" in <u>Blacks in America; Bibliogrpahical Essays</u>. 1971. pp. 26-28.

"Ridgely Torrence's and Eugene O'Neill's Negro Plays" in <u>Blacks in America; Bibliographical Essays</u>. 1971. pp. 276-277.

BLACK IMAGE IN FICTION - BIBLIOGRAPHY

"Exotic Primitivism in the White Novel" in <u>Blacks in America; Bibliographical Essays</u>. 1971. pp. 250-251.

"Novels Relating to the Negro: Novels Mainly of the Present Day, by White Authors" in <u>A Bibliography of the Negro</u>. 1928. pp. 469-471.

BLACK IMAGE IN FILM - BIBLIOGRAPHY

"Afro-Americans in Films" in <u>Blacks in America; Bibliographical Essays</u>. 1971. pp. 284-286.

BLACK IMAGE IN FILM - FILMOGRAPHY

"Blacks in Stereotyped Roles" in <u>The Afro-American Cinematic Experience</u>. 1983. pp. 221-228.

"Blaxploitation Films" in <u>The Afro-American Cinematic Experience</u>. 1983. pp. 244-245.

BLACK IMAGE IN LITERATURE - BIBLIOGRAPHY

"Black Americans as Characters in Fiction and Drama" in <u>A Comprehensive Bibliography</u>. 1976. pp. 218-220.

"Black Figures in the Writings of White Southerners: Lillian Smith and William Faulkner" in <u>Blacks in America; Bibliographical Essays</u>. 1971. pp. 265-269.

"Exotic Primitivism in the White Novel" in <u>Blacks in America; Bibliographical Essays</u>. 1971. pp. 250-253.

"The Portrayal of Blacks by White Writers" in <u>Blacks in America; Bibliographical Essays</u>. 1971. pp. 175-180.

"Racial Themes in the Writings of Poe and Melville" in <u>Blacks in America; Bibliographical Essays</u>. 1971. pp. 99-103.

BLACK IMAGE IN LITERATURE (LATIN AMERICAN)

"African Footprints in Hispanic-American Literatures," John F. Mattheus
    in Blacks in Hispanic Literature. 1977. pp. 53-64.

"The Concept of Black Awareness as a Thematic Approach in Latin American
    Literature," Antonio Olliz Boyd in Blacks in Hispanic Literatures.
    1977. pp. 65-73.

BLACK IMAGE IN LITERATURE (SPANISH)

"The Eye of the Other: Images of the Black in Spanish Literature,"
    Sylvia Wynter in Blacks in Hispanic Literature. 1977. pp. 8-19.

BLACK IMAGE IN MUSIC

Scandalize My Name; Black Imagery in American Popular Music. 1982. 594
    p.

BLACK IMAGE IN SLAVERY

"Plantation Stereotypes and Institutional Roles" in The Slave Community.
    1979. pp. 223-248.

BLACK/JEWISH COOPERATION - BIBLIOGRAPHY

"Black-Jewish Alliances" in Black-Jewish Relations. 1984. pp. 62-76.

BLACK/JEWISH RELATIONS

"Introduction" in Black-Jewish Relations. 1984. pp. ix-xv.

BLACK/JEWISH RELATIONS - BIBLIOGRAPHY

Black-Jewish Relations. 1984. 130 p.

"The Jew and the Negro" in Howard University Bibliography of African and
    Afro-American Religious Studies. 1977. pp. 367-369.

"Judaism" in Howard University Bibliography of African and Afro-American
    Religious Studies. 1977. p. 273.

BLACK LEADERSHIP FORUM

"The Black Leadership Forum" in The Negro Almanac. 1983. pp. 255-256.

BLACK MUSLIMS - BIBLIOGRAPHY

"Black Muslims" in Howard University Bibliography of African and Afro-
    American Religious Studies. 1977. pp. 210-217.

BLACK PANTHERS

"The Black Panthers" in The Negro Almanac. 1983. pp. 259-260.

BLACK PANTHERS - BIBLIOGRAPHY

"The Black Panthers" in <u>Blacks in America; Bibliographical Essays</u>. 1971. pp. 386-389.

BLACK POWER MOVEMENT

"The Black Revolution" in <u>From Slavery to Freedom</u>. 1980. pp. 463-505.

"Civil Rights Organizations and Black Power Advocates - Past and Present" in <u>The Negro Almanac</u>. 1983. pp. 223-300.

"The Time of the Whale" in <u>Before the Mayflower</u>. 1982. pp. 386-440.

BLACK POWER MOVEMENT - BIBLIOGRAPHY

"Black Cultural Ideas and Movements (The Contemporary Scene)" in <u>Afro-American History, 1</u>. 1974. pp. 748-775.

"Black Nationalism" in <u>A Comprehensive Bibliography</u>. 1976. pp. 83-90.

"Black Theology, Black Power, and Black Religion" in <u>Howard University Bibliography of African and Afro-American Religious Studies</u>. 1977. pp. 352-363.

"Racial Conflict and the Civil Rights Movement" in <u>Afro-American History, 1</u>. 1974. pp. 496-560.

BLACK STUDIES

"The Battle for Black Studies," Nathan Hare in <u>Black Scholars on Higher Education</u>. 1974. pp. 65-87.

"Developing a Relevant Afro-American Studies Program," H. Ozeri Ubamadu in <u>Black Scholars on Higher Education</u>. 1974. pp. 113-124.

"Teaching Black Studies for Social Change," James A. Banks in <u>Black Scholars on Higher Education</u>. 1974. pp. 89-111.

BLACK STUDIES - BIBLIOGRAPHY

"Afro-American Studies" in <u>The Education of Poor and Minority Children</u>. 1981. pp. 632-658.

<u>Bibliographical Guide to Black Studies Programs</u>. 1985. 120 p.

BLACK STUDIES PROGRAMS - DIRECTORY

"Afro-American Studies Programs" in <u>Black Resource Guide</u>. 1986. pp. 54-68.

BLACK UNITED FRONT

"The Black United Front" in <u>The Negro Almanac</u>. 1983. p. 257.

BLACK WOMEN ORGANIZED FOR ACTION - BIBLIOGRAPHY

"Black Women Organized for Action" in <u>The Progress of Afro-American Women</u>. 1980. p. 250.

BLACK WOMEN'S COMMUNITY DEVELOPMENT FOUNDATION - BIBLIOGRAPHY

"Black Women's Community Development Foundation" in The Progress of
    Afro-American Women. 1980. p. 250.

BLAKE, EUBIE - BIBLIOGRAPHY

"Blake, Eubie" in Black Music in America. 1981.   pp. 99-104.

BLUES MUSIC

"Blues" in Black Music. 1979. pp. 31-116.

"Blues" in The Roots of Black Music. 1982. pp. 135-144.

BLUES MUSIC - BIBLIOGRAPHY

"Blues" in Bibliography of Black Music. 1981. V. 2, pp. 88-108.

"Blues" in Jazz Bibliography. 1981. pp. 74-83.

"Blues and Blues Performers" in Afro-American Folk Culture. 1978. See
    index, p. 759.

"Selected Bibliography" in Blues Who's Who. 1979. pp. 599-609.

BLUES MUSIC - BIOGRAPHICAL DIRECTORY

Blues Who's Who. 1979. 775 p.

BLUES MUSIC - DISCOGRAPHIES - BIBLIOGRAPHY

"Discographies: Blues and Popular Music" in Bibliography of Black Music.
    1981. V. 1, pp. 26-28.

BLUES MUSIC - SONG INDEX

"Song Index" in Blues Who's Who. 1979. pp. 635-698.

BLYDEN, EDWARD WILMOT - BIBLIOGRAPHY

"Edward Wilmot Blyden's Opinion of Jews" in Black-Jewish Relations.
    1984. p. 18.

BODY BUILDERS - BIOGRAPHY - INDEX

"Body Builders" in In Black and White. 1980. See index, V. 2, p. 1122.

BODY DECORATION - BIBLIOGRAPHY

"Body Decoration and Modification" in Afro-American Folk Culture. 1978.
    pp. 759-760.

BODY SERVANTS, MILITARY - BIOGRAPHY - INDEX

"Military Service: Body Servants" in In Black and White. 1980. See
    index, V. 2, p. 1175.

BOLIVIA - BIBLIOGRAPHY

"Bolivia" in The Education of Poor and Minority Children. 1981. p. 1088.

"Bolivia" in Race and Ethnic Relations. 1980. pp. 208-209.

BOLIVIA - MUSIC - BIBLIOGRAPHY

"Bolivia" in Bibliography of Black Music. 1981. V. 3, p. 171.

BOLIVIA - SLAVERY - BIBLIOGRAPHY

"Bolivia" in Slavery: A Worldwide Bibliography. 1985. p. 139.

BONAIRE - BIBLIOGRAPHY

"Bonaire" in The Complete Caribbeana. 1977. See index, V. 4, p. 2156.

BONTEMPS, ARNA

"Arna Bontemps" in Interviews with Black Writers. 1973.

BONTEMPS, ARNA - BIBLIOGRAPHY

"Bontemps, Arna" in The Harlem Renaissance. 1982. pp. 59-62.

BOOK COLLECTING

"Fifty Years of Collecting", Dorothy Porter in Black Access. 1984. pp. xvii-xxviii.

BOOK ILLUSTRATION - BIBLIOGRAPHY

"Illustration and Illustrated Books" in 250 Years of Afro-American Art. 1981. pp. 383-386.

BOOK PUBLISHERS - DIRECTORY

"Book Publishers" in Black Resource Guide. 1986. pp. 22-23.

BOOK PUBLISHING

Gatekeepers of Black Culture: Black-Owned Book Publishing in the United States. 1983. 249 p.

BOOK PUBLISHING - BIBLIOGRAPHY

"Magazines and Books" in Black Media in America. 1984. pp. 123-134.

BOOKSTORES - DIRECTORY

"Book Stores" in Black Resource Guide. 1986. pp. 23-24.

BOTANISTS - BIOGRAPHY - INDEX

"Botanists" in In Black and White. 1980. See index, V. 2, p. 1122.

BOTSWANA - MUSIC - BIBLIOGRAPHY

"Botswana" in Bibliography of Black Music. 1981. V. 3, p. 61.

BOXING - BIBLIOGRAPHY

"Boxing" in Black Athletes. 1981. pp. 135-209.

BRADLEY, DAVID

"David Bradley," Valerie Smith in Afro-American Fiction Writers After
    1955. 1984. pp. 28-32.

BRAITHWAITE, WILLIAM STANLEY

"William Stanley Braithwaite," Kenny J. Williams in Afro-American
    Writers Before the Harlem Renaissance. 1986. pp. 7-18.

BRAND, DIONNE

"Dionne Brand," Himani Banneiji in 50 Caribbean Writers. 1986. pp. 46-
    57.

BRATHWAITE, EDWARD KAMAU

"Edward Kamau Brathwaite," Mark A. McWatt in 50 Caribbean Writers. 1986.
    pp. 58-70.

BRAXTON, ANTHONY - BIBLIOGRAPHY

"Braxton, Anthony" in Black Music in America. 1981. pp. 104-110.

BRAXTON, JOANNE M.

"Joanne M. Braxton," Edward T. Washington in Afro-American Writers After
    1955: Dramatists and Prose Writers. 1985. pp. 42-47.

BRAZIL

"Brazil" in Sex and Race. 1944. pp. 30-56.

BRAZIL - BIBLIOGRAPHY

Afro-Braziliana: A Working Bibliography. 1978. 294 p.

"Brazil" in The Education of Poor and Minority Children. pp. 1088-1092.

"Brazil" in Race and Ethnic Relations. 1980. pp. 223-243.

BRAZIL - HISTORY - BIBLIOGRAPHY

"History" in Afro-Braziliana. 1978. pp. 21-52.

BRAZIL - MUSIC - BIBLIOGRAPHY

"Brazil" in Bibliography of Black Music. 1981. V. 3, p. 171-181.

"Music, Dance and Carnival" in Afro-Braziliana. 1978. pp. 107-119.

BRAZIL - RELIGION - BIBLIOGRAPHY

"Brazil" in Howard University Bibliography of Afro-American and African
     Religious Studies. 1977. pp. 252-256.

BRAZIL - SLAVERY

"Afro-American Slave Cultue: Commentary One," Mary Karasch in Roots and
     Branches. 1979. pp. 138-141.

"Latin America's Bondmen: The Growth of Brazil's Negro Population" in
     From Slavery to Freedom. 1980. p. 71.

BRAZIL - SLAVERY - BIBLIOGRAPHY

"Brazil" in Slavery: A Worldwide Bibliography. 1985. pp. 145-169.

BROADCAST EXECUTIVES

"Prominent Black Publishers and Broadcast Executives" in The Negro
     Almanac. 1983. pp. 1218-1222.

BROADCAST GROUPS - DIRECTORY

"Broadcast Groups" in Black Resource Guide. 1986. p. 99.

BROADCASTING

"The Black Press and Broadcast Media" in The Negro Almanac. 1983. pp.
     1211-1249.

BROADCASTING - BIBLIOGRAPHY

"Broadcasting" in Black Media in America. 1984. pp. 62-66 and pp. 99-
     123.

BRODBER, ERNA

"Erna Brodber," Evelyn O'Callaghan in 50 Caribbean Writers. 1986. pp.
     71-82.

BRONC BUSTERS - BIOGRAPHY - INDEX

"Bronc Busters, Cowhands, Ropers" in In Black and White. 1980. See
     index, V. 2, p. 1122.

BROOKS, GWENDOLYN - BIBLIOGRAPHY

"Black Poetry: Gwendolyn Brooks" in Blacks in America; Bibliographical
     Essays. 1971. p. 249.

BROONZY, BIG BILL - BIBLIOGRAPHY

"Broonzy, Big Bill" in Black Music in America. 1981. pp. 110-113.

BROWN, CECIL

"Cecil Brown," Jean M. Bright in Afro-American Fiction Writers After
    1955. 1984. pp. 32-35.

BROWN, OSCAR - BIBLIOGRAPHY

"Brown, Oscar Cicero, Jr." in Black Music in America. 1981. pp. 114-
    116.

BROWN, STERLING - BIBLIOGRAPHY

"Brown, Sterling" in The Harlem Renaissance. 1982. pp. 62-64.

BROWN, WILLIAM WELLS

"William Wells Brown," Gregory Candela in Afro-American Writers Before
    the Harlem Renaissance. 1986. pp. 18-31.

BULLINS, ED

"Ed Bullins," Leslie Sanders in Afro-American Writers After 1955:
    Dramatists and Prose Writers. 1985. pp. 43-61.

BULLINS, ED - BIBLIOGRAPHY

"Black Dramatists: Ed Bullins" in Blacks in America; Bibliographical
    Essays. 1971. p. 282.

BUMBRY, GRACE - BIBLIOGRAPHY

"Bumbry, Grace" in Black Music in America. 1981. pp. 116-124.

BURROUGHS, MARGARET T.G.

"Margaret T.G. Burroughs," Mary Jane Dickerson in Afro-American Poets
    Since 1955. 1985. pp. 47-54.

BURT, GLORIA - BIBLIOGRAPHY

"Burt, Gloria" in Black Music in America. 1981. p. 124.

BURUNDI - MUSIC - BIBLIOGRAPHY

"Burundi" in Bibliography of Black Music. 1981. V. 3, p. 62.

BUSINESS

"Black Capitalism" in The Negro Almanac. 1983. pp. 551-579.

"Black Capitalism: Entrepreneurs, Consumers, and the Historical
    Evolution of the Black Market" in How Capitalism Underdeveloped
    Black America. 1983. pp. 133-167.

"Black Firsts: Business and Inventions" in Before the Mayflower. 1982.
    pp. 641-642.

"Economics and Business" in The Ebony Handbook. 1974. pp. 237-262.

BUSINESS - BIBLIOGRAPHY

"Business" in The Progress of Afro-American Women. 1980. pp. 81-84.

"The Black Entrepreneur" in A Comprehensive Bibliography. 1976. pp. 166-168.

"Economics, Employment, and Business" in Afro-American Reference. 1985. pp. 68-71.

"The Negro in Business" in A Bibliography of the Negro. 1928. pp. 491-493.

BUSINESS - CARIBBEAN - BIBLIOGRAPHY

"Industry, Business and Investments" in The Complete Caribbeana. V. 3, pp. 1509-1528.

BUSINESS - DIRECTORY

"Businesses" in Black Resource Guide. 1986. pp. 25-31.

BUSINESS - HAITI - BIBLIOGRAPHY

"Industry, Business and Investments" in The Complete Haitiana. 1982. pp. 1319-1339.

BUSINESS - HISTORY - BIBLIOGRAPHY

"Black Capitalism in the Age of Booker T. Washington" in Blacks in America; Bibliographical Essays. 1971. pp. 159-162.

BUSINESS - STATISTICS

"Business" in Facts About Blacks. 1986. pp. 18-26.

BUSINESS, JEWISH - BIBLIOGRAPHY

"Jews as Merchants in the Black Community" in Black-Jewish Relations. 1984. pp. 19-20.

BUSINESS ASSOCIATIONS - DIRECTORY

"Business Associations" in Black Resource Guide. 1986. pp. 32-35.

BUSINESS DEVELOPMENT CENTERS - DIRECTORY

"Business Development Centers" in Black Resource Guide. 1986. pp. 36-43.

BUSINESS FOUNDERS AND OWNERS - BIOGRAPHY - INDEX

"Business Founders, Owners" in In Black and White. 1980. See index, V. 2, pp. 1122-1126.

BUSINESS OFFICIALS - BIOGRAPHY - INDEX

"Business Officials" in In Black and White. 1980. See index, V. 2, pp. 1126-1127.

BUSING

"Desegregation by Forced Busing: Implications for Black Educational Development," Edward J. Hayes and Joan Franks in Beyond Identity. 1978. pp. 41-50.

BUSING - BIBLIOGRAPHY

"Busing" in The Education of Poor and Minority Children. 1981. pp. 980-984.

BUTLER, JERRY - BIBLIOGRAPHY

"Butler, Jerry" in Black Music in America. 1981. pp. 124-125.

BUTLER, OCTAVIA E.

"Octavia Butler," Margaret Anne O'Connor in Afro-American Fiction Writers After 1955. 1984. pp. 35-41.

CABINETMAKING - BIBLIOGRAPHY

"Cabinetmaking" in 250 Years of Afro-American Art. 1981. pp. 327-328.

CABLE COMPANIES - DIRECTORY

"Black-Owned Cable Companies" in Black Resource Guide. 1986. p. 98.

CABLE TELEVISION - BIBLIOGRAPHY

"Cable Television" in Black Media in America. 1984. pp. 118-123.

CAICOS ISLANDS - BIBLIOGRAPHY

"Caicos Islands" in The Complete Caribbeana. 1977. See index, V. 3, p. 2160.

CAIN, GEORGE

"George Cain," Edith Blicksilver in Afro-American Fiction Writers After 1955. 1984. pp. 41-43.

CAJUNS, BLACK - BIBLIOGRAPHY

"Cajuns, Black" in Afro-American Folk Culture. 1978. See index, p. 760.

"Zydeco" in Afro-American Folk Culture. 1978. See index, p. 806.

CALDWELL, BEN

"Ben Caldwell," Robbie Jean Walker in Afro-American Writers After 1955: Dramatists and Prose Writers. 1985. pp. 61-66.

CALIFORNIA - BIBLIOGRAPHY

"Los Angeles and California" in Afro-American Reference. 1985. pp. 215-220.

CALIFORNIA - EDUCATION - BIBLIOGRAPHY

"California" in The Education of Poor and Minority Children. 1981. pp. 208-228.

CALIFORNIA - EDUCATION, HIGHER - BIBLIOGRAPHY

"Higher Education by State: California" in The Education of Poor and Minority Children. 1981. pp. 866-872.

CALIFORNIA - GENEALOGY - BIBLIOGRAPHY

"California" in Black Genesis. 1978. pp. 243-246.

CALIFORNIA - SLAVERY - BIBLIOGRAPHY

"California" in Black Slavery in the Americas. 1982. pp. 822-824.

CALLOWAY, CAB - BIBLIOGRAPHY

"Calloway, Cab" in Black Music in America. 1981. pp. 125-127.

CALYPSO - BIBLIOGRAPHY

"Calypso Music and Dance" in Afro-American Folk Culture. 1978. See index, p. 760.

CAMEROON - MUSIC - BIBLIOGRAPHY

"Cameroon" in Bibliography of Black Music. 1981. V. 3, pp. 63-64.

CAMPBELL, JAMES EDWIN

"James Edwin Campbell," Lorenzo Thomas in Afro-American Writers Before the Harlem Renaissance. 1986. pp. 32-36.

CAMPFIRE GIRLS - BIBLIOGRAPHY

"Campfire Girls" in The Progress of Afro-American Women. 1980. pp. 250-251.

CANADA

"Canada" in The Negro Almanac 1983. pp. 1465-1466.

"Canada" in Sex and Race. 1942. V. 2, pp. 364-365.

CANADA - BIBLIOGRAPHY

"The Afro-American in Canada" in Afro-American History, 1. 1974. pp. 79-82.

"The Afro-American in Canada" in Afro-American History, 2. 1981. pp. 56-58.

"Blacks in Canada" in <u>The Education of Poor and Minority Children</u>. 1981. pp. 1096-1100.

"Canada" in <u>The Complete Caribbeana</u>. 1977. See index, V. 4, p. 2160.

CANADA - ETHNIC GROUPS - BIBLIOGRAPHY

"Canada: General" in <u>The Education of Poor and Minority Children</u>. 1981. pp. 1118-1126.

CANADA - GENEALOGY - BIBLIOGRAPHY

"Canada" in <u>Black Genesis</u>. 1978. pp. 262-263.

CANADA - SLAVERY - BIBLIOGRAPHY

"Canada" in <u>Slavery: A Worldwide Bibliography</u>. 1985. pp. 118-119.

"French North America (Canada)" in <u>Slavery</u>. 1977. p. 10.

"The Fugitive Slave in Canada" in <u>A Bibliography of the Negro</u>. 1928. pp. 339-340.

"Slavery in Canada" in <u>Bibliography of the Negro</u>. 1928. p. 341.

"Slavery in Canada" in <u>Black Slavery in the Americas</u>. 1982. pp. 760-767.

CAPE VERDE ISLANDS

"The Cape Verdean Packet Trade" in <u>Black Men of the Sea</u>. 1978. pp. 91-104.

CAPE VERDE ISLANDS - LINGUISTICS - BIBLIOGRAPHY

"Cape Verde Islands" in <u>A Bibliography of Pidgin and Creole Languages</u>. 1975. pp. 83-88.

CAPITALISM

"Black Capitalism" in <u>The Negro Almanac</u>. 1983. pp. 551-579.

"Black Capitalism: Entrepreneurs, Consumers, and the Historical Evolution of the Black Market" in <u>How Capitalism Underdeveloped Black America</u>. 1983. pp. 133-167.

CAPITALISM - HISTORY

"Capitalism, Racism and Reform" in <u>Reluctant Reformers</u>. 1975. pp. 261-296.

"Inequality and the Burden of Capitalist Democracy: A Point of View on Black History" in <u>How Capitalism Underdeveloped Black America</u>. 1983. pp. 1-19.

CAPITALISM, JEWISH - BIBLIOGRAPHY

"Jews as Merchants in the Black Community" in <u>Black-Jewish Relations</u>.

1984. pp. 19-20.

CAREERS - BIBLIOGRAPHY

"Careers" in The Education of Poor and Minority Children. 1981. pp.
    735-746.

CAREERS - DIRECTORY

Directory of Career Resources for Minorities. 1980. 335 p.

Directory of Special Programs for Minority Group Members. 1980. 612 p.

CAREW, JAN

"Jan Carew," Kwame Dawes in 50 Caribbean Writers. 1986. pp. 96-107.

CARIBBEAN

"Blacks in the Western Hemisphere: The Caribbean" in The Negro Almanac.
    1983. pp. 1469-1488.

Latin American and Caribbean Contemporary Record

CARIBBEAN - BIBLIOGRAPHIES - BIBLIOGRAPHY

"Bibliographic and Archival Resources" in The Complete Caribbeana. 1977.
    V. 2, pp. 3-33.

CARIBBEAN - BIBLIOGRAPHY

The Complete Caribbeana, 1900-1975. 1977. 4 V.

"General Caribbean" in Race and Ethnic Relations. 1980. pp. 162-168.

"Latin America and the Caribbean" in Afro-American Reference 1985. pp.
    200-214.

"Other Caribbean" in Race and Ethnic Relations. 1980. pp. 193-195.

"Present Conditions of the Negro in the West Indies and Central America"
    in A Bibliography of the Negro. 1928. pp. 637-642.

"West Indies" in The Education of Poor and Minority Children. 1981. pp.
    1350-1356.

CARIBBEAN - BIOGRAPHY - DIRECTORY

Personalities Caribbean. 1983. 1027 p.

CARIBBEAN - BLACK POPULATION - BIBLIOGRAPHY

"Population Segments: Afro-Caribbean" in The Complete Caribbeana. 1977.
    V. 1, pp. 461-488.

CARIBBEAN - CHILD DEVELOPMENT - BIBLIOGRAPHY

Child Development in the Caribbean: An Annotated Bibliography. 1984. 184 p.

CARIBBEAN - DICTIONARY

"General Section" in French and Netherlands Artilles. 1978. pp. 1-32.

Race and Ethnic Relations. 1980.

CARIBBEAN - EDUCATION - BIBLIOGRAPHY

"West Indies" in The Education of Poor and Minority Children. 1981. pp. 1350-1356.

CARIBBEAN - GENEALOGY - BIBLIOGRAPHY

"West Indies" in Black Genesis. 1978. pp. 257-261.

CARIBBEAN - HISTORY

From Columbus to Castro. 1970. 576 p.

"Trouble in the Caribbean" in From Slavery to Freedom. 1980. pp. 100-103.

CARIBBEAN - HISTORY - BIBLIOGRAPHY

"Bibliographical Notes: Seasoning in the Islands" in From Slavery to Freedom. 1980. p. 515.

"Bibliography" in Historical Dictionary of the British Caribbean. 1975. pp. 251-266.

"General History and Biography" in The Complete Caribbeana. 1977. V. 1, pp. 169-306.

"Select Bibliography" in From Columbus to Castro. pp. 516-558.

CARIBBEAN - PERIODICAL INDEX

Carindex.

CARIBBEAN - RELIGION - BIBLIOGRAPHY

"Caribbean" in Howard University Bibliography of African and Afro-American Religious Studies. 1977. pp. 256-266.

CARIBBEAN - SLAVERY - BIBLIOGRAPHY

"Caribbean" in Slavery: A Worldwide Bibliography. 1985. pp. 171-208.

"Caribbean (Non-Spanish)" in Slavery. 1977, pp. 48-55.

"Nature and Extent of Slavery in the West Indies" in A Bibliography of the Negro. 1928. pp. 267-270.

"Slavery and Emancipation" in The Complete Caribbeana. 1977. V. 1, pp.

307-341.

"Slavery in the West Indies and South America" in Howard University Bibliography of African and Afro-American Religious Studies. 1977. pp. 117-118.

"Spanish America (Caribbean)" in Slavery. 1977. pp. 42-46.

CARIBBEAN (DUTCH SPEAKING)

"Blacks in the Western Hemisphere: Netherlands Antilles" in The Negro Almanac. 1983. p. 1482.

CARIBBEAN (DUTCH SPEAKING) - BIBLIOGRAPHY

"Bibliography - Netherlands Antilles" in French and Netherlands Antilles. 1978. pp. 158-162.

"Dutch Antilles (incl. Surinam)" in Race and Ethnic Relations. 1980. pp. 187-190.

"Netherlands Antilles" in The Complete Caribbeana. 1977. See index, V. 3, pp. 2179-2180.

"Netherlands Caribbean" in The Complete Caribbeana. 1977. See index, V. 4, p. 2180.

"Netherlands Leeward Islands" in The Complete Caribbeana. 1977. See index, V. 4, pp. 2180-2181.

"Netherlands Windward Islands" in The Complete Caribbeana. 1977. See index, V. 4, p. 2181.

CARIBBEAN (DUTCH SPEAKING) - DICTIONARY

"Netherlands Antilles" in French and Netherlands Antilles. 1978. pp. 97-147.

CARIBBEAN (DUTCH SPEAKING) - SLAVERY - BIBLIOGRAPHY

"Caribbean: Dutch" in Slavery: A Worldwide Bibliography. 1985. pp. 204-207.

CARIBBEAN (ENGLISH SPEAKING) - BIBLIOGRAPHY

"Bibliography" in Historical Dictionary of the British Caribbean. 1975. pp. 251-266.

"British Caribbean" in The Complete Caribbeana. 1977. See index, V. 3, pp. 2156-2159.

"Caribbean: English" in Slavery: A Worldwide Bibliography. 1985. pp. 173-185.

"Other British West Indies," in Race and Ethnic Relations. 1980. pp. 183-187.

CARIBBEAN (ENGLISH SPEAKING) - DICTIONARY

Historical Dictionary of the British Caribbean. 1975. 266 p.

CARIBBEAN (ENGLISH SPEAKING) - HISTORY

"The British West Indies After Emancipation" in Sex and Race. 1942. V.
    2, pp. 138-144.

CARIBBEAN (FRENCH SPEAKING) - BIBLIOGRAPHY

"Bibliography - French Antilles" in French and Netherlands Antilles.
    1978. pp. 152-157.

"French Antilles" in The Complete Caribbeana. 1977. See index, pp.
    2162-2163.

"French Antilles (incl. Haiti)" in Race and Ethnic Relations. 1980. pp.
    190-193.

"French Caribbean" in The Complete Caribbeana. 1977. See index, V. 4, p.
    2163.

CARIBBEAN (FRENCH SPEAKING) - DICTIONARY

"French Antilles" in French and Netherlands Antilles. 1978. pp. 33-96.

CARIBBEAN (FRENCH SPEAKING) - SLAVERY - BIBLIOGRAPHY

"French" in Slavery: A Worldwide Bibliography. 1985. pp. 194-204.

CARIBBEAN (SPANISH SPEAKING) - SLAVERY - BIBLIOGRAPHY

"Caribbean: Spanish" in Slavery: A Worldwide Bibliography. 1985. pp.
    185-193.

CARIBBEAN EMBASSIES - DIRECTORY

"Caribbean Embassies" in Black Resource Guide. 1986. pp. 77-78.

CARIBBEAN REGION - BIBLIOGRAPHY

"Intraregional Issues" in The Complete Caribbeana. V. 2, pp. 1281-1308.

CARIBBEAN STUDIES - LIBRARY COLLECTIONS

"Library Resources on Caribbean Peoples," Alma Jordan in Ethnic
    Collections. 1983. pp. 202-229.

CARIBBEAN SUPPORT ORGANIZATIONS - DIRECTORY

"Support Organizations" in Black Resource Guide. 1986. p. 79.

CARIBS, BLACK - BIBLIOGRAPHY

"Black Caribs" in Afro-American Folk Culture. 1978. See index, p. 758.

"Population Segments: Amerindian and Black Carib" in The Complete
    Caribbeana. 1977. V. 1, pp. 509-543.

CARNIVAL - BIBLIOGRAPHY

"Carnival" in Afro-American Folk Culture. 1978. See index, p. 761.

CARRIACOU - BIBLIOGRAPHY

"Carriacou" in The Complete Caribbeana. 1977. See index, V. 4, p. 2160.

CARRINGTON, TERRI LYNNE - BIBLIOGRAPHY

"Carrington, Terri Lynne" in Black Music in America. 1981. p. 127.

CARROLL, DIAHANN - BIBLIOGRAPHY

"Carroll, Diahann" in Black Music in America. 1981. pp. 128-131.

CARTER, MARTIN WYLDE

"Martin Wylde Carter," Lloyd A. Brown in 50 Caribbean Writers. 1986. pp.
    108-114.

CARTHAGE

"Negroes in Ancient Rome and Carthage" in Sex and Race. 1944. V. 1, pp.
    86-90.

CARTOONISTS - BIOGRAPHY - INDEX

"Artists: Cartoon" in In Black and White. 1980. See index, V. 2, p.
    1114.

CATHOLIC CHURCH - CIVIL RIGHTS MOVEMENT - BIBLIOGRAPHY

"The Church, Synagogue and Integration: Roman Catholic" in Howard
    University Bibliography of African and Afro-American Religious
    Studies. 1977. pp. 320-323.

CATHOLIC CHURCH - RACE RELATIONS - BIBLIOGRAPHY

"Roman Catholic" in Howard University Bibliography of African and Afro-
    American Religious Studies. 1977. pp. 285-290.

CATHOLIC CHURCH - SLAVERY - BIBLIOGRAPHY

"Slavery, Negroes and the Church: Roman Catholic" in Howard University
    Bibliography of African and Afro-American Religious Studies. 1977.
    pp. 144-145.

CAYMAN ISLANDS

"Blacks in the Western Hemisphere: Cayman Islands (Grand Cayman, Little
    Cayman, Cayman Brac" in The Negro Almanac. 1983. p. 1483.

CAYMAN ISLANDS - BIBLIOGRAPHY

"Cayman Islands" in The Complete Caribbeana. 1977. See index, V. 4, p. 2160.

CELLISTS - BIOGRAPHY - INDEX

"Musicians: Instrumental: Cello" in In Black and White. 1980. See index, V. 2, p. 1185.

CENTRAL AMERICA - AUTHORS

Central American Writers. 1984. 149 p.

CENTRAL AMERICA - BIBLIOGRAPHY

"Central America" in Race and Ethnic Relations. 1980. pp. 203-206.

"Present Conditions of the Negro in the West Indies and Central America" in A Bibliography of the Negro. 1928. pp. 637-642.

CENTRAL AMERICA - LITERATURE - BIBLIOGRAPHY

Central American Writers. 1984. 149 p.

CENTRAL AMERICA - RELIGION - BIBLIOGRAPHY

"Religious Development of the Negro in Central and South America" in Howard University Bibliography of African and Afro-American Religious Studies. 1977. p. 252-268.

CENTRAL AMERICA - SLAVERY - BIBLIOGRAPHY

"Central America" in Slavery: A Worldwide Bibliography. 1985. pp. 130-132.

"Slavery in Central and South America" in Black Slavery in the Americas. 1982. pp. 539-606.

"Spanish America (Mainland)" in Slavery. 1977. pp.

CHAD - MUSIC - BIBLIOGRAPHY

"Chad" in Bibliography of Black Music. 1981. V. 3, p. 65.

CHARLES, RAY - BIBLIOGRAPHY

"Charles, Ray" in Black Music in America. 1981. pp. 131-142.

CHEMISTS - BIOGRAPHY - INDEX

"Chemists" in In Black and White. 1980. See index, V. 2, p. 1127.

CHESAPEAKE AREA - SLAVERY - BIBLIOGRAPHY

"Chesapeake" in Slavery: A Worldwide Bibliography. pp. 80-89.

CHESNUTT, CHARLES WADDELL - BIBLIOGRAPHY

"Charles Waddell Chesnutt," William L. Andrews in <u>Afro-American Writers Before the Harlem Renaissance</u>. 1986. pp. 36-51.

"Black Fiction at the Turn of the Century: Charles Waddell Chesnutt and Paul Laurence Dunbar" in <u>Blacks in America; Bibliographical Essays</u>. 1971. pp. 174-175.

<u>CHI ETA PHI SORORITY - BIBLIOGRAPHY</u>

"Chi Eta Phi Sorority" in <u>The Progress of Afro-American Women</u>. 1980. p. 251.

<u>CHICAGO - EDUCATION - BIBLIOGRAPHY</u>

"Chicago" in <u>The Education of Poor and Minority Children</u>. 1981. pp. 260-273.

<u>CHICANO STUDIES - LIBRARY COLLECTIONS</u>

"Chicano Collections of Library Resources" Joseph B. Olvera, Evelyn Escatiola, Benjamin Ocon and Albert Tovas in <u>Ethnic Collections</u>. 1983. pp. 75-100.

<u>CHILD DEVELOPMENT - BIBLIOGRAPHY</u>

<u>Black Child Development in America</u>. 1979. 470 p.

<u>Research in Black Child Development</u>. 1982. 737 p.

<u>CHILD DEVELOPMENT - CARIBBEAN - BIBLIOGRAPHY</u>

<u>Child Development in the Caribbean</u>. 1984. 184 p.

<u>CHILD PRODIGIES - BIOGRAPHY - INDEX</u>

"Child Prodigies" in <u>In Black and White</u>. 1980. See index, V. 2, pp. 1127-1128.

<u>CHILD REARING - BIBLIOGRAPHY</u>

"Child Rearing and Motherhood" in <u>The Progress of Afro-American Women</u>. 1980. pp. 138-144.

<u>CHILDREN</u>

"Black Father and Child Interactions," John L. McAdoo in <u>Black Men</u>. 1981. pp. 115-130.

"Living Arrangements of Children" in <u>The Negro Almanac</u>. 1983. pp. 477-478.

"Moms, Dads, and Boys: Race and Sex Differences in the Socialization of Male Children," Walter R. Allen in <u>Black Men</u>. 1981. pp. 99-114.

<u>CHILDREN - BIBLIOGRAPHIES - BIBLIOGRAPHY</u>

"Children: Bibliographies" in <u>The Education of Poor and Minority</u>

<u>Children</u>. 1981. pp. 171-174.

CHILDREN - BIBLIOGRAPHY

<u>Black Children and Their Families</u>. 1976. 103 p.

"Black Family and Children" in <u>The Black Family in the United States</u>.
    1986. pp. 73-74, 103-109 and 177-184.

"Children and Youths" in <u>Afro-American Reference</u>. 1985. p. 174.

"Children" in <u>Afro-American Folk Culture</u>. 1978. See index, p. 761.

"Children: General" in <u>The Education of Poor and Minority Children</u>.
    1981. pp. 93-171.

CHILDREN - BIOLOGY - BIBLIOGRAPHY

"Children: Biological Factors" in <u>The Education of Poor and Minority
    Children</u>. 1981. pp. 29-36.

CHILDREN - EDUCATION

"Schooling and Black Children's Images of the Future" in <u>Beyond
    Identity</u>. 1978. pp. 13-25.

CHILDREN - HAITI - BIBLIOGRAPHY

"Population Categories: Afro-Haitian Men, Women and Children" in <u>The
    Complete Haitiana</u>. 1982. pp. 561-575.

CHILDREN - LANGUAGE SOCIALIZATION

"Television's Impact on Black Children's Language: An Exploration,"
    Molefi Kete Asante in <u>Contemporary Black Thought</u>. 1980. pp. 181-
    194.

CHILDREN, ADOPTED - BIOGRAPHY - INDEX

"Adopted Children" in <u>In Black and White</u>. 1980. See index, V. 2, p.
    1110.

CHILDREN'S LITERATURE - BIBLIOGRAPHY

"Literature for Children and Youths" in <u>Afro-American Reference</u>. 1985.
    pp. 148-149.

"A Selected Bibliography: Juvenile" in <u>The Negro Almanac</u>. 1983. pp.
    1505-1507.

CHILDRESS, ALICE

"Alice Childress," Trudier Harris in <u>Afro-American Writers After 1955:
    Dramatists and Prose Writers</u>. 1985. pp. 66-79.

CHILE

"The Black Experience in Chile," William F. Sater. <u>Slavery and Race Relations in Latin America</u>. 1974. pp. 13-50.

"Uruguay, Argentina, Paraguay, Chile" in <u>Sex and Race</u>. 1944. pp. 57-65.

CHILE - BIBLIOGRAPHY

"Chile" in <u>The Education of Poor and Minority Children</u>. 1981. p. 1126.

"Chile" in <u>Race and Ethnic Relations</u>. 1980. pp. 209-210.

CHILE - MUSIC - BIBLIOGRAPHY

"Chile" in <u>Bibliography of Black Music</u>. 1981. V. 3, p. 181.

CHILE - SLAVERY - BIBLIOGRAPHY

"Chile" in <u>Slavery: A Worldwide Bibliography</u>. 1985. p. 139.

CHINA

"Who Were the First Chinese?" in <u>Sex and Race</u>. 1944. V. 1, pp. 67-68.

CHINESE AMERICANS - EDUCATION - BIBLIOGRAPHY

"Chinese Americans" in <u>The Education of Poor and Minority Children</u>. 1981. pp. 579-588.

CHIROPODISTS - BIOGRAPHY - INDEX

"Chiropodists" in <u>In Black and White</u>. 1980. See index, V. 2, p. 1128.

CHORAL MUSIC - BIBLIOGRAPHY

<u>Choral Music by Afro-American Composers</u>. 1981. 167 p.

CHORAL MUSIC - DISCOGRAPHY

"Selected Bibliography" in <u>Choral Music by Afro-American Composers</u>. 1981. pp.146-163.

CHOREOGRAPHERS - DIRECTORIES

<u>Directory of Blacks in the Performing Arts</u>. 1978. 428 p.

CHRONOLOGY

<u>Black Chronology: From 4000 B.C. to the Abolition of the Slave Trade</u>. 1983. 312 p.

"Chronology: A Historical Review" in <u>The Negro Almanac</u>. 1983. pp. 1-93.

"Chronology of Events - 1984" in <u>The State of Black America, 1985</u>. pp. 191-223.

"Chronology of Events - 1985" in <u>The State of Black America, 1986</u>. pp. 183-212.

"Historical Record: Chronology of Contemporary Events, 1954-1973" in The Ebony Handbook. 1974. pp. 88-121.

CHURCH

"The Ambiguous Politics of the Black Church" in How Capitalism Underdeveloped Black America. 1983. pp. 195-214.

"Church Participation in a Community of Black Immigrants: A Social Space Analysis," Bobby M. Wilson in Contemporary Black Thought. 1980. pp. 195-280.

"Family and Church: Enduring Institutions" in Long Memory. 1982. pp. 70-113.

CHURCH - BIBLIOGRAPHY

"Bibliography: Family and Church: Enduring Institutions" in Long Memory. 1982. pp. 429-432.

"Black Family and the Black Church" in The Black Family in the United States. 1986. pp. 129-130.

"Church" in The Study and Analysis of Black Politics. 1973. pp. 22-24.

CHURCH - CIVIL RIGHTS - BIBLIOGRAPHY

"The Church and the Civil Rights Movement" in Blacks in America; Bibliographical Essays. 1971. pp. 325-331.

"The First Negro Churches" in A Bibliography of the Negro. 1928. p. 405.

CHURCH - EDUCATION - BIBLIOGRAPHY

"Church" in The Education of Poor and Minority Children. 1981. pp. 827-834.

CHURCH - HISTORY - BIBLIOGRAPHY

"The Antebellum Black Church" in Blacks in America; Bibliographical Essays. 1971. pp. 81-86.

"The Black Church, 1865-1915" in Blacks in America; Bibliographical Essays. 1971. pp. 153-157.

"The Black Church in an Era of Urbanization" in Blacks in America; Bibliographical Essays. 1971. pp. 205-209.

CHURCH OF THE BRETHREN - CIVIL RIGHTS MOVEMENT - BIBLIOGRAPHY

"The Church, Synagogue and Integration: Church of the Brethren" in Howard University Bibliography of African and Afro-American Religious Studies. 1977. p. 315.

CITIES - BIBLIOGRAPHY

"Negro Communities" in A Bibliography of the Negro. 1928. pp. 488-489.

CITIES - HISTORY

"Urban Problems" in From Slavery to Freedom. 1980. pp. 308-313.

CITY FOUNDERS - BIOGRAPHY - INDEX

"Settlers, Founders of Cities, Colonizers" in In Black and White. 1980.
See index, V. 2, p. 1233.

CITY GOVERNMENT OFFICIALS - BIOGRAPHY - INDEX

"City, County Government Officials" in In Black and White. 1980. See
index, V. 2, pp. 1128-1130.

CIVIL RIGHTS

"Beyond Civil Rights," Glenn C. Lowry in The State of Black America,
1986. pp. 163-174.

"Ceremonies in Civil Rights: A Thirty-Year Retrospective on the Law and
Race," Derrick Bell in The State of Black America, 1984. pp. 119-
141.

CIVIL RIGHTS - BIBLIOGRAPHY

"Civil Rights and Legal Status" in Afro-American Reference. 1985. pp.
63-66.

"Discussions Relating to Negroes and Civil Rights" in A Bibliography of
the Negro. 1928. pp. 533-536.

CIVIL RIGHTS AGENCIES

"State and Federal Agencies with Civil Rights Responsibilities" in The
Negro Almanac. 1983. pp. 298-300.

CIVIL RIGHTS MOVEMENT

"Civil Rights Organizations and Black Power Advocates Past and Present"
in The Negro Almanac. 1983. pp. 223-300.

"The Civil Rights Revolution, 1945-1960: The Gods Brings Threads to Web
Begun," William H. Chafe in Reshaping America. 1982. pp. 67-100.

"The Time of the Whale" in Before the Mayflower. 1982. pp. 386-440.

CIVIL RIGHTS MOVEMENT - BIBLIOGRAPHY

"The Church and the Civil Rights Movement" in Blacks in America;
Bibliographical Essays. 1971. pp. 325-331.

"The Civil Rights Movement" in Blacks in America; Bibliographical
Essays. 1971. pp. 314-325.

"The Civil Rights Movement" in A Comprehensive Bibliography. 1976. pp.

66-83.

"The Civil Rights Movement, 1955-1964" in Black Rhetoric. 1966. pp. 102-104.

"The Civil Rights Movement, 1954-1967" in Howard University Bibliography of African and Afro-American Religious Studies. 1977. pp. 315-343.

"Congress, the Executive and Civil Rights" in Blacks in America; Bibliographical Essays. 1971. pp. 303-310.

"Racial Conflict and the Civil Rights Movement" in Afro-American History, 1. 1974. pp. 496-560.

"Racial Conflict and the Civil Rights Movement" in Afro-American History, 2. 1981. pp. 173-187.

CIVIL RIGHTS ORGANIZATIONS

"Civil Rights Organizations" in The Negro Almanac. 1983. pp. 247-261.

CIVIL RIGHTS ORGANIZATIONS - DIRECTORIES

"Civil Rights Organizations" in Black Resource Guide. 1986. pp. 52-53.

The National Civil Rights Directory. 1979. 183 p.

"National Private Organizations with Civil Rights Programs" in The Negro Almanac. 1983. pp. 295-298.

CIVIL RIGHTS ORGANIZATIONS - JEWISH PARTICIPATION - BIBLIOGRAPHY

"Jews in Civil Rights Organizations" in Black-Jewish Relations. 1984. pp. 27-33.

CIVIL WAR

"Civil War" in From Slavery to Freedom. 1980. pp. 205-226.

"The Jubilee War: Witnesses and Warriors" in Before the Mayflower. 1982. pp. 187-215.

CIVIL WAR - BIBLIOGRAPHY

"The Abortive Revolution of Equality: The Civil War and Reconstruction" in Blacks in America; Bibliographical Essays. 1971. pp. 111-113.

"Bibliographical Notes: Civil War" in From Slavery to Freedom. 1980. pp. 527-528.

"Civil War" in Black Rhetoric. 1976. pp. 78-79.

"Civil War and Emancipation" in Afro-American History, 1. 1974. pp. 279-325.

"Civil War and Emancipation" in Afro-American History, 2. 1981. pp. 116-124.

"Civil War and Emancipation of the Negro" in A Bibliography of the Negro. 1928. pp. 365-369.

"Slavery and the Civil War" in Black Slavery in the Americas. 1982. pp. 1507-1568.

CIVIL WAR - BIOGRAPHY - INDEX

"Military Service: Civil War" in In Black and White. 1980. See index, V. 2, pp. 1175-1176.

CIVIL WAR - CONFEDERACY - BIBLIOGRAPHY

"Blacks in the Confederacy" in Blacks in America; Bibliographical Essays. 1971. pp. 113-115.

CIVIL WAR - JEWISH PARTICIPATION - BIBLIOGRAPHY

"Jews in the American Civil War" in Black-Jewish Relations. 1984. pp. 25-27 and 90-91.

CIVIL WAR - UNION ARMY - BIBLIOGRAPHY

"Black Soldiers in the Union Army" in Blacks in America; Bibliographical Essays. 1971. pp. 115-116.

CIVILIZATION - AFRICAN INFLUENCES

"Africa's Relevance to Modern Civilization: Past Influences and Future Trends" Ali A. Mazrui in The Negro Impact on Western Civilization. 1970. pp. 467-488.

CLARKE, AUSTIN

"Austin Clarke," Daryl Cumber Dance in 50 Caribbean Writers. 1986. pp. 115-121.

CLASSICAL MUSIC - BIBLIOGRAPHY

"Blacks in Opera and Symphonic Music" in Blacks in America; Bibliographical Essays. 1971. pp. 290-293.

"Negro Composers of Classicial Music and Examples of Spirituals Classically Arranged by Both White and Negro Authors" in A Bibliography of the Negro. 1928. pp. 440-441.

CLASSICAL MUSIC - DISCOGRAPHIES - BIBLIOGRAPHY

"Discographies: Concert Music and Opera" in Bibliography of Black Music. 1981. V. 1, p. 29.

CLASSICAL MUSICIANS

"Black Classical Musicians" in The Negro Almanac. 1983. pp. 1127-1147.

CLEAVER, ELDRIDGE - BIBLIOGRAPHY

"Eldridge Cleaver's Opinion of Jews" in <u>Black-Jewish Relations</u>. 1984. p. 89.

CLERGY - BIOGRAPHY

<u>Biographical Sketches of our Pulpit</u>. 1888. 216 p.

<u>Black Apostles at Home and Abroad</u>. 1982. 321 p.

CLERGY - BIOGRAPHY - INDEX

"Clergy" in <u>In Black and White</u>. 1980. See index, V. 2, pp. 1130-1132.

CLERKS - BIOGRAPHY - INDEX

"Clerks" in <u>In Black and White</u>. 1980. See index, V. 2, p. 1132.

CLIFTON, LUCILLE

"Lucille Clifton," Wallace R. Peppers in <u>Afro-American Poets Since 1955</u>. 1985. pp. 55-60.

CLOTHING - SLAVERY - BIBLIOGRAPHY

"Slave Clothing" in <u>Black Slavery in the Americas</u>. 1982. pp. 1159-1161.

CLUBS - BIBLIOGRAPHY

"Clubs, Associations and Societies" in <u>Afro-American Folk Culture</u>. 1978. See index, p. 764.

COALITIONS - BIBLIOGRAPHY

"A New Black Coalition," Joseph L. Amprey Jr. in <u>Black Scholars on Higher Education</u>. 1974. pp. 335-352.

COAST GUARD - BIOGRAPHY - INDEX

"Military Service: Coast Guard" in <u>In Black and White</u>. 1980. See index, V. 2, p. 1176.

COBB, ARNETT CLEOPHUS - BIBLIOGRAPHY

"Cobb, Arnett Cleophus" in <u>Black Music in America</u>. 1981. p. 142.

COBB, CHARLES E.

"Charles E. Cobb, Jr.," Clara R. Williams in <u>Afro-American Writers Since 1955, Dramatists and Prose Writers</u>. 1985. pp. 60-64.

CODES, WRITING - BIBLIOGRAPHY

"Writing, Secret Systems" in <u>Afro-American Folk Culture</u>. 1978. See index, p. 806.

COLE, NAT KING - BIBLIOGRAPHY

"Cole, Nat King" in <u>Black Music in America</u>. 1981. pp. 142-156.

COLEMAN, ORNETTE - BIBLIOGRAPHY

"Coleman, Ornette" <u>Black Music in America</u>. 1981. pp. 156-168.

COLERIDGE-TAYLOR, SAMUEL - BIBLIOGRAPHY

"Coleridge-Taylor, Samuel" in <u>Black Music in America</u>. 1981. pp. 168-169.

COLLEGE AND UNIVERSITY PRESIDENTS - BIOGRAPHY - INDEX

"College, University, Seminary Presidents" in <u>In Black and White</u>. 1980. See index, V. 2, pp. 1132-1133.

COLLYMORE, FRANK

"Frank Collymore," Edward Baugh in <u>50 Caribbean Writers</u>. 1986. pp. 122-132.

COLOMBIA

"Peru, Ecuador, Colombia, Panama" in <u>Sex and Race</u>. V. 2, pp. 66-71.

COLOMBIA - BIBLIOGRAPHY

"Colombia" in <u>The Education of Poor and Minority Children</u>. 1981. pp. 1133-1134.

"Colombia" in <u>Race and Ethnic Relations</u>. 1980. pp. 210-213.

COLOMBIA - HISTORY

"Manumission, Libres and Black Resistance: The Colombian Choco, 1680-1810," William F. Sharp in <u>Slavery and Race Relations in Latin America</u>. 1974. pp. 89-111.

COLOMBIA - MUSIC - BIBLIOGRAPHY

"Colombia" in <u>Bibliography of Black Music</u>. 1981. V. 3, pp. 182-183.

COLOMBIA - SLAVERY - BIBLIOGRAPHY

"Colombia" in <u>Slavery: A Worldwide Bibliography</u>. 1985. pp. 133-136.

COLONIAL PERIOD

"Blacks in Colonial and Revolutionary America" in <u>The Negro Almanac</u>. 1983. pp. 789-826.

COLONIAL PERIOD - BIBLIOGRAPHY

"The Black Experience in Colonial America" in <u>Afro-American History, 1</u>. pp. 83-102. 1974.

"The Black Experience in Colonial America" in <u>Afro-American History, 2</u>.

1981. pp. 59-68. 1981.

COLONIALISM - HISTORY

"Capitalism, Racism and Reform" in Reluctant Reformers. 1975. pp. 261-296.

COLONIZATION - AFRICA - BIBLIOGRAPHY

"European Governments and African Colonization" in A Bibliography of the Negro. 1928. pp. 125-165.

COLONIZATION MOVEMENTS - BIBLIOGRAPHY

"Colonization" in A Bibliography of the Negro. 1928. pp. 358-364.

"Colonization as a Proposed Solution to the Race Problem" in Blacks in America; Bibliographical Essays. 1971. p. 88-89.

COLORADO - EDUCATION - BIBLIOGRAPHY

"Colorado" in The Education of Poor and Minority Children. 1981. pp. 228-230.

COLORADO - EDUCATION, HIGHER - BIBLIOGRAPHY

"Colorado" in The Education of Poor and Minority Children. 1981. p. 873.

COLORADO - SLAVERY - BIBLIOGRAPHY

"Colorado" in Black Slavery in the Americas. 1982. p. 824.

COLORED WOMEN'S CIVIC LEAGUE - BIBLIOGRAPHY

"Colored Women's Civic League" in The Progress of Afro-American Women. 1980. p. 251.

COLTER, CYRUS

"Cyrus Colter," Helen Houston in Afro-American Fiction Writers After 1955. 1984. pp. 48-52.

"Cyrus Colter" in Interviews with Black Writers. 1973. pp. 16-33.

COLTRANE, JOHN

"Coltrane, John William" in Black Music in America. 1981. pp. 169-181.

COMEDIANS - BIOGRAPHY

"Comedians" in In Black and White. 1980. See index, V. 2, p. 1133.

COMMUNICATION

"The Communication Person in Society," Molefi Kete Asante in Contemporary Black Thought. 1982. pp. 15-28.

"The Cultural Dimensions of the Right to Communicate," Njoku E. Awa in
   Contemporary Black Thought. 1980. pp. 80-92.

"Global Information and Communications: New Explorations," Abdulai S.
   Vandi in Contemporary Black Thought. 1980. pp. 29-42.

"Guilt - Provocation: A Strategy in Black Rhetoric," Dorothy Rennington
   in Contemporary Black Thought. 1980. pp. 29-42.

Handbook of Intercultural Communication. 1979. 469 p.

"International/Intercultural Relations," Molefi Kete Asante in
   Contemporary Black Thought. 1980. pp. 43-58.

COMMUNICATION - BIBLIOGRAPHY

Black Rhetoric. 1976. 376 p.

"Communications/Media Works" in Black Media in America. 1984. pp. 1-52.

"Communications/Public Relations" in Black Media in America. 1984. pp.
   66-68.

"Speaking, Ways of (Styles of Talk)" in Afro-American Folk Culture.
   1978. See index, p. 798.

COMMUNICATION - CARIBBEAN - BIBLIOGRAPHY

"Public Utilities and Communication" in The Complete Caribbeana. V. 3,
   pp. 1595-1610.

COMMUNICATION - EDUCATION - BIBLIOGRAPHY

"Communication in the Classroom" in Black Rhetoric. 1976. pp. 57-58.

COMMUNICATION - HAITI - BIBLIOGRAPHY

"Public Utilities and Communication" in The Complete Haitiana. 1982. pp.
   1387-1394.

COMMUNICATION, INTERRACIAL - BIBLIOGRAPHY

"Communication, Interracial" in Black Rhetoric. 1976. pp. 52-54.

COMMUNICATION, NONVERBAL - BIBLIOGRAPHY

"Communication, Nonverbal" in Black Rhetoric. 1976. pp. 58-59.

"Non-verbal Communication (Kinesics and Proxemics)" in Afro-American
   Folk Culture. 1978. See index, p. 784.

COMMUNISM

"Socialists, Communists and Self-Determination" in Reluctant Reformers.
   1975. pp. 217-259.

COMMUNISM - BIBLIOGRAPHY

"Blacks and Communism" in Blacks in America; Bibliographical Essays.
     1971. pp. 231-234.

COMMUNITY - BIBLIOGRAPHY

"Black Life-Styles in the Ghetto" in Blacks in America; Bibliographical
     Essays. 1971. pp. 396-404.

"Community" in The Education of Poor and Minority Children. 1981. pp.
     835-861.

"The Urban Situation" in A Comprehensive Bibliography. 1976. pp. 133-
     144.

COMMUNITY CONTROL OF EDUCATION - BIBLIOGRAPHY

"Parent Participation" in The Education of Poor and Minority Children.
     1981. pp. 843-848.

COMPENSATORY EDUCATION - BIBLIOGRAPHY

"Compensatory Education" in The Education of Poor and Minority Children.
     1981. pp. 692-706.

COMPOSERS - BIOGRAPHY

"Biographical Sketches" in Choral Music by Afro-American Composers.
     1981. pp. 131-141.

"Black Classical Musicians" in The Negro Almanac. 1983. pp. 1127-1147.

COMPOSERS - BIOGRAPHY - INDEX

"Musicians: Composers, Song Writers" in In Black and White. 1980. See
     index, V. 2, pp. 1181-1183.

COMPOSERS - DIRECTORIES

Directory of Blacks in the Performing Arts. 1978. 428 p.

COMPOSERS, FOLK - BIBLIOGRAPHY

"Musicians and Composers" in Afro-American Folk Culture. 1978. See
     index, p. 783.

COMPUTER EMPLOYEES AND OFFICIALS - BIOGRAPHY - INDEX

"Computer Related Careers" in In Black and White. 1980. See index, V. 2,
     p. 1133.

COMPUTER TECHNOLOGY EDUCATION

"Modern Technology and Urban Schools," Robert E. Fullilove, III in The
     State of Black America, 1985. pp. 37-64.

CONCERT MUSIC - BIBLIOGRAPHY

"Concert Music" in Bibliography of Black Music. 1983. V. 2, pp. 80-86.

"Discographies: Concert Music and Opera" in Bibliography of Black Music. 1981. V. 1, p. 29.

CONDUCTORS, MUSICAL - BIOGRAPHY

"Black Classical Musicians" in The Negro Almanac. 1983. pp. 1127-1147.

CONDUCTORS, MUSICAL - BIOGRAPHY - INDEX

"Musicians: Conductors, Choral Leaders" in In Black and White. 1980. See index, V. 2, p. 1183.

CONDUCTORS, MUSICAL - DIRECTORIES

Directory of Blacks in the Performing Arts. 1981. 428 p.

CONFESSIONS - LEGAL CASES

"Important Cases: Forced Confessions" in The Negro Almanac. 1983. pp. 310-311.

CONGO - MUSIC - BIBLIOGRAPHY

"Congo" in Bibliography of Black Music. 1981. V. 3, p. 66.

CONGREGATIONAL CHURCH - CIVIL RIGHTS MOVEMENT - BIBLIOGRAPHY

"The Church, Synagogue and Integration: Congregational (United Church of Christ)" in Howard University Bibliography of African and Afro-American Religious Studies. 1977. pp. 315-316.

CONGREGATIONAL CHURCH - RACE RELATIONS - BIBLIOGRAPHY

"Congregational (United Church of Christ)" in Howard University Bibliography of African and Afro-American Religious Studies. 1977. pp. 271-272.

CONGREGATIONAL CHURCH - SLAVERY - BIBLIOGRAPHY

"Slavery, Negroes and the Church: Congregational (United Church of Christ)" in Howard University Bibliography of African and Afro-American Religious Studies. 1977. pp. 129-132.

CONGRESS

"The Black Congress" in The Negro Almanac. 1983. pp. 364-365.

CONGRESS ON RACIAL EQUALITY

"Congress on Racial Equality" in The Negro Almanac. 1983. p. 255.

CONGRESS ON RACIAL EQUALITY - BIBLIOGRAPHY

"CORE's Opinion of Jews" in Black-Jewish Relations. 1984. p. 89.

CONGRESSIONAL BLACK CAUCUS

"The Congressional Black Caucus" in The Negro Almanac. 1983. pp. 361-363.

CONGRESSIONAL REPRESENTATIVES

"Biographies of Current Black Representatives" in The Negro Almanac. 1983. pp. 365-376.

CONGRESSIONAL REPRESENTATIVES - DIRECTORY

"Members of Congress" in Black Resource Guide. 1986. pp. 167-168.

CONGRESSIONAL REPRESENTATIVES - HISTORY

"Black Congressmen of the Past" in The Negro Almanac. 1983. pp. 382-394.

CONNECTICUT - EDUCATION - BIBLIOGRAPHY

"Connecticut" in The Education of Poor and Minority Children. 1981. pp. 230-233.

CONNECTICUT - EDUCATION, HIGHER - BIBLIOGRAPHY

"Higher Education by State: Connecticut" in The Education of Poor and Minority Children. 1081. pp. 873-874.

CONNECTICUT - GENEALOGY - BIBLIOGRAPHY

"Connecticut" in Black Genesis. 1978. pp. 150-154.

CONNECTICUT - SLAVERY - BIBLIOGRAPHY

"Connecticut" in Black Slavery in the Americas. 1982. pp. 772-774.

CONSTITUTIONAL HISTORY - BIBLIOGRAPHY

"Nullification of the Fifteenth Amendment: The Disenfranchisment Movement" in Blacks in America; Bibliographical Essays. 1971. pp. 135-137.

"Origins of Legal Equality: The Fourteenth and Fifteenth Amendments" in Blacks in America; Bibliographical Essays. 1971. pp. 123-125.

CONSTRUCTION WORKERS - BIOGRAPHY - INDEX

"Construction Workers, Laborers" in In Black and White. 1980. See index, V. 2, pp. 1133-1134.

CONSUMERS

"Black Capitalism: Entrepreneurs, Consumers, and the Historical
,   Evolution of the Black Market" in How Capitalism Underdeveloped Black America. 1983. pp. 133-167.

CONSUMERS - BIBLIOGRAPHY

"The Black Consumer" in <u>A Comprehensive Bibliography</u>. 1976. pp. 165-166.

"Black Consumers" in <u>The Economics of Minorities</u>. 1976. pp. 105-107.

"Consumerism" in <u>Black Media in America</u>. 1984. pp. 68-75.

"Marketing/Consumerism" in <u>Black Media in America</u>. 1984. pp. 135-161.

CONSUMERS - STATISTICS

"Consumerism" in <u>Facts About Blacks</u>. 1986. pp. 30-37.

CONTEST WINNERS - BIOGRAPHY - INDEX

"Contest Winners" in <u>In Black and White</u>. 180. See index, V. 2, p. 1134.

COOKING - BIBLIOGRAPHY

"Foods and Cooking" in <u>Afro-American Folk Culture</u>. 1978. See index, p. 774.

COOKING - BRAZIL - BIBLIOGRAPHY

"African Influence on Brazilian Cooking" in <u>Afro-Braziliana</u>, 1978. p. 79.

COOKING - CARIBBEAN - BIBLIOGRAPHY

"Food and Nutrition" in <u>The Complete Caribbeana</u>. V. 2, pp. 1001-1024.

COOKING - HAITI - BIBLIOGRAPHY

"Food and Nutrition" in <u>The Complete Haitiana</u>. V. 2, pp. 957-970.

COOKS - BIOGRAPHY - INDEX

"Culinary Artists" in <u>In Black and White</u>. 1980. See index, V. 2, p. 1135.

COOPERATIVES - HAITI - BIBLIOGRAPHY

"Cooperatives" in <u>The Complete Haitiana</u>. 1982. V. 2, pp. 1447-1452.

CORN ISLANDS

"Blacks in the Western Hemisphere: Corn Islands" in <u>The Negro Almanac</u>. 1983. p. 1485.

CORNET PLAYERS - BIOGRAPHY - INDEX

"Musicians: Instrumental: Cornet" in <u>In Black and White</u>. 1980. See index, V. 2, p. 1185.

CORNISH, SAM

"Sam Cornish," Jon Woodson in <u>Afro-American Poets Since 1955</u>. 1985. pp. 64-69.

CORPORATE BOARDS

"Blacks on Some Boards of Major Corporations" in <u>Facts About Blacks</u>.
    1980. pp. 11-14.

CORRECTIONAL INSTITUTIONAL OFFICERS - BIOGRAPHY - INDEX

"Protective Services: Correctional Institutions" in <u>In Black and White</u>.
    1980. See index, V. 2, p. 1224.

CORROTHERS, JAMES D.

"James D. Corrothers," Richard Yarborough in <u>Afro-American Writers</u>
    <u>Before the Harlem Renaissance</u>. 1986. pp. 52-62.

CORTEZ, JAYNE

"Jayne Cortez," Jon Woodson in <u>Afro-American Poets Since 1955</u>. 1985. pp.
    69-74.

COSMETICIANS - BIOGRAPHY - INDEX

"Cosmeticians" in <u>In Black and White</u>. 1980. See index, V. 2, p. 1159.

COSTA RICA - BIBLIOGRAPHY

"Costa Rica" in <u>The Complete Caribbeana</u>. 1977. See index, V. 4, p. 2160.

"Costa Rica" in <u>The Education of Poor and Minority Children</u>. 1981. p.
    1134.

COSTA RICA - MUSIC - BIBLIOGRAPHY

"Costa Rica" in <u>Bibliography of Black Music</u>. 1983. V. 3, p. 183.

COTTER, JOSEPH S., JR.

"Joseph Seamon Cotter, Jr.," James Robert Payne in <u>Afro-American Writers</u>
    <u>Before the Harlem Renaissance</u>. 1986. pp. 70-73.

COTTER, JOSEPH S., SR.

"Joseph Seamon Cotter, Sr.," A. Russell Brooks in <u>Afro-American Writers</u>
    <u>Before the Harlem Renaissance</u>. 1986. pp. 62-70.

COUNSELORS - BIBLIOGRAPHY

"Counselors" in <u>The Education of Poor and Minority Children</u>. 1981. pp.
    680-684.

"Guidance and Career Counseling" in <u>The Progress of Afro-American Women</u>.
    1980. p. 115.

COUNTY GOVERNMENT OFFICIALS - BIOGRAPHY - INDEX

"City, County Government Officials" in <u>In Black and White</u>. 1980. See
    index, V. 2, pp. 1128-1130.

COWHANDS - BIOGRAPHY - INDEX

"Bronc Busters, Cowhands, Ropers" in In Black and White. 1980. See
    index, V. 2, p. 1122.

CRAFT WORKERS - BIOGRAPHY - INDEX

"Craftsmen" in In Black and White. 1980. See index, V. 2, p. 1134.

CRAFTS - BIBLIOGRAPHY

"Crafts-Contemporary" in 250 Years of Afro-American Art. 1981. pp. 354-
    355.

CRAFTS - HISTORY

"The Manual Arts," Cedric Dover in The Other Slaves. 1978. pp. 221-225.

CRAFTS - HISTORY - BIBLIOGRAPHY

"Crafts-Traditional" in 250 Years of Afro-American Art. 1981. pp. 355-
    360.

CRAFTSMANSHIP - HISTORY

"Negro Craftsmanship in Early America," Leonard P. Stavisky in The Other
    Slaves. 1978. pp. 193-203.

"The Origins of Negro Craftsmanship in Colonial America," Leonard P.
    Stavisky in The Other Slaves. 1978. pp. 183-191.

"Negro Craftsmen and Artists of Pre-Civil War Days," James Porter in The
    Other Slaves. 1978. pp. 209-220.

CREOLE CASE - BIBLIOGRAPHY

"Noted Law Suits Relating to the Status of Slaves: Creole Case" in A
    Bibliography of the Negro. 1928. p. 344.

CREOLE LANGUAGES - BIBLIOGRAPHY

A Bibliography of Pidgin and Creole Languages. 1975. 804 p.

"Creole Studies" in The Complete Haitiana. 1982. V. 1, pp. 779-798.

CRIME

"Black Crime: A Reexamination of the Alcohol Recidivism Hypothesis,"
    Kenneth A. Johnson in Contemporary Black Thought. 1980. pp. 209-
    222.

"Race, Masculinity and Crime" in Black Masculinity. 1982. pp. 39-53.

"Victims of Crime" in The Negro Almanac. 1983. pp. 484-485.

CRIME - BIBLIOGRAPHY

"Crime and Delinquency" in The Progress of Afro-American Women. 1980.
    pp. 195-196.

"Crime and Delinquency Studies" in A Bibliography of the Negro. 1928. p.
    615.

"Criminology and Juvenile Delinquency" in Afro-American Reference. 1985.
    pp. 66-67.

"A General View of Crime as it Relates to the Negro" in A Bibliography
    of the Negro. 1928. pp. 543-546.

CRIMINAL JUSTICE

"American Archipelago: Blacks and Criminal Justice" in Long Memory.
    1982. pp. 227-260.

"Black Prisoners and Punishment in a Racist Capitalist State" in How
    Capitalism Underdeveloped Black America. 1983. pp. 105-130.

"Crime, Law Enforcement and Criminal Justice" in Ebony Handbook. 1974.
    pp. 225-235.

CRIMINAL JUSTICE - BIBLIOGRAPHY

"Bibliography: American Archipelago: Blacks and Criminal Justice" in
    Long Memory. 1982. pp. 441-445.

CRIMINAL REHABILITATION - BIBLIOGRAPHY

"Rehabilitation" in The Progress of Afro-American Women. 1980. pp. 203-
    205.

CRUZ, VICTOR HERNANDEZ

"Victor Hernandez Cruz," Pamela Masingale Lewis in Afro-American Poets
    Since 1955. 1985. pp. 74-84.

CUBA

"Blacks in the Western Hemisphere: Cuba" in The Negro Almanac. 1983. pp.
    1471-1473.

"Cuba, Puerto Rico, Surinam" in Sex and Race. 1942. V. 2, pp. 80-90.

"The Gradual Integration of the Black in Cuba: Under the Colony, the
    Republic, and the Revolution," Marianne Masferrer and Carmelo
    Mesa-Lago in Slavery and Race Relations in Latin America. 1974. pp.
    348-384.

CUBA - BIBLIOGRAPHY

"Cuba" in The Education of Poor and Minority Children. 1981. pp. 1134-
    1137.

"Cuba" in Race and Ethnic Relations. 1980. pp. 168-172.

CUBA - HISTORY

"Slavery, Race, and Social Structure in Cuba During the Nineteenth
    Century," Franklin W. Knight in Slavery and Race Relations in Latin
    America. 1974. pp. 204-227.

CUBA - MUSIC - BIBLIOGRAPHY

"Cuba" in Bibliography of Black Music. 1981. V. 3, p. 137-142.

CULLEN, COUNTEE - BIBLIOGRAPHY

"Black Poetry: Countee Cullen" in Blacks in America; Bibliographical
    Essays. 1971. pp. 246-247.

"Cullen, Countee" in The Harlem Renaissance. 1982. pp. 64-75.

CULT LEADERS - BIOGRAPHY - INDEX

"Cult Leaders" in In Black and White. 1980. See index, V. 2, p. 1135.

CULTS, RELIGIOUS - BIBLIOGRAPHY

"Cults and Sects, General" in Howard University Bibliography of African
    and Afro-American Religious Studies. 1977. pp. 205-209.

CULTURAL HISTORY - BIBLIOGRAPHY

"Development of an Afro-American Community" (1865-1900) in Afro-American
    History, 1. 1974. pp. 398-407.

"Development of an Afro-American Community" (1865-1900) in Afro-American
    History, 2. 1981. pp. 142-143.

"The Elements of Black Society" (Colonial Period) in Afro-American
    History, 1. 1974. pp. 33-45.

"The Elements of Black Society" (Colonial Period) in Afro-American
    History, 2. 1981. pp. 62-66.

"Social and Cultural History" in Afro-American History, 1. 1974. pp.
    33-45.

"Social and Cultural History" in Afro-American History, 2. 1981. pp.
    19-32.

CULTURAL NATIONALISM - BIBLIOGRAPHY

"Black Cultural Ideas and Movements (The Contemporary Scene)" in Afro-
    American History, 1. 1974. pp. 748-775.

CULTURE

"Agenda for Action: Black Art and Letters, 1972," Margaret Walker
    Alexander in The Ebony Handbook. 1974. pp. 432-436.

"Arts and Letters" in The Ebony Handbook. 1974. pp. 431-462.

"The Black Arts Movement," Larry Neal in <u>Afro-American Writers After
    1955: Dramatists and Prose Writers</u>. 1985. pp. 293-300.

"Contributions of the Negro Press to American Culture," William C.
    Spragens in <u>The Negro Impact on Western Civilization</u>. 1970. pp.
    173-194.

CULTURE - BIBLIOGRAPHY

<u>Afro-American Folk Culture</u>. 1978. 2 V., 814, 814 p.

"Black Cultural Ideas and Movements" in <u>Afro-American History, 2</u>. 1981.
    pp. 259-273.

"Blacks in American Culture, 1900-1970" in <u>Blacks in America;
    Bibliographical Essays</u>. 1971. pp. 239-300.

"Contributions to American Culture" in <u>Afro-American History, 2</u>. pp.
    40-43.

"Identity Individual and Collective" in <u>Black Separatism; a
    Bibliography</u>. 1976. pp. 42058.

"Literature, Art, and Music" in <u>Black Rhetoric</u>. 1976. pp. 109-113.

"A Selected Bibliography: General" in <u>The Negro Almanac</u>. 1983. pp.
    1489-1492.

"Towards a Black Aesthetic" in <u>Blacks in America; Bibliographical
    Essays</u>. 1971. pp. 263-265.

"Traditions in Afro-American Culture" in <u>Afro-American History, 1</u>. 1974.
    pp. 3-82.

"With a Sense of Pride: Black Cultural and Intellectual History" in
    <u>Blacks in the Humanities</u>. 1986. pp. 161-168.

CULTURE - DICTIONARY

<u>Dictionary of Black American Culture</u>. 1973. 493 p.

<u>The Harlem Renaissance</u>. 1984. 476 p.

CULTURE - SLAVERY

"Culture" in <u>The Slave Community</u>. 1979. pp. 105-148.

CULTURE - SLAVERY - BIBLIOGRAPHY

"Slave Culture" in <u>Black Slavery in the Americas</u>. 1982. pp. 1295-1389.

CULTURE, AFRICAN - BIBLIOGRAPHY

"African Laws and Customs" in <u>A Bibliography of the Negro</u>. 1928. pp.
    51-65.

"Bibliographical Notes: The African Way of Life" in <u>From Slavery to</u>

Freedom. 1980. p. 513.

CULTURE, AFRICAN - HISTORY

"The African Way of Life: The Arts" in From Slavery to Freedom. 1980. pp. 24-28.

CULTURE, CARIBBEAN - BIBLIOGRAPHY

"Cultural Change" in The Complete Caribbeana. 1977. V. 2, pp. 837-843.

"Cultural Continuities" in The Complete Caribbeana. 1977. V. 2, pp. 651-670.

CULTURE, HAITIAN - BIBLIOGRAPHY

"Values and Norms" in The Complete Haitiana. 1982. V. 2, pp. 645-656.

CURACAO - BIBLIOGRAPHY

"Curacao" in The Complete Caribbeana. 1977. See index, V. 4, p. 2161.

CURACAO - MUSIC - BIBLIOGRAPHY

"Curacao and Aruba" in Bibliography of Black Music. 1981. V. 3, p. 143.

DALE, CLAMMA - BIBLIOGRAPHY

"Dale, Clamma" in Black Music in America. 1981. p. 181.

DANCE

"Afro-American Music and Dance," Mohan Lal Sharma in The Negro Impact on Western Civilization. 1970. pp. 139-158.

DANCE - BIBLIOGRAPHY

"Dance" in Afro-American Reference. 1985. pp. 98-99.

"Dance" in The Progress of Afro-American Women. 1980. pp. 19-20.

"Dance, Dance Music and Songs" in Afro-American Folk Culture, 1978. See index, pp. 765-766.

"Jazz and Dance" in Jazz Bibliography. 1981. p. 319.

"Music and Dance" in A Comprehensive Bibliography. 1976. pp. 256-261.

"Slave Culture: Dance" in Black Slavery in the Americas. 1982. pp. 1368-1373.

DANCE, AFRICAN

"Dance and Music" in The Roots of Black Music. 1982. pp. 101-106.

DANCE, BRAZILIAN - BIBLIOGRAPHY

"Music, Dance, and Carnival" in Afro-Braziliana; a Working Bibliography. 1978. pp. 107-119.

DANCE, HAITIAN - BIBLIOGRAPHY

"Music and Dance" in The Complete Haitiana. 1982. V. 1, pp. 799-806.

DANCE TEACHERS - BIOGRAPHY - INDEX

"Dance Teachers" in In Black and White. 1980. See index, V. 2, p. 1135.

DANCERS - BIBLIOGRAPHY

"Dance" in The Progress of Afro-American Women. 1980. pp. 19-20.

DANCERS - BIOGRAPHY - INDEX

"Dancers" in In Black and White. 1980. See index, V. 2, pp. 1135-1137.

DANCERS - DIRECTORIES

Directory of Blacks in the Performing Arts. 1978. 428 p.

DANNER, MARGARET ESSE

"Margaret Esse Danner," June M. Aldridge in Afro-American Poets Since 1955. 1985. pp. 84-89.

DATHORNE, O.R.

"O.R. Dathorne," Leota S. Lawrence in 50 Caribbean Writers. 1986. pp. 133-144.

DAUGHTER ELKS - BIBLIOGRAPHY

"Daughter Elks" in The Progress of Afro-American Women. 1980. pp. 251-252.

DAVIS, MILES - BIBLIOGRAPHY

"Davis, Miles Dewey, Jr." in Black Music in America. 1981. pp. 182-202.

DAVIS, OSSIE

"Ossie Davis," Michael E. Greene in Afro-American Writers After 1955: Dramatists and Prose Writers. 1985. pp. 80-86.

DAVIS, OSSIE - BIBLIOGRAPHY

"Black Dramatists: Ossie Davis" in Blacks in America; Bibliographical Essays. 1971. p. 282.

DAWES, NEVILLE

"Neville Dawes," Edward Baugh in 50 Caribbean Writers. 1986. pp. 141-150.

D'COSTA, JEAN

"Jean D'Costa," Joyce Johnson in 50 Caribbean Writers. 1986. pp. 160-
    165.

DE BOISSIERE, RALPH

"Ralph De Boissiere," Reinhard W. Sander in 50 Caribbean Writers. 1986.
    pp. 151-159.

DEITIES, BLACK - HISTORY

"Black Gods and Messiahs" in Sex and Race. 1944. V. 1, pp. 265-271.

DELANY, MARTIN R.

"Martin Robinson Delany," Carol Marsh-Lockett in Afro-American Writers
    Before the Harlem Renaissance. 1986. pp. 74-80.

DELANY, SAMUEL R.

"Samuel R. Delany," Sandra Y. Govan in Afro-American Fiction Writers
    After 1955. 1984. pp. 52-59.

DELAWARE - EDUCATION - BIBLIOGRAPHY

"Delaware" in The Education of Poor and Minority Children. 1981. pp.
    233-234.

DELAWARE - EDUCATION, HIGHER - BIBLIOGRAPHY

"Higher Education by State: Delaware" in The Education of Poor and
    Minority Children. 1981. p. 874.

DELAWARE - GENEALOGY - BIBLIOGRAPHY

"Delaware" in Black Genesis. 1978. pp. 189-190.

DELAWARE - SLAVERY - BIBLIOGRAPHY

"Delaware" in Black Slavery in the Americas. 1982. pp. 831-834.

DE LISSER, HERBERT GEORGE

"Herbert George De Lisser," Rhonda Cobham in 50 Caribbean Writers. 1986.
    pp. 166-177.

DELTA SIGMA THETA SORORITY - BIBLIOGRAPHY

"Delta Sigma Theta Sorority" in The Progress of Afro-American Women.
    1980. pp. 252-253.

DEMBY, WILLIAM

"William Demby" in Interviews with Black Writers. 1973. pp. 34-53.

"William Demby," Margaret Perry in Afro-American Fiction Writers After

<u>1955</u>. 1984. pp. 59-64.

DEMOCRATIC NATIONAL COMMITTEE BLACK CAUCUS - DIRECTORY

"Black Caucus of the Democratic National Committee" in <u>Black Resource Guide</u>. 1986. pp. 155-156.

DEMOCRATIC PARTY - BIBLIOGRAPHY

"Blacks and the Democratic Party" in <u>The Study and Analysis of Black Politics</u>. 1973. pp. 29-30.

DEMOGRAPHY

"Black Demography: A Review Essay" in <u>Demography of the Black Population</u>. 1983. pp. 3-31.

"Growth and Distribution of the Black Population" in <u>The Negro Almanac</u>. 1983. pp. 445-474.

DEMOGRAPHY - BIBLIOGRAPHY

<u>Demography of the Black Population in the United States</u>. 1984. 354 p.

"Statistics, Demography and Migration" in <u>Afro-American Reference</u>. 1985. pp. 87-92.

DEMOGRAPHY - CARIBBEAN - BIBLIOGRAPHY

"Demography and Human Resources" in <u>The Complete Caribbeana</u>. 1977. V. 1, pp. 345-373.

DEMOGRAPHY - HAITI - BIBLIOGRAPHY

"Demography and Human Resources" in <u>The Complete Haitiana</u>. 1982. V. 1, pp. 553-560.

DEMOGRAPHY - SLAVERY

"Statistics on Slaves and Slavery: Observations and Tables" in <u>The Slave Community</u>. 1979. pp. 336-366.

DEMOGRAPHY - SLAVERY - BIBLIOGRAPHY

"Slave Demography" in <u>Black Slavery in the Americas</u>. 1982. pp. 1107-1121.

DENT, TOM

"Tom Dent," Lorenzo Thomas in <u>Afro-American Writers After 1955: Dramatists and Prose Writers</u>. 1985. pp. 86-92.

DENTISTS - BIBLIOGRAPHY

"Dentistry" in <u>The Progress of Afro-American Women</u>. 1980. p. 215.

DENTISTS - BIOGRAPHY - INDEX

"Dentists" in In Black and White. 1980. See index, V. 2, p. 1137.

DERMATOLOGISTS - BIOGRAPHY - INDEX

"Dermatologists" in In Black and White. 1980. See index, V. 2, p. 1137.

DESEGRATION - BIBLIOGRAPHY

"Jews' Opinion on Desegregation" in Black-Jewish Relations. 1984. p. 92.

DESIGNERS - BIBLIOGRAPHY

"Designers" in The Progress of Afro-American Women. 1980. pp. 84-85.

DESIGNERS - BIOGRAPHY - INDEX

"Designers" in In Black and White. 1980. See index, V. 2, pp. 1137-1139.

DESIRADE - BIBLIOGRAPHY

"Desiderade" in The Complete Caribbeana. 1972. See index, V. 4, p. 2162.

DETECTIVES - BIOGRAPHY - INDEX

"Detectives, Investigators" in In Black and White. 1980. See index, V. 2, p. 1139.

DEVEAUX, ALEXIS

"Alexis Deveaux," Priscilla R. Ramsey in Afro-American Prose Writers After 1955: Dramatists and Prose Writers. 1985. pp. 92-96.

DEVELOPMENT - HAITI - BIBLIOGRAPHY

"Rural Development and Evaluation of Development Projects" in The Complete Haitiana. 1982. V. 2, pp. 1453-1500.

DIALECT IN LITERATUE - BIBLIOGRAPHY

"Discussions of the Negro in Literature: Negro Dialect" in A Bibliography of the Negro. 1928. pp. 454-455.

DIASPORA

"The African Diaspora," Philip D. Curtin in Roots and Branches. 1979. pp. 1-17.

"Black America as a Mobilizing Diaspora," Locksley Edmondson in Modern Diasporas in International Politics. 1986. pp. 164-211.

"Blacks in the Western Hemisphere" in The Negro Almanac. 1976. pp. 1125-1144.

DIASPORA - BIBLIOGRAPHY

"Haitians Abroad" in The Complete Haitiana. 1982. V. 2, pp. 609-624.

"West Indians Abroad" in The Complete Caribbeana. 1977. V. 1, pp. 615-
647.

DIETICIANS - BIOGRAPHY - INDEX

"Dieticians, Home Economists, Nutritionists" in In Black and White.
1980. See index, V. 2, p. 1139.

DIPLOMATS - BIOGRAPHY - INDEX

"Ambassadors, Diplomats" in In Black and White. 1980. See index, V. 2,
pp. 1111-1112.

DISCIPLES OF CHRIST - CIVIL RIGHTS MOVEMENT - BIBLIOGRAPHY

"The Church, Synagogue and Integration; Disciples of Christ (Christian
Churches)" in Howard University Bibliography of African and Afro-
American Religious Studies. 1977. p. 316.

DISCIPLES OF CHRIST - RACE RELATIONS - BIBLIOGRAPHY

"Disciples of Christ" in Howard University Bibliography of African and
Afro-American Religious Studies. 1977. pp. 272-273.

DISCIPLES OF CHRIST - SLAVERY - BIBLIOGRAPHY

"Slavery, Negroes and the Church: Disciples of Christ: Christian
Churches" in Howard University Bibliography of African and
African-American Religious Studies. 1977. p. 132.

DISTRICT OF COLUMBIA - EDUCATION - BIBLIOGRAPHY

"District of Columbia" in The Education of Poor and Minority Children.
1981. pp. 234-241.

DISTRICT OF COLUMBIA - EDUCATION, HIGHER - BIBLIOGRAPHY

"Higher Education by State: District of Columbia" in The Education of
Poor and Minority Children. 1981. pp. 874-877.

DISTRICT OF COLUMBIA - GENEALOGY - BIBLIOGRAPHY

"District of Columbia" in Black Genesis. 1978. pp. 125-129.

DISTRICT OF COLUMBIA - SLAVERY - BIBLIOGRAPHY

"District of Columbia" in Black Slavery in the Americas. 1982. pp. 834-
836.

DOCUMENTARIES - FILMOGRAPHY

"Documentaries" in The Afro-American Cinematic Experience. pp. 245-248.

DOCUMENTS - FEDERAL RECORDS

"Federal Appointment Papers and Black History," James D. Walker in
Afro-American History; Sources for Research. 1981. pp. 59-64.

"National Archives and Federal Records" in Black Genesis. 1978. pp. 24-28.

"Saving Federal Records for Research," Harold T. Rinkett in Afro-American History; Sources for Research. 1981. pp. 9-18.

DOCUMENTS - MILITARY RECORDS

"Military Records for Nonmilitary History," Preston E. Ames in Afro-American History; Sources for Research. 1981. pp. 65-73.

"War Records" in Black Genesis. 1978. pp. 29-33.

DOCUMENTS - PAPERS (PERSONAL)

"The National Historical Publications and Records Commission's Committee on the Publication of Papers Relating to Blacks," Edgar A. Toppin in Afro-American History; Sources for Research. 1981. pp. 113-120.

DODSON, OWEN

"Owen Dodson" in Interviews with Black Writers. 1973. pp. 54-61.

DOLL MANUFACTURES - BIBLIOGRAPHY

"Doll Manufacturers" in The Progress of Afro-American Women. 1980. p. 87.

DOMESTIC WORKERS - BIBLIOGRAPHY

"Domestic Workers" in The Progress of Afro-American Women. 1980. pp. 87-91.

DOMINICA - BIBLIOGRAPHY

"Dominica" in The Complete Caribbeana. 1977. See index, V. 4, pp. 2162.

DOMINICAN REPUBLIC

"Blacks in the Western Hemisphere: Dominican Republic" in The Negro Almanac. 1983. pp. 1473-1475.

"The Dominican Republic" in Sex and Race. 1942. V. 2, pp. 91-96.

DOMINICAN REPUBLIC - BIBLIOGRAPHY

"Dominican Republic" in The Complete Caribbeana. 1977. See index, p. 2162.

"Dominican Republic" in Race and Ethnic Relations. 1980. pp. 172-173.

"Haiti-Dominican Republic Frontier Issues" in The Complete Haitiana. 1982. V. 2, pp. 1179-1185.

DOMINICAN REPUBLIC - MUSIC - BIBLIOGRAPHY

"Dominican Republic" in Bibliography of Black Music. 1981. V. 3, pp.

144-145.

DOUGLASS, FREDERICK

"Frederick Douglass," Russell K. Hinely in Afro-American Writers Before
     the Harlem Renaissance. 1986. pp. 80-91.

DOZENS - BIBLIOGRAPHY

"Speech Play" in Afro-American Folk Culture. 1978. See index, p. 798.

"Verbal and Musical Dueling" in Afro-American Folk Culture. 1978. See
     index, pp. 803-804.

DRAFTERS - BIOGRAPHY - INDEX

"Draftsmen" in In Black and White. 1980. See index, V. 2, p. 1139.

DRAMA - ANTHOLOGIES - BIBLIOGRAPHY

"Drama: General Studies - Play Collections" in Afro-American Poetry and
     Drama. 1979. pp. 272-275.

DRAMA - BIBLIOGRAPHY

"Afro-American Drama, 1850-1975" in Afro-American Poetry and Drama.
     1979. pp. 249-293.

Black Playwrights, 1823-1977: An Annotated Bibliography of Plays. 1977.
     319 p.

"Drama: General Studies - Bibliographies" in Afro-American Poetry and
     Drama. 1979. pp. 271-272.

"Dramas Having Negro Characters or Dealing with Negro Life (Authors
     Whites and Negroes)" in A Bibliography of the Negro. 1928. pp.
     447-451.

"General Bibliography' in Black American Playwrights. 1976. pp. 217-273.

"General Bibliography" in More Black American Playwrights. 1978. pp.
     213-306.

"Individual Writers: Original Works and Criticism: Drama" in A
     Comprehensive Bibliography. 1976. pp. 250-254.

DRAMA - COLLECTIONS - BIBLIOGRAPHY

"Drama: General Studies - Library Resources" in Afro-American Poetry and
     Drama. 1979. pp. 267-268.

DRAMA - HISTORY AND CRITICISM

"Black Drama" in A Critical Introduction to Twentieth Century American
     Drama, Volume 1, 1900-1940. 1982. pp. 237-255.

DRAMA - HISTORY AND CRITICISM - BIBLIOGRAPHY

"Drama: General Studies: Critical Studies" in <u>Afro-American Poetry and Drama</u>. 1979. pp. 275-295.

"Individual Writers: Original Works and Criticism: Drama" in <u>A Comprehensive Bibliography</u>. 1976. pp. 250-254.

"Literary History and Criticism: Theatre and Film" in <u>A Comprehensive Bibliography</u>. 1976. pp. 215-218.

DRAMA - INDEX

<u>Index to Black American Literary Anthologies</u>. 1979. 219 p.

DRAMA - PERIODICALS - BIBLIOGRAPHY

"Drama: General Studies - Periodicals" in <u>Afro-American Poetry and Drama</u>. 1979. pp. 268-271.

DRAMA, FOLK - BIBLIOGRAPHY

"Drama" in <u>Afro-American Folk Culture</u>. 1978. See index, p. 770.

DRAMATISTS - BIBLIOGRAPHY

<u>Black American Playwrights, 1800 to the Present: A Bibliography</u>. 1976. 295 p.

"Black Dramatists" in <u>Blacks in America; Bibliographical Essays</u>. 1971. pp. 280-281.

"Drama: Individual Authors" in <u>Afro-American Poetry and Drama</u>. 1979. pp. 297-493.

<u>More Black American Playwrights: A Bibliography</u>. 1978. 328 p.

DRAMATISTS - BIOGRAPHY - INDEX

"Dramatists" in <u>In Black and White</u>. 1980. See index, V. 2, pp. 1139-1140.

DRED SCOTT CASE - BIBLIOGRAPHY

"Dred Scott Case" in <u>A Bibliography of the Negro</u>. 1928 p. 345.

DRUMMERS - BIOGRAPHY - INDEX

"Musicians: Instrumental: Drums, Percussion" in <u>In Black and White</u>. 1980. See index, V. 2, pp. 1185-1186.

DRUMS - BIBLIOGRAPHY

"Drums and Drumming" in <u>Afro-American Folk Culture</u>. 1978. See index, p. 771.

DUBOIS, W. E. B.

"W.E.B. DuBois," Addison Gayle in <u>Afro-American Writers Before the</u>

Harlem Renaissance. 1986. pp. 92-105.

DUBOIS, WILLIAM EDWARD BURGHARDT - BIBLIOGRAPHY

"Accommodation and Protest in Black Thought - Protest: W.E.B. DuBois" in
Blacks in America; Bibliographical Essays. 1971. pp. 152-153.

"DuBois, William Edward" in The Harlem Renaissance. 1982. pp. 75-77.

"W.E.B. DuBois' Opinion of Jews" in Black-Jewish Relations. 1984. pp. 19
and 96.

Writings by W.E.B. DuBois in Non-Periodical Literature, 1982. 302 p.

Writings by W.E.B. DuBois in Periodicals Edited by Others, 1982. 4
volumes.

DUE PROCESS - LEGAL CASES

"Important Cases: Due Process" in The Negro Almanac. 1983. pp. 304-305.

DUMAS, HENRY

"Henry Dumas," Carolyn A. Mitchell in Afro-American Poets Since 1955.
1985. pp. 89-99.

DUNBAR, PAUL LAURENCE

"Paul Laurence Dunbar," Doris Lucas Laryea in Afro-American Writers
Before the Harlem Renaissance. 1986. pp. 106-122.

DUNBAR, PAUL LAURENCE - BIBLIOGRAPHY

"Black Fiction at the Turn of the Century: Charles Waddell Chestnutt and
Paul Laurence Dunbar" in Blacks in America; Bibliographical Essays.
1971. pp. 174-175.

DUNCAN, TODD - BIBLIOGRAPHY

"Duncan, Todd," in Black Music in America. 1981. pp. 202-203.

DUTCH LANGUAGE - CREOLE - BIBLIOGRAPHY

"Dutch-Based Creoles" in A Bibliography of Pidgin and Creole Languages.
1975. pp. 316-317.

DUTCH REFORMED CHURCH - SLAVERY - BIBLIOGRAPHY

"Slavery, Negroes and the Church: Reformed Church" in Howard University
Bibliography of African and Afro-American Religious Studies. 1977.
p. 144.

EAST INDIANS - CARIBBEAN - BIBLIOGRAPHY

"Population Segments: East Indian" in The Complete Caribbeana. 1977. pp.
489-507.

EASTERN ORTHODOX CHURCH - RACE RELATIONS - BIBLIOGRAPHY

"Eastern Orthodox" in Howard University Bibliography of African and
    Afro-American Religious Studies. 1977. p. 273.

EBON

"Ebon (Leo Thomas Hale/Ebon Dooley)," Rhonda V. Wilcox in Afro-American
    Poets Since 1955. 1985. pp. 99-103.

ECOLOGY - BIBLIOGRAPHY

"Black Migration, Urbanization and Ecology" in Black Demography in the
    United States. 1983. pp. 235-298.

ECOLOGY - CARIBBEAN - BIBLIOGRAPHY

"Geography and Ecology" in The Complete Caribbeana. V. 3, pp. 1871-1911.

ECOLOGY - HAITI - BIBLIOGRAPHY

"Geography and Ecology" in The Complete Haitiana. 1982. V. 1, pp. 97-
    112.

ECONOMIC CONDITIONS - BIBLIOGRAPHY

"Description and Causes of Black Economic Inequality" in The Economics
    of Minorities. 1976. pp. 3-29.

"Economic Conditions" in The Progress of Afro-American Women. 1980. pp.
    55-57.

"The General Economic Conditions of Negroes" in A Bibliography of the
    Negro. 1928. pp. 490-491.

"Social, Political and Economic Conditions" in Afro-American History, 2.
    1981. pp. 217-259.

"Social, Political and Economic Dimensions" in Afro-american History, 2.
    1981. pp. 159-168.

"The Social, Political and Economic Situation" in Afro-American History,
    1. 1974. pp. 460-490.

"The Social, Political and Economic Situation" in Afro-American History,
    1. 1974. pp. 628-748.

ECONOMIC DEVELOPMENT - BIBLIOGRAPHY

"Economic Development of the Black Community" in The Economics of
    Minorities. 1976. pp. 81-102.

ECONOMIC HISTORY - CARIBBEAN - BIBLIOGRAPHY

"Plantation Economics and the Sugar Complex" in The Complete Caribbeana.
    1977. V. 3, pp. 1417-1438.

ECONOMICS

"The Black Role in the Economy," Mabel M. Smythe in The Black American Reference Book. 1976. pp. 207-250.

"The Economic Status of Black America - Is There a Recovery?" Denys Vaughn-Cooke in The State of Black America, 1984. pp. 1-23.

"Economic Status of Blacks, 1985," David Swinton in The State of Black America, 1986. pp. 1-21.

"Economics and Business" in The Ebony Handbook. 1974. pp. 237-262.

"The Economics of Hope and Despair" in Long Memory. 1982. pp. 195-226.

"Income, Earnings and Incidence of Poverty" in The Negro Almanac. 1983. pp. 645-678.

"Racial Perspectives in Economics," Thaddeus H. Spratlen in Contemporary Black Thought. 1980. pp. 126-137.

ECONOMICS - BIBLIOGRAPHY

"Bibliography: The Economics of Hope and Despair" in Long Memory. 1982. pp. 438-441.

"Black Family and Economics" in The Black Family in the United States. 1986. pp. 74-75, 109.

"The Economic Context" in Afro-American History, 2. 1981. pp. 249-259.

"Economic Discrimination" in The Education of Poor and Minority Children. 1981. pp. 746-750.

"The Economic Order: Black Enterprise, Black Workers and Income" in Black Separatism; a Bibliography. 1976. pp. 109-117.

"The Economic Status of Black Americans" in Blacks in America; Bibliographical Essays. 1971. pp. 340-350.

"Economic Studies" in A Bibliography of the Negro. 1928. pp. 615-618.

"Economics" in A Comprehensive Bibliography. 1976. pp. 144-171.

"Economics, Employment, and Business" in Afro-American Reference. 1985. pp. 68-71.

"Economics: General" in A Comprehensive Bibliography. 1976. pp. 168-171.

The Economics of Minorities. 1976. 212 p.

"Economy and Income" in The Education of Poor and Minority Children. 1981. pp. 729-735.

"A Selected Bibliography: Economics" in The Negro Almanac. 1983. pp. 1524-1526.

ECONOMICS - CARIBBEAN - BIBLIOGRAPHY

"General Economics" in The Complete Caribbeana. V. 3, pp. 1355-1416.

ECONOMICS - HAITI - BIBLIOGRAPHY

"General Economics" in The Complete Haitiana. 1982. V. 2. pp. 1269-1296.

ECONOMICS - HISTORY

"Inequality and the Burden of Capitalist Democracy: A Point of View on
    Black History" in How Capitalism Underdeveloped Black America.
    1980. pp. 1-19.

ECONOMICS - HISTORY - BIBLIOGRAPHY

"Economic History" in Afro-American History, 1. 1974. pp. 45-49.

"Economic History" in Afro-American History, 2. 1981. pp. 32-36.

"Social and Economic Dimensions" (1865-1900) in Afro-American History,
    2. 1981. pp. 143-149.

"The Social and Economic Situation (Reconstruction and its Aftermath)"
    in Afro-American History, 1. pp. 407-420.

"Social, Political and Economic Dimensions" in Afro-American History, 2.
    pp. 159-168.

ECONOMICS - POLITICAL ASPECTS - BIBLIOGRAPHY

"Economic Programs" in The Study and Analysis of Black Politics. 1973.
    p. 120.

ECONOMICS, COOPERATIVE - HISTORY - BIBLIOGRAPHY

"Social Welfare Organizations and Fraternal Societies" in Blacks in
    America; Bibliographical Essays. 1971. pp. 157-159.

ECONOMISTS - BIOGRAPHY - INDEX

"Economists" in In Black and White. 1980. See index, V. 2, p. 1140.

ECUADOR

"Peru, Ecuador, Colombia, Panama" in Sex and Race. 1942. V. 2, pp. 66-
    71.

ECUADOR - BIBLIOGRAPHY

"Ecuador" in The Education of Poor and Minority Children. 1981. p. 1139.

"Ecuador" in Race and Ethnic Relations. 1980. pp. 213-214.

ECUADOR - MUSIC - BIBLIOGRAPHY

"Ecuador" in Bibliography of Black Music. 1981. V. 3, p. 184.

ECUADOR - SLAVERY - BIBLIOGRAPHY

"Ecuador" in Slavery: A Worldwide Bibliography. 1985. p. 138.

EDITORS - BIOGRAPHY - INDEX

"Editors" in In Black and White. 1980. See index, V. 2, pp. 1140-1142.

EDUCATION

"The Battle for Education" in Long Memory. 1982. pp. 261-294.

"The Black Male's Struggle for an Education," James M. Patten in Black
    Men. 1981.

"The Destruction of Black Education" in How Capitalism Underdeveloped
    Black America. 1983. pp. 215-228.

"Educating Black Americans," Regina Goff in The Black American Reference
    Book. 1976. pp. 410-452.

"Education" in The Ebony Handbook. 1974. pp. 124-178.

"Equity and Excellence: An Educational Imperative," Charles D. Moody,
    Sr. in The State of Black America, 1986. pp. 23-42.

"Milestones in the History of Education of the Negro in the United
    States," Joseph S. Roucek in The Negro Impact on Western
    Civilization. 1970. pp. 195-230.

"Modern Technology and Urban Schools," Robert E. Fullilove, III in The
    State of Black America, 1985. pp. 37-64.

"Perspectives on Black Education" in The Negro Almanac. 1983. pp. 711-
    781.

"Schooling and Black Children's Images of the Future," Roy A. Weaver in
    Beyond Identity. 1978. pp. 13-25.

"The State of Urban Education," Faustine C. Jones-Wilson in The State of
    Black America, 1984. pp. 95-118.

EDUCATION - AFRICA - BIBLIOGRAPHY

"The Education of the Native" in A Bibliography of the Negro. 1928. pp.
    232-237.

EDUCATION - BIBLIOGRAPHY

Afro-American Education, 1907-1932. 1984. 178 p.

"Bibliography: The Battle for Education" in Long Memory. 1982. pp. 445-
    447.

Black Authors and Education. 1980. 103 p.

"Black Family and Education" in The Black Family in the United States.

1986. pp. 75, 109 and 185-187.

"Education" in <u>Afro-American Folk Culture</u>. 1978. See index, pp. 771-772.

"Education" in <u>Afro-American Reference</u>. 1985. pp. 162-169.

"Education" in <u>Black Rhetoric</u>. 1976. pp. 59-63.

"Education" in <u>A Comprehensive Bibliography</u>. 1976. pp. 111-132.

"Education" in <u>The Progress of Afro-American Women</u>. 1980. pp. 58-75.

"Education" in <u>The Study and Analysis of Black Politics</u>. 1973. pp. 117-119.

<u>The Education of Poor and Minority Children</u>. 1981. 1563 p.

"Educational Studies" in <u>A Bibliography of the Negro</u>. 128 pp. 618-620.

"General Discussions of the Education of the Negro" in <u>A Bibliography of the Negro</u>. 1928. pp. 420-422.

"A Selected Bibliography: Education" in <u>The Negro Almanac</u>. 1983. pp. 1503-1505.

EDUCATION - CARIBBEAN - BIBLIOGRAPHY

"Education" in <u>The Complete Caribbeana</u>. 1977. V. 2, pp. 1043-1107.

EDUCATION - DESEGREGATION

"Desegregation and Black Child Development," J. John Harris in <u>Contemporary Black Thought</u>. 1980. pp. 259-272.

EDUCATION - DESEGREGATION - BIBLIOGRAPHY

"Children: Desegregation Effects" in <u>The Education of Poor and Minority Children</u>. 1981. pp. 70-87.

"Since Brown V. Board of Education: Black Education Since 1954" in <u>Blacks in America; Bibliographical Essays</u>. 1971. pp. 331-340.

EDUCATION - ECONOMIC ASPECTS - BIBLIOGRAPHY

"Public Finance" in <u>The Education of Poor and Minority Children</u>. 1981. pp. 803-810.

"Quality and Economic Returns of Black Education" in <u>The Economics of Minorities</u>. 1976. pp. 45-55.

"School and Livelihood" in <u>The Education of Poor and Minority Children</u>. 1981. pp. 729-735.

EDUCATION - FIRST FACTS

"Black Firsts: Education" in <u>Before the Mayflower</u>. 1982. pp. 633-634.

EDUCATION - HISPANIC AMERICANS - BIBLIOGRAPHY

"Other Spanish-Speaking Peoples" in The Education of Poor and Minority
    Children. 1981. pp. 490-502.

EDUCATION - HISTORY

"Chronology of Black Education" in The Negro Almanac. 1983. pp. 723-735.

"Philanthropy and Self-Help" in From Slavery to Freedom. 1980. pp. 268-
    294.

"Trends in Education" in From Slavery to Freedom. 1980. pp. 402-412.

EDUCATION - HISTORY - BIBLIOGRAPHY

Afro-American Education, 1907-1932. 1984. 178 p.

"Black Education, 1877-1915" in Blacks in America; Bibliographical
    Essays. 1971. pp. 162-165.

"The Education of the Negro Before the Civil War" in A Bibliography of
    the Negro. 1928. pp. 416-417.

"The Education of the Negro During the Civil War Period" in A
    Bibliography of the Negro. 1928. p. 418.

"The Education of the Negro During the Reconstruction Period" in A
    Bibliography of the Negro. 1928. pp. 418-420.

"Freedmen's Education During the Civil War and Reconstruction" in Blacks
    in America; Bibliographical Essays. 1971. pp. 119-121.

"History" in The Education of Poor and Minority Children. 1981. pp. 3-
    28.

"Mind of the Slave: Slave Education" in Black Slavery in the Americas.
    1982. pp. 1421-1430.

EDUCATION - LEGAL CASES

"Important Legal Cases: Education" in The Negro Almanac. 1983. pp. 305-
    309.

EDUCATION - PHILANTHROPY - BIBLIOGRAPHY

"Boards and Foundations Carrying on Educational Work Among Negroes" in A
    Bibliography of the Negro. 1928. pp. 422-423.

EDUCATION - STATISTICS

"Education" in Facts About Blacks. 1980. pp. 5-7.

EDUCATION, ELEMENTARY AND SECONDARY - BIBLIOGRAPHY

"Education: Segregation and Desegregation - Elementary and Secondary
    School" in Black Separatism; a Bibliography. 1976. pp. 59-71.

"The Elementary Education of the Negro" in <u>A Bibliography of the Negro</u>. 1928. pp. 423-424.

"Schools" in <u>The Study and Analysis of Black Politics</u>. 1973. p. 24.

"The Secondary and Industrial Education of the Negro" in <u>A Bibliography of the Negro</u>. 1928. pp. 424-427.

EDUCATION, ELEMENTARY AND SECONDARY - LAW

"Elementary and Secondary Education Act" in <u>The Negro Almanac</u>. 1983. pp. 747-748.

EDUCATION, HIGHER

"Black Males in Higher Education," John E. Fleming in <u>Black Men</u>. 1981. pp. 215-227.

<u>Black Scholars on Higher Education in the 70's</u>. 1974. 392 p.

"Black Students in White Universities Revisited," Elois Scott in <u>Contemporary Black Thought</u>. 1980. pp. 273-294.

"Blacks in Colleges" in <u>The Negro Almanac</u>. 1983. pp. 752-758.

"Cleavages and Contradictions in White Institutions," Roosevelt Johnson in <u>Black Scholars on Higher Education</u>. 1974. pp 1-6.

"Helping Minority Students to Excel in University-level Mathematics and Science Courses: The Professional Development Program at the University of California, Berkeley," Katharyn Culler in <u>The State of Black America, 1985</u>. pp. 225-231.

"Higher Education and the Black American: An Overview," James M. Rosser in <u>Black Scholars on Higher Education</u>. 1974. pp. 241-255.

"Urban America and Crucial Issues Facing Higher Education," Robert L. Green in <u>Black Scholars on Higher Education</u>. 1974. pp. 191-214.

"Vignettes on White Academia," Roosevelt Johnson in <u>Black Scholars on Higher Education</u>. 1974. pp. 1-34.

EDUCATION, HIGHER - ADMINISTRATION

"Reflections and Notes on Styles and Attitudes in Higher Education Administration," King V. Cheek, Jr. in <u>Black Scholars on Higher Education</u>. 1974. pp. 353-370.

EDUCATION, HIGHER - BIBLIOGRAPHY

<u>Black Higher Education in the United States</u>. 1978. 268 p.

"Education: Segregation and Desegregation - Higher Education" in <u>Black Separatism; a Bibliography</u>. 1976. pp. 71-94.

"Higher Education" in <u>The Education of Poor and Minority Children</u>. 1981. pp. 862-977.

"Higher Education and Black Scholarship" in <u>Blacks in America;</u>
    <u>Bibliographical Essays</u>. 1971. pp. 121-218.

"The Higher Education of the Negro" in <u>A Bibliography of the Negro</u>.
    1928. pp. 427-428.

EDUCATION, HIGHER - COMMUNITY SERVICE

"Public Service: The Role of Black Professionals and Black College and
    University Personnel in Public Service, Direct Services to the
    Community," Arthur T. L. Simmons in <u>Black Scholars on Higher</u>
    <u>Education</u>. 1974. pp. 293-299.

EDUCATION, HIGHER - COMPENSATORY PROGRAMS

"Compensatory Educational Programs: Is There a Place in Higher
    Education?" Randolph Bracy in <u>Black Scholars on Higher Education</u>.
    1974. pp. 277-284.

"Compensatory Programs for Blacks: A Study," Roosevelt Johnson in <u>Black</u>
    <u>Scholars on Higher Education</u>. 1974. pp. 257-275.

"Special Programs: The Need for a Concept and Commitment, Not a Name,"
    Roosevelt Johnson in <u>Black Scholars on Higher Education</u>. 1974. pp.
    285-291.

EDUCATION, HIGHER - FACULTY

"Second Class Citizens and the Academic Community," Roosevelt Johnson in
    <u>Black Scholars on Higher Education</u>. 1974. pp. 10-16.

"Southeastern Black Library Educators," Herman L. Totten in <u>The Black</u>
    <u>Librarian in the Southeast</u>. 1980. pp. 198-211.

EDUCATION, HIGHER - HAITI - BIBLIOGRAPHY

"Higher Education" in <u>The Complete Haitiana</u>. 1982. V. 2, pp. 1025-1033.

EDUCATION, HIGHER - LAW

"The Higher Education Act of 1965" in <u>The Negro Almanac</u>. 1983. pp. 748-
    749.

"The Higher Education Amendments of 1968" in <u>The Negro Almanac</u>. 1983.
    pp. 749-750.

EDUCATION, HIGHER - PERSONNEL

"Conflicts of Black Personnel in White Higher Education," Roosevelt
    Johnson in <u>Black Scholars on Higher Education</u>. 1974. pp. 6-10.

"Human Resources Development - an Emerging Role for Black Professionals
    in Higher Education," Theo James Pinnock in <u>Black Scholars on</u>
    <u>Higher Education</u>. 1974. pp. 301-314.

EDUCATION, HIGHER - STUDENT SERVICES

"Mandamus for Change in Student Services," Lawrence F. Davenport in
Black Scholars on Higher Education. 1974. pp. 323-334.

EDUCATION, INDUSTRIAL - BIBLIOGRAPHY

"The Secondary and Industrial Education of the Negro" in A Bibliography
of the Negro. 1928. pp. 424-427.

EDUCATION, RURAL - HAITI - BIBLIOGRAPHY

"Rural Education" in The Complete Haitiana. 1982. V. 2, pp. 983-1003.

EDUCATION, URBAN - HAITI - BIBLIOGRAPHY

"Urban Education" in The Complete Haitiana. 1982. V. 2, pp. 1005-1024.

EDUCATIONAL ADMINISTRATORS AND EMPLOYEES, FEDERAL - BIOGRAPHY - INDEX

"Federal Education Program Administrators, Employees" in In Black and
White. 1980. See index, V. 2, pp. 1146-1147.

EDUCATIONAL ADMINISTRATORS - BIOGRAPHY - INDEX

"Educational Administrators, Consultants" in In Black and White. 1980.
See index, V. 2, pp. 1142-1143.

EDUCATIONAL CONSULTANTS - BIOGRAPHY - INDEX

"Educational Administrators, Consultants" in In Black and White. 1980.
See index, V. 2, pp. 1142-1143.

EDUCATIONAL DEVELOPMENT

"Educational Needs: Implications for Black Educational Development" in
Beyond Identity. 1978. pp. 51-99.

EDUCATIONAL INSTITUTION FOUNDERS - BIOGRAPHY - INDEX

"Educational Institute Founders" in In Black and White. 1980. See index,
V. 2, p. 1143.

EDWARDS, JUNIUS

"Junius Edwards," Australia Henderson in Afro-American Fiction Writers
After 1955. 1984. pp. 65-67.

EGYPT - HISTORY

"Ethiopia and Egypt" in The African Background Outlined. 1936. pp. 20-
30.

EGYPT - MUSIC - BIBLIOGRAPHY

"Egypt" in Bibliography of Black Music. 1981. V. 3, pp. 67-68.

EGYPTIAN LANGUAGE - CREOLE - BIBLIOGRAPHY

"Egyptian: Creole Orgin Theory" in A Bibliography of Pidgin and Creole Languages. 1975. pp. 53-55.

EISENHOWER, DWIGHT D. - BIBLIOGRAPHY

"The Eisenhower Administration" in Blacks in America; Bibliographical Essays. 1971. pp. 305-307.

ELDER, LONNE

"Lonne Elder, III," Wilsonia E.D. Cherry in Afro-American Writers After 1955: Dramatists and Prose Writers. 1985. pp. 97-104.

ELLINGTON, DUKE - BIBLIOGRAPHY

"Ellington, Duke" in Black Music in America. 1981. pp. 203-262.

ELLISON, RALPH

"Ralph Ellison" in Interviews with Black Writers. 1973. pp. 62-77.

ELLISON, RALPH - BIBLIOGRAPHY

"After Protest: Black Writers in the 1950s and 1960s - Ralph Ellison" in Blacks in America; Bibliographical Essays. 1971. pp. 259-260.

EMANCIPATION - BIBLIOGRAPHY

"The Civil War and Emancipation" in Afro-American History, 1. 1974. pp. 279-325.

"The Civil War and Emancipation" in Afro-American History, 2. 1981. pp. 116-124.

"Civil War and the Emancipation of the Negro" in A Bibliography of the Negro. 1928. pp. 365-369.

"Slave Law: Emancipation" in Black Slavery in the Americas. 1982. pp. 740-759.

EMANCIPATION - CARIBBEAN - BIBLIOGRAPHY

"Slavery and Emancipation" in The Complete Caribbeana. V. 1, p. 307-341.

EMANCIPATION - HAITI - BIBLIOGRAPHY

"Slavery, Marronage and Emancipation, 1492-1803" in The Complete Haitiana. V. 1, pp. 277-368.

EMANCIPATION MOVEMENTS - CARIBBEAN - BIBLIOGRAPHY

"Emancipation in the West Indies" in A Bibliography of the Negro. 1928. pp. 271-274.

EMANCIPATION MOVEMENTS - SOUTH AMERICA - BIBLIOGRAPHY

"Emancipation in South America" in A Bibliography of the Negro. 1928.

pp. 278-279.

EMANUEL, JAMES ANDREW

"James Andrew Emanuel," Douglas Watson in <u>Afro-American Poets Since</u>
   <u>1955</u>. pp. 103-117.

EMPLOYMENT

"Employment and Labor" in <u>The Ebony Handbook</u>. 1974. pp. 263-329.

"Employment, Unemployment and the Labor Force" in <u>The Negro Almanac</u>.
   1983. pp. 581-644.

"The High-Tech Revolution and Its Implication for Black Employment,"
   Charles L. Betsey and Bruce H. Dunson in <u>The State of Black</u>
   <u>America, 1984</u>. pp. 25-42.

EMPLOYMENT - BIBLIOGRAPHY

"Blacks and the Manpower Policies of the Business Community" in <u>The</u>
   <u>Economics of Minorities</u>. 1976. pp. 111-130.

"Economics, Employment and Business" in <u>Afro-American Reference</u>. 1985.
   pp. 68-71.

"Employment" in <u>A Comprehensive Bibliography</u>. 1976. pp. 144-157.

"Employment" in <u>The Progress of Afro-American Women</u>. 1980. pp. 76-131.

EMPLOYMENT - CARIBBEAN - BIBLIOGRAPHY

"Employment and Labor Issues" in <u>The Complete Caribbeana</u>. V. 3, pp.
   1529-1559.

EMPLOYMENT - HAITI - BIBLIOGRAPHY

"Employment and Labor Issues" in <u>The Complete Haitiana</u>. 1982. V. 2, pp.
   1341-1353.

EMPLOYMENT - LEGAL CASES

"Important Cases: Employment" in <u>The Negro Almanac</u>. 1983. pp. 318-319.

ENCYCLOPEDIA

<u>Encyclopedia of Black America</u>. 1981. 921 p.

ENGINEERING ORGANIZATIONS - DIRECTORY

"Science, Engineering and Health Organizations" in <u>Black Resource Guide</u>.
   1986. pp. 203-206.

ENGINEERS - BIBLIOGRAPHY

"Engineering" in <u>The Progress of Afro-American Women</u>. 1980. p. 92.

ENGINEERS - BIOGRAPHY - INDEX

"Engineers" in In Black and White. 1980. See index, V. 2, pp. 1143-1144.

ENGLAND - SLAVERY - BIBLIOGRAPHY

"England" in Slavery: A Worldwide Bibliography. 1985. pp. 320-321.

ENGLISH LANGUAGE - CREOLE - BIBLIOGRAPHY

"West African Pidgin English" in A Bibliography of Pidgin and Creole
    Languages. 1975. pp. 345-360.

ENTERTAINERS

"The Black Entertainer in the Performing Arts" in The Negro Almanac.
    1983. pp. 1077-1126.

"The Negro's Contribution to the World of Entertainment," Calvin A.
    Claudel in The Negro Impact on Western Civilization. 1970. pp.
    231-250.

ENTERTAINERS - BIOGRAPHY - INDEX

"Entertainers" in In Black and White. 1980. See index, V. 2, p. 1144.

ENTERTAINERS - DIRECTORY

"Entertainers" in Black Resource Guide. 1986. pp. 47-48.

ENTERTAINERS - FILMOGRAPHY

"Blacks as Entertainers" in The Afro-American Cinematic Experience.
    1983. pp. 229-232.

ENTERTAINMENT - FIRST FACTS

"Black Firsts: Entertainment" in Before the Mayflower. 1982. pp. 622-
    625.

EPISCOPAL CHURCH - SLAVERY - BIBLIOGRAPHY

"Slavery, Negroes and the Church: Protestant Episcopal and Anglican" in
    Howard University Bibliography of African and Afro-American
    Religious Studies. 1977. pp. 143-144.

EQUIANO, OLAUDAH

"Olaudah Equiano (Gustanus Vassa)," Wilfred D. Samuels in Afro-American
    Writers Before the Harlem Renaissance. 1986. pp. 123-129.

ETHNIC GROUPS - CARIBBEAN - BIBLIOGRAPHY

"Population Segments: Others" in The Complete Caribbeana. V. 1, pp.
    559-572.

ETHNIC GROUPS - HAITI - BIBLIOGRAPHY

"Population Categories: Other Ethnic Groups" in <u>The Complete Haitiana</u>.
    1982. V. 1, pp. 577-594.

ETHNIC LIBRARY MATERIALS

"Criteria for the Evaluation of Ethnic Materials," Wendell Wray in
    <u>Ethnic Collections</u>. 1983. pp. 24-35.

ETHNIC STUDIES - ORGANIZATIONS

"Forging a Partnership with Professional Ethnic Associations," John C.
    Tyson in <u>Ethnic Collections</u>. 1983. pp. 310-317.

ETHNOLOGY, AFRICAN - BIBLIOGRAPHY

"African Peoples" in <u>A Bibliography of the Negro</u>. 1928. pp. 38-50.

ETHNOMUSICOLOGY - BIBLIOGRAPHY

"Ethnomusicology" in <u>Bibliography of Black Music</u>. 1981. V. 3, pp. 3-8.

EVANGELISTS - BIOGRAPHY - INDEX

"Evangelists" in <u>In Black and White</u>. 1980. See index, V. 2, p. 1145.

EVANS, MARI

"Mari Evans," Wallace R. Peppers in <u>Afro-American Poets Since 1955</u>. pp.
    117-123.

EXECUTIVE RECRUITERS - DIRECTORY

"Executive Recruiters" in <u>Black Resource Guide</u>. 1986. p. 80.

EXPATRIOTS - BIOGRAPHY - INDEX

"Expatriots" in <u>In Black and White</u>. 1980. See index, V. 2, p. 1145.

EXPLORERS

"Negro Contributions to the Exploration of the Globe," Ronald W. Davis
    in <u>The Negro Impact on Western Civilization</u>. 1970. pp. 33-50.

EXPLORERS - BIOGRAPHY - INDEX

"Explorers" in <u>In Black and White</u>. 1980. See index, V. 2, p. 1145.

EXPLORERS, AFRICAN

"African Seafarers and Discoverers" in <u>Black Men of the Sea</u>. 1978. pp.
    1-6.

FAIR, RONALD L.

"Ronald L. Fair," R. Baxter Miller in <u>Afro-American Fiction Writers
    After 1955</u>. 1984. pp. 67-76.

FAMILY

"The Black Family" in The Negro Almanac. 1983. pp. 475-525.

"The Black Family," Joseph H. Douglass and Mabel M. Smythe in The Black American Reference Book. 1976. pp. 316-340.

"The Black Family Today and Tomorrow," James D. McGhee in The State of Black America, 1985. pp. 1-20.

"Black Father and Child Interactions," John L. McAdoo in Black Men. 1981. pp. 115-130.

"Black Unwed Adolescent Fathers," Leo E. Hendricks in Black Men. 1981. pp. 131-140.

"Family and Church: Enduring Institutions" in Long Memory. 1982. pp.

"Moms, Dads, and Boys: Race and Sex Differences in the Socialization of Male Children," Walter R. Allen in Black Men. 1981. pp. 99-114.

"A Profile of the Black Single Female-Headed Household," James D. McGhee in The State of Black America, 1984. pp. 43-67.

"Teenage Pregnancy: The Implications for Black Americas," Joyce A. Ladner in The State of Black America, 1986. pp. 65-84.

FAMILY - BIBLIOGRAPHY

"Bibliography: Family and Church: Enduring Institutions" in Long Memory. 1982. pp. 429-432.

The Black Family in the United States: A Revised, Updated, Selectively Annotated Bibliography. 1986. 234 p.

"The Black Family in Urban America" in Blacks in America; Bibliographical Essays. 1971. pp. 364-372.

"Black Nuptiality, Family and Fertility Outside Marriage" in Black Demography in the United States. 1983. pp. 80-108.

"Family" in Afro-American Reference. 1985. pp. 171-174.

"Family Life" in The Progress of Afro-American Women. 1980. pp. 132-162.

FAMILY - CARIBBEAN - BIBLIOGRAPHY

"Socialization, Family and Kinship" in The Complete Caribbeana. 1977. V. 1, pp. 417-442.

FAMILY - HAITI - BIBLIOGRAPHY

"Socialization, Family and Kinship" in The Complete Haitiana. 1982. V. 2, pp. 833-842.

FAMILY - HISTORY

"Slave Family and its Legacies," Herbert G. Gutman in Roots and Branches. 1979. pp. 183-199.

FAMILY - HISTORY - DOCUMENTATION

"Familial Values of Freedmen and Women," Herbert G. Gutman in Afro-American History; Sources for Research. 1981. pp. 139-147.

FAMILY - SLAVERY

"The Slave Family" in The Slave Community. 1979. pp. 149-191.

FAMILY - SLAVERY - BIBLIOGRAPHY

"Black Family and Slavery" in The Black Family in the United States. 1986. pp. 63-72, 95-102 and 175.

"Slave Family: General" in Black Slavery in the Americas. 1982. pp. 1200-1219.

FAMILY - STATISTICS

"The Black Family (Tables)" in The Negro Almanac. 1983. pp. 493-524.

FAMILY PLANNING - BIBLIOGRAPHY

"Black Family Planning" in The Black Family in the United States. 1986. pp. 131-133.

FAMILY PLANNING - CARIBBEAN - BIBLIOGRAPHY

"Fertility and Family Planning" in The Complete Caribbeana. 1972. V. 2, pp. 1143-1156.

FAMILY PLANNING - HAITI - BIBLIOGRAPHY

"Fertility and Family Planning" in The Complete Haitiana. 1982. pp. 977-980.

FARMERS

"Blacks in Agriculture" in The Negro Almanac. 1983. pp. 555-557.

"Decline of Black Family Farmers" in The Negro Almanac. 1983. p. 481.

FARMERS - BIOGRAPHY - INDEX

"Farmers, Ranchers" in In Black and White. 1980. See index, V. 2, pp. 1145-1146.

FARMING

"Farms and Farming" in The Ebony Handbook. 1974. pp. 331-341.

FARMING - BIBLIOGRAPHY

"Farming" in The Progress of Afro-American Women. 1980. pp. 92-93.

FASHIONS - BIBLIOGRAPHY

"Fashions" in The Progress of Afro-American Women. 1980. pp. 174-176.

FAUSET, JESSIE - BIBLIOGRAPHY

"Fauset, Jessie" in The Harlem Renaissance. 1982. pp. 77-81.

FEDERAL BUREAU OF INVESTIGATION - BIOGRAPHY - INDEX

"Protective Services: FBI, Secret Service" in In Black and White. 1980.
    See index, V. 2, p. 1224.

FEDERAL COUNCIL OF CHURCHES - BIBLIOGRAPHY

"Federal Council of Churches" in Howard University Bibliography of
    African and Afro-American Religious Studies. 1977. pp. 293-295.

FEDERAL GOVERNMENT OFFICIALS - BIOGRAPHY - INDEX

"Federal, National, Government Officials" in In Black and White. 1980.
    See index, V. 2, pp. 1147-1148.

FEDERATION OF COLORED WOMEN'S CLUBS - BIBLIOGRAPHY

"Federation of Colored Women's Clubs" in The Progress of Afro-American
    Women. 1980. pp. 253-255.

FEMINISM - BIBLIOGRAPHY

"Women's Rights and Feminist Movement" in The Progress of Afro-American
    Women. 1980. pp. 348-356.

FEMINISM - HISTORY

"Woman Suffrage: Feminism and White Supremacy in Reluctant Reformers.
    1975. pp. 127-172.

FERTILITY - BIBLIOGRAPHY

"Black Nuptiality, Family and Fertility Outside of Marriage" in Black
    Demography in the United States. 1983. pp. 80-108.

FERTILITY - CARIBBEAN - BIBLIOGRAPHY

"Fertility and Family Planning" in The Complete Caribbeana. 1977. V. 2,
    pp. 1143-1156.

FESTIVALS - BIBLIOGRAPHY

"Festivals" in Afro-American Folk Culture. 1978. See index, p. 773.

FICTION

Afro-American Fiction Writers After 1955. 1984. 350 p.

FICTION - BIBLIOGRAPHY

The Afro-American Novel 1965-1975. 1977. 214 p.

"After Protest: Black Writers in the 1950s and 1960s" in Blacks in
    America; Bibliographical Essays. 1971. pp. 256-265.

Black American Fiction: A Bibliography. 1978. 351 p.

"Black Social Fiction: The Protest School" in Blacks in America;
    Bibliographical Essays. 1971. pp. 253-256.

"Individual Writers: Original Works and Criticism: Fiction" in A
    Comprehensive Bibliography. 1976. pp. 220-245.

"Literary History and Criticism: Fiction" in A Comprehensive
    Bibliography. 1976. pp. 212-214.

"Literature-Fiction" in Afro-American Reference. 1985. pp. 143-146.

"Novels by Negro Authors Treating Mainly of the Present" in A
    Bibliography of the Negro. 1928. pp. 471-472.

FICTION - INDEX

Index to Black American Literary Anthologies. 1979. 219 p.

FICTION - SHORT STORIES - COLLECTIONS - BIBLIOGRAPHY

"Books of Short Stories by Negro Authors" in A Bibliography of the
    Negro. 1928. pp. 463-464.

FICTION (WHITE AUTHORS) - BIBLIOGRAPHY

"Books of Short Stories by White Authors Relating to the Negro" in A
    Bibliography of the Negro. 1928. pp. 461-463.

"Novels by White Authors Relating to the Negro" in A Bibliography of the
    Negro. 1928. pp. 464-471.

FIELDS, JULIA

"Julia Fields," Mary Williams Burger in Afro-American Poets Since 1955.
    1985. pp. 123-131.

FIGUEROA, JOHN JOSEPH MARIA

"John Joseph Maria Figueroa," Pamela C. Mordecai in 50 Caribbean
    Writers. 1986. pp. 178-186.

FILM

"The Black in Films" in The Negro Almanac. 1983. pp. 1185-1210.

FILM - ATHLETES - FILMOGRAPHY

"Documentaries on Black Athletes" in Black Athletes in the U.S. 1981.
    pp. 253-254.

FILM - BIBLIOGRAPHY

The Afro-American Cinematic Experience: An Annotated Bibliography and
    Filmography. 1983. 260 p.

"Afro-Americans in Films" in Blacks in America; Bibliographical Essays.
    1971. pp. 284-286.

"Audio-Visual Materials: Writing on Film" in Black Women and Religion.
    1980. p. 99.

"Motion Pictures" in Afro-American Reference. 1985. pp. 153-156.

"Motion Pictures and Films" in The Progress of Afro-American Women. 1980
    pp. 23-25.

"Theater and Film Industry" in The Progress of Afro-American Women.
    1980. pp. 345-347.

FILM - HISTORY AND CRITICISM - BIBLIOGRAPHY

"Literary History and Criticism: Theatre and Film" in A Comprehensive
    Bibliography. 1976. pp. 215-218.

FILM - MUSIC - INDEX

"Film Index" in Blues Who's Who. 1979. pp. 611-616.

FILM MAKERS - BIOGRAPHY - INDEX

"Filmmakers" in In Black and White. 1980. See index, V. 2, p. 1148.

FILMOGRAPHY

"Black Independent Films" in The Afro-American Cinematic Experience.
    1983. pp. 233-238.

"Documentaries" in The Afro-American Cinematic Experience. 1983. pp.
    245-248.

"Educational Films with Black Themes" in The Negro Almanac. 1983. pp.
    758-765.

"Films Featuring Black Actors or With Black Themes" in The Negro
    Almanac. 1983. pp. 1189-1210.

"Major Films in the Afro-American Cinematic Experience" in The Afro-
    American Cinematic Experience. 1983. pp. 181-210.

Women of Color: A Filmography of Minority and Third World Women. 1985.
    338 p.

FILMSTRIPS - HARLEM RENAISSANCE - BIBLIOGRAPHY

"Filmstrips" in The Harlem Renaissance. 1982. pp. 203-204.

FINANCE - CARIBBEAN - BIBLIOGRAPHY

"Monetary Issues" in The Complete Caribbeana. V. 3, pp. 1611-1623.

FINANCE - HAITI - BIBLIOGRAPHY

"Banking and Monetary Issues" in The Complete Haitiana. 1982. V. 2, pp. 1395-1420.

FINANCIAL INSTITUTIONS

"The Potential and Problems of Black Financial Institutions," William D. Bradford in The State of Black America, 1985. pp. 127-142.

FIRE FIGHTERS - BIBLIOGRAPHY

"Firefighting" in The Progress of Afro-American Women. 1980. p. 93.

FIRE FIGHTERS - BIOGRAPHY - INDEX

"Protective Services: Fire Fighter" in In Black and White. 1980. See index, V. 2, p. 1224.

FIRST FACTS

"Black Firsts" in Before the Mayflower. 1982. pp. 613-642.

"Black Firsts: A Compilation of Interesting Debut Events" in The Negro Almanac. 1983. pp. 1357-1366.

Famous First Facts. 1972. 212 p.

FIRST FACTS - BIOGRAPHY - INDEX

"Firsts" in In Black and White. 1980. See index, V. 2, pp. 1148-11.

"One-of-a-Kind" in In Black and White. 1980. See index, V. 2, pp. 1198-1202.

FISHER, RUDOLPH - BIBLIOGRAPHY

"Fisher, Rudolph" in The Harlem Renaissance. 1982. pp. 83-86.

FISHERMEN

"Menhaden Men" in Black Men of the Sea. 1978. pp. 105-113.

"Watermen" in Black Men of the Sea. pp. 39-47.

FISHERMEN, AFRICAN

"African Fishermen and Traders" in Black Men of the Sea. 1978. pp. 7-15.

FISHING - CARIBBEAN - BIBLIOGRAPHY

"The Fishing Industry" in The Complete Caribbeana. V. 3, pp. 1655-1667.

FISHING - HAITI - BIBLIOGRAPHY

"The Fishing Industry" in The Complete Haitiana. 1982. V. 2, pp. 1431-1433.

FISK UNIVERSITY - MUSIC EDUCATION - BIBLIOGRAPHY

"Fisk University" in Bibliography of Black Music. 1984. V. 4, pp. 98-101.

FITZGERALD, ELLA - BIBLIOGRAPHY

"Fitzgerald, Ella" in Black Music in America. 1981. pp. 264-278.

FLACK, ROBERTA - BIBLIOGRAPHY

"Flack, Roberta" in Black Music in America. 1981. pp. 278-282.

FLIGHT ATTENDANTS - BIOGRAPHY - INDEX

"Flight Attendants" in In Black and White. 1980. See index, V. 2, p. 1158.

FLORIDA - EDUCATION - BIBLIOGRAPHY

"Florida" in The Education of Poor and Minority Children. 1981. pp. 241-246.

FLORIDA - EDUCATION, HIGHER - BIBLIOGRAPHY

"Higher Education by State: Florida" in The Education of Poor and Minority Children. 1981. pp. 877-878.

FLORIDA - GENEALOGY - BIBLIOGRAPHY

"Florida" in Black Genesis. 1978. pp. 130-132.

FLORIDA - LIBRARIANS

"Black Librarians in Florida," Joseph H. Reason in The Black Librarian in the Southeast. 1976. pp. 25-31.

FLORIDA - SLAVERY - BIBLIOGRAPHY

"Florida" in Black Slavery in the Americas. 1982. pp. 880-888.

"Florida" in Slavery: A Worldwide Bibliography. 1985. pp. 113-114.

FLORISTS - BIBLIOGRAPHY

"Florists" in The Progress of Afro-American Women. 1980. p. 93.

FLORISTS - BIOGRAPHY - INDEX

"Florists" in In Black and White. 1980. See index, V. 2, p. 1158.

FLUGELHORN PLAYERS - BIOGRAPHY - INDEX

"Musicians: Instrumental: Flugelhorn" in In Black and White. 1980. See index, V. 2, p. 1186.

FLUTISTS - BIOGRAPHY - INDEX

"Musicians: Instrumental: Flute" in In Black and White. 1980. See index,
     V. 2, p. 1186.

FOLK CULTURE - BIBLIOGRAPHY

Afro-American Folk Culture. 1978. 2 V.

FOLK CULTURE, AFRICAN

"Legend, Magic, Myth and Symbolism" in The Roots of Black Music. 1982.
     pp. 93-96.

FOLK MUSIC - BIBLIOGRAPHY

"Dance, Dance Music and Songs" in Afro-American Folk Culture. 1978. See
     index, 765-766.

"Folk Music Studies" in A Bibliography of the Negro. 1928. p. 620.

"Music" in Afro-American Folk Culture. 1978. See index, pp. 781-782.

"Spirituals and Earlier Folk Music" in Bibliography of Black Music.
     1981. V. 2, pp. 34-64.

FOLK MUSIC - CARIBBEAN - BIBLIOGRAPHY

"Folk Music of the Negro in the West Indies and South America" in A
     Bibliography of the Negro. 1928. pp. 648-649.

FOLK MUSIC - COLLECTIONS - BIBLIOGRAPHY

"Collections of Negro Folk Songs: Collections of Secular Songs" in A
     Bibliography of the Negro. 1928. pp. 433-434.

FOLK MUSIC - DISCOGRAPHIES - BIBLIOGRAPHY

"Discographies Folk Music" in Bibliography of Black Music. 1981. V. 1,
     p. 30.

FOLK MUSIC - HISTORY AND CRITICISM - BIBLIOGRAPHY

"Discussions of Negro Folk Songs" in A Bibliography of the Negro. 1928.
     pp. 437-439.

FOLK MUSIC - SPIRITUALS - COLLECTIONS - BIBLIOGRAPHY

"Collections of Negro Folk Songs: Collections of Religious Songs" in A
     Bibliography of the Negro. 1928. pp. 434-437.

FOLK MUSICIANS - BIBLIOGRAPHY

"Musicians and Composers" in Afro-American Folk Culture. 1978. See
     index, p. 783.

FOLK TALES - BIBLIOGRAPHY

"Tales and Tale Telling" in Afro-American Folk Culture. 1978. See index,
    pp. 800-801.

FOLKLORE - BIBLIOGRAPHY

"Bibliography of Folklore in America; Afro-American Folklore," Charles
    Perdue in Folk Festivals; a Handbook for Organization and
    Management. 1982. pp. 269-273.

"Folklore" in Afro-American Reference. 1985. pp. 99-105.

"Folklore" in Black Slavery in the Americas. 1982. pp. 1339-1367.

"Folklore" in A Comprehensive Bibliography. 1976. pp. 254-256.

"Folklore of the Negro in the United States" in A Bibliography of the
    Negro. 1928. pp. 430-432.

"Literature (Novels, Drama, Poetry) with Folkloric Content" in Afro-
    American Folk Culture. 1978. See index, pp. 778-779.

"Shuckin' and Jivin': Blacks in Folklore" in Blacks in the Humanities.
    1986. pp. 75-84.

FOLKLORE, AFRICAN - BIBLIOGRAPHY

"African Folklore" in A Bibliography of the Negro. 1928. pp. 101-110.

FOLKLORE, BELIZEAN - BIBLIOGRAPHY

"Folklore" in Belize. 1980. pp. 97-98.

FOLKLORE, BRAZILIAN - BIBLIOGRAPHY

"Folklore: Mythology, Legends, Costumes and Festivals" in Afro-
    Braziliana. 1978. pp. 91-105.

FOLKLORE, CARIBBEAN - BIBLIOGRAPHY

"Folklore of the Negro in the West Indies and South America" in A
    Bibliography of the Negro. 1928. pp. 646-647.

FOLKLORE, SOUTH AMERICAN - BIBLIOGRAPHY

"Folklore of the Negro in the West Indies and South America" in A
    Bibliography of the Negro. 1928. pp. 646-647.

FOOD WORKERS - BIBLIOGRAPHY

"Dietetics and Food Service" in The Progress of Afro-American Women.
    1980. pp. 85-87.

FOOTBALL - BIBLIOGRAPHY

"Articles: Football" in Black Athletes. 1981. pp. 210-218.

FOREIGN RELATIONS

"Black Participation in U.S. Foreign Relations" Hugh Smythe and Elliott
    Skinner in The Black American Reference Book. 1976. pp. 638-647.

FOREIGN RELATIONS - HAITI - BIBLIOGRAPHY

"Haiti - U.S. Relations" in The Complete Haitiana. 1982. V. 2, pp.
    1217-1265.

FORESTERS - BIOGRAPHY - INDEX

"Foresters" in In Black and White. 1980. See index, V. 2, p. 1158.

FORREST, LEON

"Leon Forrest," Johanna L. Grimes in Afro-American Fiction Writers After
    1955. 1984. pp. 77-83.

FORTEN, CHARLOTTE

"Charlotte L. Forten," Trudier Harris in Afro-American Writers Before
    the Harlem Renaissance. 1986. pp. 130-139.

FOSTER PARENTS - BIOGRAPHY - INDEX

"Foster Parents" in In Black and White. 1980. See index, V. 2, p. 1158.

FOUNDATIONS

"Blacks and American Foundations: Two Views," Vernon E. Jordan and
    Ernest Kaiser in The Black American Reference Book. 1976. pp. 480-
    491.

FRANCE

"Miscegenation in France" in Sex and Race. 1944. V. 1, pp. 221-240.

FRANCE - BIBLIOGRAPHY

"France" in The Complete Caribbeana. 1977. See index, V. 4, p. 2162.

"France" in The Education of Poor and Minority Children. 1981. pp.
    1141-1150.

FRANCE - SLAVE TRADE - BIBLIOGRAPHY

"Atlantic - French" in Slavery: A Worldwide Bibliography. 1985. pp.
    371-376.

"France" in Slavery: A Worldwide Bibliography. 1985. pp. 319-320.

FRANKLIN, ARETHA - BIBLIOGRAPHY

"Franklin, Aretha Louise" in Black Music in America. 1981. pp. 282-289.

FRATERNITIES - DIRECTORY

"Fraternities" in <u>Black Resource Guide</u>. 1986. p. 88.

FREE AFRICAN SOCIETY

"The Free African Society" in <u>The Negro Almanac</u>. 1983. p. 258.

FREE BLACKS IN ANTEBELLUM U.S.

"The Founding of Black America" in <u>Before the Mayflower</u>. 1982. pp. 54-85.

"Quasi-Free Negroes" in <u>From Slavery to Freedom</u>. 1980. pp. 157-179.

"Rich Negroes with White Wives During Slavery" in <u>Sex and Race</u>. 1942. V. 2, pp. 242-248.

"An Unsecure People: Free Negroes in America" in <u>Long Memory</u>. 1982.

FREE BLACKS IN ANTEBELLUM U.S. - BIBLIOGRAPHY

"Antebellum Free Blacks and Southern Abolitionism" in <u>The American South</u>, 1986. V. 1, pp. 142-151.

"Bibliographical Notes: Quasi-Free Negroes" in <u>From Slavery to Freedom</u>. 1980. pp. 523-525.

"Bibliography: An Unsecure People: Free Negroes in America" in <u>Long Memory</u>. 1982. pp. 427-432.

"The Free Black Community" in <u>Afro-American History, 1</u>. 1974. pp. 256-279.

"The Free Black Community: in <u>Afro-American History, 2</u>. 1981. pp. 110-116.

"The Free Negro" in <u>A Bibliography of the Negro</u>. 1928. pp. 352-357.

"Slave Law: Free Blacks" in <u>Black Slavery in the Americas</u>. 1982. pp. 695-740.

FREE BLACKS IN ANTEBELLUM U.S. - NEW YORK - CENSUS

<u>Free Black Heads of Household</u>. 1981. 301 p.

FREE BLACKS IN ANTEBELLUM U.S. - NORTH - BIBLIOGRAPHY

"Slaves and Black Freemen in the Northern Colonies" in <u>Blacks in America; Bibliographical Essays</u>. 1971. pp. 44-45.

FREE BLACKS IN ANTEBELLUM U.S. - SOUTH - BIBLIOGRAPHY

"Free Blacks in the Antebellum South" in <u>Blacks in America; Bibliographical Essays</u>. 1971. pp. 69-70.

"Slaves and Free Blacks in the Antebellum South" in <u>Blacks in America; Bibliographical Essays</u>. 1971. pp. 42-44.

FREEDMEN - BIBLIOGRAPHY

"The Black Freedmen" in Blacks in America; Bibliographical Essays. 1971.
pp. 117-119.

FREEDMEN - DOCUMENTATION

"Familial Values of Freedmen and Women," Herbert G. Gutman in Afro-
American History; Sources for Research. 1981. pp. 139-147.

FREEDMEN'S BUREAU

"Freedmen's Bureau Records: Texas, a Case Study," Barry A. Crouch in
Afro-American History; Sources for Research. 1981. pp. 74-94.

FRENCH AND INDIAN WARS - BIOGRAPHY - INDEX

"Military Service, French, Indian Wars" in In Black and White. 1980. See
index, V. 2, p. 1176.

FRENCH GUIANA

"Blacks in the Western Hemisphere: French Guiana" in The Negro Almanac.
1983. pp. 1480-1481.

FRENCH GUIANA - BIBLIOGRAPHY

"French Guiana" in The Complete Caribbeana. 1977. See index, V. 3, pp.
2163-2164.

FRENCH GUIANA - LINGUISTICS - BIBLIOGRAPHY

"Guyane Francaise (French Guiana)" in A Bibliography of Pidgin and
Creole Languages. 1975. pp. 275-277.

FRENCH HORN PLAYERS - BIOGRAPHY - INDEX

"Musicians: Instrumental: French Horn" in In Black and White. 1980. See
index, V. 2, p. 1186.

FRONTERIZO DIALECT - BIBLIOGRAPHY

"Dialecto Fronterizo" in A Bibliography of Pidgin and Creole Languages.
1975. p. 63.

FRONTIER PERSONS - BIOGRAPHY - INDEX

"Frontiersmen" in In Black and White. 1980. See index, V. 2, p. 1158.

FUGITIVE SLAVE LAW - BIBLIOGRAPHY

"The Fugitive Slave Law" in A Bibliography of the Negro. 1928. pp. 333-
335.

FULLER, CHARLES H.

"Charles H. Fuller," Ethel W. Githi in Afro-American Writers After 1955:

<u>Dramatists and Prose Writers</u>. 1985. pp. 104-109.

FUNERAL DIRECTORS - BIOGRAPHY - INDEX

"Funeral Directors" in <u>In Black and White</u>. 1980. See index, V. 2, pp. 1158-1159.

FUTURE

<u>Blacks in the Year 2000</u>. 1981. 70 p.

"The Challenge of America in the Year 2000," Robert Theobald in <u>Blacks in the Year 2000</u>. 1981. pp. 31-38.

"Probable Development of the Black American Condition," Charles V. Hamilton in <u>Blacks in the Year 2000</u>. 1981. pp. 39-43.

GABON - MUSIC - BIBLIOGRAPHY

"Gabon" in <u>Bibliography of Black Music</u>. 1981. V. 3, p. 72.

GAINES, ERNEST

"Ernest Gaines" in <u>Interviews with Black Writers</u>. 1973. pp. 78-93.

"Ernest J. Gaines," Keith E. Byerman in <u>Afro-American Fiction Writers After 1955</u>. 1984. pp. 84-96.

GAMBIA - MUSIC - BIBLIOGRAPHY

"Gambia" in <u>Bibliography of Black Music</u>. 1981. V. 3, p. 73.

GAMES - BIBLIOGRAPHY

"Games" in <u>Afro-American Folk Culture</u>. 1978. See index, pp. 774-775.

GAMES, SINGING - BIBLIOGRAPHY

"Singing, Games" in <u>Afro-American Folk Culture</u>. 1978. See index, p. 791.

GARVEY, MARCUS - BIBLIOGRAPHY

"Black Nationalism: Marcus Garvey" in <u>Blacks in America; Bibliographical Essays</u>. 1971. pp. 203-205.

<u>Marcus Garvey</u>. 1980. 1924.

"Marcus Garvey's Opinion of Jews" in <u>Black-Jewish Relations</u>. 1984. p. 34 and 93.

GAYE, MARVIN - BIBLIOGRAPHY

"Gaye, Marvin" in <u>Black Music in America</u>. 1981. pp. 289-292.

GENEALOGY

<u>Ethnic Genealogy</u>. 1983. 440 p.

GENEALOGY - BIBLIOGRAPHY

Black Genesis. 1978. 328 p.

"Genealogy" in Afro-American Reference. 1985. pp. 36-37.

GENEALOGY - DOCUMENTATION

"Genealogy of Afro-Americans," Alex Haley in Afro-American History;
    Sources for Research. 1981. pp. 148-158.

GENOCIDE - BIBLIOGRAPHY

"Black Family and Genocide" in The Black Family in the United States.
    1986. p. 115.

GEOGRAPHY - CARIBBEAN - BIBLIOGRAPHY

"Geography and Ecology" in The Complete Caribbeana. V. 3, pp. 1871-1911.

GEOGRAPHY - HAITI - BIBLIOGRAPHY

"Geography and Ecology" in The Complete Haitiana. 1982. V. 1, pp. 97-
    112.

GEOLOGISTS - BIOGRAPHY - INDEX

"Geologists" in In Black and White. 1980. See index, V. 2, p. 1159.

GEOLOGY - CARIBBEAN - BIBLIOGRAPHY

"Geology and Land Forms" in The Complete Caribbeana. V. 2, pp. 1671-
    1733.

GEOLOGY - HAITI - BIBLIOGRAPHY

"Geology and Land Forms" in The Complete Haitiana. 1981. V. 1, pp. 119-
    125.

GEORGIA - EDUCATION, HIGHER - BIBLIOGRAPHY

"Higher Education by State: Georgia" in The Education of Poor and
    Minority Children. 1981. pp. 879-880.

GEORGIA - GENEALOGY - BIBLIOGRAPHY

"Georgia" in Black Genesis. 1978. pp. 51-67.

GEORGIA - LIBRARIANS

"Georgia, Peaches and Cream - Afro-American Librarians in the State of
    Georgia," Casper LeRoy Jordan in The Black Librarian in the
    Southeast. 1976. pp. 32-36.

GEORGIA - SLAVERY - BIBLIOGRAPHY

"Colonial Slavery: The Carolinas and Georgia" in <u>From Slavery to Freedom</u>. 1980. pp. 58-60.

"Georgia" in <u>Black Slavery in the Americas</u>. 1982. pp. 888-905.

GERMAN LANGUAGE - PIDGIN - BIBLIOGRAPHY

"Germanic Languages: Pidgin Orgigin Theory" in <u>A Bibliography of Pidgin and Creole Languages</u>. 1975. p. 57.

GERMANY

"Negro-White Mixing in Germany, Ancient and Modern" in <u>Sex and Race</u>. 1944. V. 1, pp., 176-195.

GERMANY - BIBLIOGRAPHY

"The Germanies" in <u>The Education of Poor and Minority Children</u>. 1981. pp. 1150-1158.

GHANA - HISTORY

"Kumbi" in <u>The African Background Outlined</u>. 1936. pp. 30-42.

GHANA - MUSIC - BIBLIOGRAPHY

"Ghana" in <u>Bibliography of Black Music</u>. 1981. V. 3, pp. 74-79.

GILLESPIE, DIZZY - BIBLIOGRAPHY

"Gillespie, Dizzy" in <u>Black Music in America</u>. 1981. pp. 293-309.

GIOVANNI, NIKKI

"Nikki Giovanni," Mozella G. Mitchell in <u>Afro-American Poets Since 1955</u>. 1985. pp. 135-151.

GIRL SCOUTS - BIBLIOGRAPHY

"Girl Scouts" in <u>The Progress of Afro-American Women</u>. 1980. pp. 255-257.

GOINES, DONALD

"Donald Goines," Greg Goode in <u>Afro-American Fiction Writers After 1955</u>. 1984. pp. 96-100.

GOLF - BIBLIOGRAPHY

"Golf" in <u>Black Athletes</u>. 1981. pp. 219-222.

GOSPEL MUSIC

"Gospel" in <u>Black Music</u>. 1979. pp. 147-158.

GOSPEL MUSIC - BIBLIOGRAPHY

"Gospel Music" in <u>Bibliography of Black Music</u>. 1981. V. 2, pp. 109-116.

"Spirituals and Gospel Music" in <u>Jazz Bibliography</u>. 1981. pp. 84-89.

GOVERNMENT - HAITI - BIBLIOGRAPHY

"Politics and Government" in <u>The Complete Haitiana</u>. 1982. V. 2, pp. 1037-1117.

GOVERNMENT AID

"The Federal Government and Assistance Programs" in <u>The Negro Almanac</u>. 1983. pp. 679-709.

GOVERNMENT DOCUMENTS

"United States Government Publications as Sources for Ethnic Materials," Barbara J. Ford and Laurel Minott in <u>Ethnic Collections</u>. 1983. pp. 46-62.

GOVERNMENT OFFICIALS

"Past and Present Appointed Government Officials and Appointees" in <u>The Negro Almanac</u>. 1983. pp. 417-441.

GOVERNMENT OFFICIALS - BIBLIOGRAPHY

"Politics and Government" in <u>The Progress of Afro-American Women</u>. 1980. pp. 283-291.

GRAFFITI - BIBLIOGRAPHY

"Graffiti" in <u>Afro-American Folk Culture</u>. 1978. See index, p. 775.

GRAN COLOMBIA - SLAVERY - BIBLIOGRAPHY

"New Grenada and Gran Colombia" in <u>Slavery: A Worldwide Bibliography</u>. 1985. pp. 132-133.

GRAVE DECORATION - BIBLIOGRAPHY

"Grave Decoration" in <u>250 Years of Afro-American Art</u>. 1981. pp. 368-369.

GREAT BRITAIN

"The Mixing of Whites and Blacks in the British Isles" in <u>Sex and Race</u>. 1944. V. 1, pp. 196-220.

GREAT BRITAIN - BIBLIOGRAPHY

"Great Britain: Blacks" in <u>The Education of Poor and Minority Children</u>. 1981. pp. 1165-1172.

"United Kingdom" in <u>The Complete Caribbeana</u>. 1977. See index, V. 4, p. 2191.

GREAT BRITAIN - EDUCATION, HIGHER - BIBLIOGRAPHY

"Great Britain: Higher Education" in <u>The Education of Poor and Minority</u>

Children. 1981. pp. 1177-1178.

GREAT BRITAIN - SLAVE TRADE - BIBLIOGRAPHY

"Atlantic - English" in Slavery: A Worldwide Bibliography. 1985. pp.
    364-368.

GREECE (ANCIENT)

"The Negro in Ancient Greece" in Sex and Race. 1944. V. 1, pp. 79-85.

GRENADA - BIBLIOGRAPHY

"Grenada" in The Complete Caribbeana. 1977. See index, V. 4, p. 2168.

GRENADINES - BIBLIOGRAPHY

"Grenadines" in The Complete Caribbeana. 1977. See index, V. 4, p. 2169.

GRIGGS, SUTTON E.

"Sutton Elbert Griggs," Betty E. Taylor Thompson in Afro-American
    Writers Before the Harlem Renaissance. 1986. pp. 140-148.

GRIMKE, ANGELINA WELD

"Angelina Weld Grimke," Michael Greene in Afro-American Writers Before
    the Harlem Renaissance. 1986. pp. 149-155.

GRIMKE, ANGELINA WELD - BIBLIOGRAPHY

"Grimke, Angeline Weld" in The Harlem Renaissance. 1982. pp. 86-87.

GUADELOUPE

"Blacks in the Western Hemisphere: Guadeloupe (Basse-Terre, Grand
    Terre)" in The Negro Almanac. 1983. p. 1481.

"Haiti, Martinique, Guadeloupe" in Sex and Race. 1942. V. 1, pp. 97-121.

GUADELOUPE - BIBLIOGRAPHY

"Guadeloupe" in The Complete Caribbeana. 1977. See index, V. 4, p. 2169.

GUATEMALA - MUSIC - BIBLIOGRAPHY

"Guatemala" in Bibliography of Black Music. 1981. V. 3, p. 184.

GUINEA - MUSIC - BIBLIOGRAPHY

"Guinea" in Bibliography of Black Music. 1981. V. 3, p. 80.

GUINEA BISSAU - LINGUISTICS - BIBLIOGRAPHY

"Guine" in A Bibliography of Pidgin and Creole Languages. 1975. pp. 89-
    90.

GUINEA-BISSAU - MUSIC - BIBLIOGRAPHY

"Guinea-Bissau" in Bibliography of Black Music. 1981. V. 3, p. 81.

GUITARISTS - BIOGRAPHY - INDEX

"Musicians: Instrumental: Guitar" in In Black and White. 1980. See
    index, V. 2, p. 1186.

GULLAH AND SEA ISLAND CULTURE - BIBLIOGRAPHY

"Gullah and Sea Island Culture" in Afro-American Folk Culture. 1978. See
    index, p. 776.

GUNN, BILL

"Bill Gunn," Ilona Leki in Afro-American Writers After 1955: Dramatists
    and Prose Writers. 1985. pp. 109-114.

GUY, ROSA

"Rosa Guy," Leota S. Lawrence in Afro-American Fiction Writers After
    1955. 1984. pp. 101-106.

GUYANA

"Blacks in the Western Hemisphere: Guyana" in The Negro Almanac. 1983.
    pp. 1475-1476.

GUYANA - BIBLIOGRAPHY

"British Guiana/Guyana" in Race and Ethnic Relations. 1980. pp. 214-216.

"Guyana" in The Complete Caribbeana. 1977. See index, V. 4, pp. 2171-
    2172.

"Guyana" in The Education of Poor and Minority Children. 1981. pp.
    1207-1208.

GUYANA - MUSIC - BIBLIOGRAPHY

"Guyana" in Bibliography of Black Music. 1981. V. 3, p. 185.

HAIR STYLISTS - BIOGRAPHY - INDEX

"Hairstylists, Cosmeticians" in In Black and White. 1980. See index, V.
    2, p. 1159.

HAITI

"Blacks in the Western Hemisphere: Haiti" in The Negro Almanac. 1983.
    pp. 1476-1477.

"Haiti, Martinique, Guadeloupe" in Sex and Race. 1942, V. 2, pp. 97-121.

HAITI - BIBLIOGRAPHIES - BIBLIOGRAPHY

"Bibliographic and Archival Resources" in The Complete Haitiana. 1982.
   V. 1, pp. 5-30.

HAITI - BIBLIOGRAPHY

"Bibliography" in Historical Dictionary of Haiti. 1977. pp. 116-124.

The Complete Haitiana. 1982. 1562 p.

Haiti. 1983. 177 p.

"Haiti" in The Education of Poor and Minority Children. 1981. p. 1208.

"Haiti" in Race and Ethnic Relations. 1980. pp. 173-175.

HAITI - EDUCATION - BIBLIOGRAPHY

"Educational System" in The Complete Haitiana. 1982. V. 2, pp. 981-1033.

HAITI - HISTORY - BIBLIOGRAPHY

"Contemporary Period, 1935-1980" in The Complete Haitiana. 1982, V, 1,
   pp. 471-497.

"General History, 1492-1980" in The Complete Haitiana. 1982. V. 1, pp.
   185-275.

"Post-Independence, 1804-1914" in The Complete Haitiana. 1982. V. 1, pp.
   369-414.

HAITI - HISTORY - DICTIONARY

Historical Dictionary of Haiti. 1977. 124 p.

HAITI - LINGUISTICS - BIBLIOGRAPHY

"Haiti" in A Bibliography of Pidgin and Creole Languages. 1975. pp.
   224-253.

HAITI - MUSIC - BIBLIOGRAPHY

"Haiti" in Bibliography of Black Music. 1981. V. 3. pp. 146-149.

"Music and Dance" in The Complete Haitiana. 1982. V. 1, pp. 799-806.

HAITI - U.S. OCCUPATION - BIBLIOGRAPHY

"U.S. Occupation of Haiti, 1915-1934" in The Complete Haitiana. 1982. V.
   1, pp. 415-469.

HALEY, ALEX

"Alex Haley," Marilyn Kern-Foxworth in Afro-American Writers After 1955:
   Dramatists and Prose Writers. 1985. pp. 115-119.

HAMILTON, VIRGINIA

"Virginia Hamilton," Jane Ball in <u>Afro-American Fiction Writers After</u>
     <u>1955</u>. 1984. pp. 107-110.

HAMMOND, JUPITER

"Jupiter Hammond," Sondra A. O'Neale in <u>Afro-American Writers Before the</u>
     <u>Harlem Renaissance</u>. 1986. pp. 156-163.

HAMPTON INSTITUTE - MUSIC EDUCATION - BIBLIOGRAPHY

"Colleges and Universities: Hampton Institute" in <u>Bibliography of Black</u>
     <u>Music</u>. 1984. V. 4, pp. 101-102.

HANCOCK, HERBIE - BIBLIOGRAPHY

"Hancock, Herbie" in <u>Black Music in America</u>. 1981. pp. 315-320.

HANDICAPPED ACHIEVERS - BIOGRAPHY - INDEX

"In spite of Handicaps" in <u>In Black and White</u>. 1980. See index, V. 2,
     pp. 1160-1161.

HANDY, WILLIAM C. - BIBLIOGRAPHY

"Handy, William Christopher" in <u>Black Music in America</u>. 1981. pp. 315-
     320.

HANSBERRY, LORRAINE

"Lorraine Hansberry," Steven R. Carter in <u>Afro-American Writers After</u>
     <u>1955: Dramatists and Prose Writers</u>. 1984. pp. 120- 134.

HANSBERRY, LORRAINE - BIBLIOGRAPHY

"Black Dramatists: Lorraine Hansberry" in <u>Blacks in America;</u>
     <u>Bibliographical Essays</u>. 1971. pp. 282-283.

HARLEM - ART - BIBLIOGRAPHY

"Harlem" in <u>250 Years of Afro-American Art</u>. 1981. pp. 369-379.

HARLEM - JEWS - BIBLIOGRAPHY

"Jews in New York City and Harlem" in <u>Black-Jewish Relations</u>. 1984. pp.
     23-25.

HARLEM RENAISSANCE

<u>From DuBois to Van Vechten</u>. 1981. 218 p.

"Introduction" in <u>The Harlem Renaissance</u>. 1982. pp. xv-xxxlx.

HARLEM RENAISSANCE - BIBLIOGRAPHY

"The Harlem Renaissance" in <u>Blacks in America; Bibliographical Essays</u>.
     1971. pp. 142-243.

The Harlem Renaissance. 1982. 272 p.

HARMONICA PLAYERS - BIOGRAPHY - INDEX

"Musicians: Instrumental: Harmonica" in In Black and White. 1980. See
    index, V. 2, pp. 1186-1187.

HARPER, FRANCES ELLEN WATKINS

"Frances Ellen Watkins Harper," Maryemma Graham in Afro-American Writers
    Before the Harlem Renaissance. 1986. pp. 164-173.

HARPER, MICHAEL S.

"Michael Harper" in Interviews With Black Writers. 1973. pp. 94-107.

"Michael S. Harper," Norris B. Clark in Afro-American Poets Since 1955.
    pp. 152-166.

HARPISTS - BIOGRAPHY - INDEX

"Instrumental Musicians, Harp, Harpischord" in In Black and White. 1980.
    See index, V. 2, p. 1187.

HARRIS, WILSON

"Wilson Harris," Anthony Boxill in 50 Caribbean Writers. 1986. pp. 187-
    197.

HARRISON, PAUL CARTER

"Paul Carter Harrison," Steven R. Carter in Afro-American Writers After
    1955: Dramatists and Prose Writers. 1985. pp. 134-139.

HAWAII - EDUCATION - BIBLIOGRAPHY

"Hawaii" in The Education of Poor and Minority Children. 1981. pp. 252-
    257.

HAWAII - EDUCATION, HIGHER - BIBLIOGRAPHY

"Higher Education by State: Hawaii" in The Education of Poor and
    Minority Children. 1981. p. 881.

HAWKINS, WALTER EVERETTE

"Walter Everette Hawkins," Dickson D. Bruce in Afro-American Writers
    Before the Harlem Renaissance. 1986. pp. 174-181.

HAYDEN, ROBERT

"Robert Hayden" in Interviews With Black Writers. 1973. pp. 108-123.

HAYNES, LEMUEL

"Biographical Sketch" in Lemuel Haynes. 1984. pp. 9-17.

HAYNES, LEMUEL - BIBLIOGRAPHY

Lemuel Haynes. 1984. 138 p.

HEADS OF STATE - BIOGRAPHY - INDEX

"Heads of State" in In Black and White. 1980. See index, V. 2, p. 1159.

HEALTH

"The Black Family: Health Care" in The Negro Almanac. 1983. pp. 483-484.

"Health Status," Lawrence E. Gary in Black Men. 1981.

HEALTH - AFRICA - BIBLIOGRAPHY

"Health Problems in Africa" in A Bibliography of the Negro. 1928. pp. 227-231.

HEALTH - BIBLIOGRAPHY

"Black Family and Health" in The Black Family in the United States. 1986. pp. 75-76 and 189-190.

"Black Health and Mortality" in Black Demography in the United States. pp. 203-234.

"Health" in The Progress of Afro-American Women. 1980. pp. 176-182.

"Health: Physical" in A Comprehensive Bibliography. 1976. pp. 184-186.

"Health Problems of Negroes" in A Bibliography of the Negro. 1928. pp. 508-527.

"Medicine and Health Care" in Afro-American Reference. 1985. pp. 188-193.

HEALTH - BRAZIL

"Medicine and Health" in Afro-Braziliana. 1978.   pp. 71-73.

HEALTH - CARIBBEAN - BIBLIOGRAPHY

"Health and Public Health" in The Complete Caribbeana. V. 2, pp. 865-1000.

HEALTH - HAITI - BIBLIOGRAPHY

"Public Health" in The Complete Haitiana. 1982. V. 2, pp. 905-952.

HEALTH ORGANIZATIONS - DIRECTORY

"Science, Engineering and Health Organizations" in Black Resource Guide. 1986. pp. 203-206.

HEALTH SERVICES

"Human Needs and Human Services: A Research Agenda," June Jackson Christmas in <u>Blacks in the Year 2000</u>. 1981. pp. 45-56.

HEARD, NATHAN C.

"Nathan C. Heard," Richard Yarborough in <u>Afro-American Fiction Writers After 1955</u>. 1984. pp. 110-115.

HEARNE, JOHN

"John Hearne," David Engledew in <u>50 Caribbean Writers</u>. 1986. pp. 198-206.

HEATH, ROY A. K.

"Roy A. K. Heath," Mark A. McWatt in <u>50 Caribbean Writers</u>. 1986. pp. 207-216.

HEIRS - BIOGRAPHY - INDEX

"Inheritors" in <u>In Black and White</u>. 1980. See index, V. 2, p. 1161.

HENDERSON, DAVID

"David Henderson," Terry Joseph Cole in <u>Afro-American Poets Since 1985</u>. 1985. pp. 166-171.

HERCULES, FRANK E. M.

"Frank E. M. Hercules," Carol P. Marsh in <u>Afro- American Fiction Writers After 1955</u>. 1984. pp. 115-119.

"Frank E. M. Hercules," Carol P. Marsh in <u>50 Caribbean Writers</u>. 1986. pp. 217-223.

HERNTON, CALVIN C.

"Calvin C. Hernton," Anthony S. Magistrale in <u>Afro-American Writers After 1955: Dramatists and Prose Writers</u>. 1985. pp. 139-146.

HERO MEDAL RECIPIENTS - BIOGRAPHY - INDEX

"Hero Medal Recipients" in <u>In Black and White</u>. 1980. See index, V. 2, p. 1159.

HIMES, CHESTER - BIBLIOGRAPHY

"Black Social Fiction: The Protest School - Chester Himes" in <u>Blacks in America; Bibliographical Essays</u>. 1971. p. 255.

HINES, EARL "FATHA" - BIBLIOGRAPHY

"Hines, Earl Kenneth (Fatha)" in <u>Black Music in America</u>. 1981. pp. 320-331.

HISPANIC AMERICANS - EDUCATION - BIBLIOGRAPHY

"Other Spanish-Speaking Peoples" in The Education of Poor and Minority Children. 1980. pp. 490-502.

HISPANIC AMERICANS - LIBRARY SERVICES

"Library Services to the Spanish Speaking and Data Base Development," Roberto Cabello-Argandona in Ethnic Collections. 1983. pp. 101-118.

HISTORIANS - BIOGRAPHY - INDEX

"Historians" in In Black and White. 1980. See index, V. 2, pp. 1159-1160.

HISTORICAL LANDMARKS

"Historic Landmarks of Black America" in The Negro Almanac. 1983. pp. 171-222.

"Where to See the Black Maritime Heritage" in Black Men of the Sea. 1978. pp. 125-131.

HISTORIOGRAPHY

"The Black American and the New Viewpoints in Black American History," Joseph Roucek in The Negro Impact on Western Civilization. pp. 1-22.

"Discovering Black American History," John Hope Franklin in The Negro Impact on Western Civilization. 1970. pp. 23-32.

HISTORIOGRAPHY - BIBLIOGRAPHY

"Historiography" in A Comprehensive Bibliography. 1976. pp. 65-66.

HISTORIOGRAPHY - CARIBBEAN

Study of the Historiography of the British West Indies. 1980. 181 p.

HISTORIOGRAPHY - SLAVERY - BIBLIOGRPAHY

"Historiography, Method, Historical Criticism" in Black Slavery in the Americas. 1982. pp. 50-154.

HISTORY

Before the Mayflower. 1982. 681 p.

"A Brief History," John Hope Franklin in Black American Reference Book. 1976. pp. 1-89.

From Slavery to Freedom. 1980. 554 p.

"Inequality and the Burden of Capitalist Democracy: A Point of View on Black History" in How Capitalism Underdeveloped Black America. 1983. pp. 1-19.

Long Memory. 1982. 486 p.

HISTORY - ANTEBELLUM PERIOD - BIBLIOGRAPHY

"History: Antebellum" in A Comprehensive Bibliography. 1976. pp. 51-59.

"Slavery and Freedom (1783-1865)" in Afro-American History, 2. 1981. pp. 69-124.

HISTORY - BIBLIOGRAPHY

Afro-American History, 1. 1974. 856 p.

Afro-American History, 2. 1981. 394 p.

"Bibliographical Notes" in From Slavery to Freedom. 1980. pp. 507-546.

"Histories Written by Negroes" in A Bibliography of the Negro. 1928. pp. 472-473.

"History" in Afro-American Reference. 1985. pp. 38-45.

"History" in The Progress of Afro-American Women. 1980. pp. 183-190.

"History: Civil War to the Present" in A Comprehensive Bibliography. 1976. pp. 59-65.

"History, General" in Black Rhetoric. 1976. pp. 64-67.

"History: General" in A Comprehensive Bibliography. pp. 47-51.

"Select Bibliography" in Before the Mayflower. 1982. pp. 643-662.

"A Selected Bibliography: History" in The Negro Almanac. 1983. pp. 1492-1497.

HISTORY - CHRONOLOGY

Black Chronology from 4000 B.C. to the Abolition of the Slave Trade. 1983. 312 p.

"Landmarks and Milestones" in Before the Mayflower. 1982. pp. 441-611.

"Selected Chronology of Events in Black History as Related to Founding of Black Journals" in Black Journals of the United States. 1982. pp. 381-409.

HISTORY - DICTIONARY

Dictionary of Black American Culture. 1973. 493 p.

HISTORY - DOCUMENTS

Afro-American History; Sources for Research. 1981. 236 p.

"Significant Documents in Afro-American History (1688-1975)" in The Negro Almanac. 1983. pp. 95-169.

HISTORY - LOCAL AND REGIONAL - DIRECTORIES

"Name Index by State" in Index to the American Slave. 1981. pp. 77-143.

HISTORY - MARXIST PERSPECTIVES - BIBLIOGRAPHY

"Marxist Historians on Blacks in the Civil War and Reconstruction" in Blacks in America; Bibliographical Essays. 1971. pp. 131-132.

HISTORY - POST RECONSTRUCTION PERIOD

"Blacks" in The Rise of Industrial America. 1984. pp. 614-660.

HISTORY - POST RECONSTRUCTION PERIOD - BIBLIOGRAPHY

"Post-Reconstruction, 1877-1895" in Black Rhetoric. 1976. pp. 2-94.

"Reconstruction and its Aftermath, 1865-1900" in Afro-American History, 1. 1974. pp. 326-420.

"Reconstruction and its Afermath, 1865-1900" in Afro-American History, 2. 1981. pp. 125-149.

HISTORY - PRECOLUMBIAN - BIBLIOGRAPHY

"Archaeology and Pre-Columbian History" in The Complete Haitiana. 1982. V. 1, pp. 177-184.

HISTORY - PRIMARY RESOURCES

"Significant Documents in Afro-American History" in The Negro Almanac. 1983. pp. 95-169.

HISTORY - TWENTIETH CENTURY

"From Booker T. Washington to Martin Luther King, Jr." in Before the Mayflower. 1982. pp. 326-386.

"The Time of the Whale" in Before the Mayflower. 1982. pp. 386-440.

HISTORY - TWENTIETH CENTURY - BIBLIOGRAPHY

"Afro-American Society in the Twentieth Century" in Afro-American History, 1. pp. 421-495.

"Afro-American Society in the Twentieth Century" in Afro-American History, 2. pp. 150-172.

"The Cold War Era, 1945-1955" in Black Rhetoric. 1976. pp. 101-102.

"The Contemporary Scene (Since 1945)" in Afro-American History, 1. pp. 496-775.

"The Contemporary Scene (Since 1945)" in Afro-American History, 2, 1981. pp. 173-273.

"The Era of Booker T. Washington, 1895-1915" in Black Rhetoric. 1976. pp. 95-97.

"From Booker T. Washington to the New Deal, 1915-1933" in Black
     Rhetoric. 1976. pp. 97-99.

HISTORY, AFRICAN

The African Background Outlined. 1936. 478 p.

"The African Past" in Before the Mayflower. 1982. pp. 3-27.

"Land of Their Fathers" in From Slavery to Freedom. 1980. pp. 3-14.

HISTORY, AFRICAN - BIBLIOGRAPHY

"African Background of American Slaves" in Black Slavery in the
     Americas. 1982. pp. 337-374.

"African Civilizations" in A Bibliography of the Negro. 1928. pp. 28-37.

"Bibliographical Notes: Land of Their Fathers" in From Slavery to
     Freedom. 1980. 512 p.

HOAGLAND, EVERETT H.

"Everett H. Hoagland, III," Linda E. Scott in Afro-American Poets Since
     1955. 1985. pp. 171-176.

HODGE, MERLE

"Merle Hodge," Leota S. Lawrence in 50 Caribbean Writers. 1986. pp.
     224-228.

HOLDEN CASE - BIBLIOGRAPHY

"Noted Law Suits Relating to the Status of Slaves: Holden Case," in A
     Bibliography of the Negro. 1928. pp. 345-346.

HOLIDAY, BILLIE - BIBLIOGRAPHY

"Holiday, Billie" in Black Music in America. 1981. pp. 331- 341.

HOLINESS CHURCH - BIBLIOGRAPHY

"Holiness and Pentacostal Churches" in Howard University Bibliography of
     African and Afro-American Religious Studies. 1977. pp. 204-205.

HOME ECONOMISTS - BIOGRAPHY - INDEX

"Dieticians, Home Economists, Nutritionists" in In Black and White.
     1980. See index, V. 2, p. 1139.

HOMOSEXUALITY

"Color Attraction and Homosexuality" in Sex and Race. 1944. V. 3, pp.
     126-133.

"Homosexuality and the Black Male" in Black Masculinity. 1982. pp. 87-
     97.

HOMOSEXUALITY - BIBLIOGRAPHY

"Black Family and Homosexuality" in The Black Family in the United
    States. 1986. p. 115.

HOPKINS, LINDA - BIBLIOGRAPHY

"Hopkins, Linda" in Black Music in America. 1981. pp. 341-342.

HOPKINS, PAULINE ELIZABETH

"Pauline Elizabeth Hopkins," Jane Campbell in Afro-American Writers
    Before the Harlem Renaissance. 1986. pp. 182-189.

HORNE, LENA - BIBLIOGRAPHY

"Horne, Lena" in Black Music in America. 1981. pp. 342-347.

HORTON, GEORGE MOSES

"George Moses Horton," William Carroll in Afro-American Writers Before
    the Harlem Renaissance. 1986. pp. 190-201.

HOSPITAL WORKERS - BIBLIOGRAPHY

"Hospital Workers" in The Progress of Afro-American Women. 1980. p. 216.

HOSPITALS - DIRECTORY

"Hospitals" in Black Resource Guide. 1986. pp. 90-91.

HOTEL INDUSTRY - BIBLIOGRAPHY

"Hotel Industry" in The Progress of Afro-American Women. 1980. p. 115.

HOUSING

"The Black Family: Housing" in The Negro Almanac. 1983. pp. 481-482.

"Housing" in The Ebony Handbook. 1974. pp. 343-351.

"National Housing Policies and Black America: Trends, Issues and
    Implications," John O. Calmore in The State of Black America, 1986.
    pp. 115-149.

HOUSING - BIBLIOGRAPHY

"Black Family and Housing" in The Black Family in the United States.
    1986. pp. 115-118.

"Blacks in Residential Housing Markets" in The Economics of Minorities.
    1976. pp. 69-78.

"Housing" in The Education of Poor and Minority Children. 1981. pp.
    835-843.

"Housing" in A Comprehensive Bibliography. 1976. pp. 157-164.

"Housing and Urban Conditions" in <u>Afro-American Reference</u>. 1985. pp. 71-73.

"Housing for Black Americans" in <u>Blacks in America; Bibliographical Essays</u>. 1971. pp. 350-364.

"The Negro and Segregation in Residential Areas" in <u>A Bibliography of the Negro</u>. 1928. pp. 539-541.

HOUSING - CARIBBEAN - BIBLIOGRAPHY

"Housing and Architecture" in <u>The Complete Caribbeana</u>. V. 3, pp. 1157-1167.

HOUSING - HAITI - BIBLIOGRAPHY

"Housing and Architecture" in <u>The Complete Haitiana</u>. 1982. V. 2, pp. 1437-1441.

HOUSING - LEGAL CASES

"Important Cases: Housing (Right of Sale and Restrictive Covenants)" in <u>The Negro Almanac</u>. 1983. pp. 311-313.

HOUSING - SLAVERY - BIBLIOGRAPHY

"Slave Housing" in <u>Black Slavery in the Americas</u>. 1982. pp. 1153-1159.

HOWARD UNIVERSITY - MUSIC EDUCATION - BIBLIOGRAPHY

"Colleges and Universities: Howard University" in <u>Bibliography of Black Music</u>. 1984. p. 103.

HUGHES, LANGSTON - BIBLIOGRAPHY

"Black Dramatists: Langston Hughes" in <u>Blacks in America; Bibliographical Essays</u>. 1971. p. 283.

"Black Poetry - Langston Hughes" in <u>Blacks in America; Bibliographical Essays</u>. 1971. p. 247.

"Hughes, Langston" in <u>The Harlem Renaissance</u>. 1982. pp. 87-100.

HUMAN BIOLOGY - CARIBBEAN - BIBLIOGRAPHY

"Human Biology" in <u>The Complete Caribbeana</u>. 1977. V. 2, pp. 847-864.

HUMAN BIOLOGY - HAITI - BIBLIOGRAPHY

"Human Biology and Anthropology" in <u>The Complete Haitiana</u>. 1982. V. 2, pp. 899-904.

HUMAN RESOURCES - CARIBBEAN - BIBLIOGRAPHY

"Demography and Human Resources" in <u>The Complete Caribbeana</u>. 1977. V. 1, pp. 345-373.

HUMAN RESOURCES - HAITI - BIBLIOGRAPHY

"Demography and Human Resources" in The Complete Haitiana. 1982. V. 1,
     pp. 553-560.

HUMANITIES - BIBLIOGRAPHY

Blacks in the Humanities. 1986. 209 p.

HUMES, HELEN - BIBLIOGRAPHY

"Humes, Helen" in Black Music in America. pp. 348-349.

HUNTER, ALBERTA - BIBLIOGRAPHY

"Hunter, Alberta" in Black Music in America. 1981. p. 349.

HUNTER, KRISTIN

"Kristin Hunter," Sondra O'Neale in Afro-American Fiction Writers After
     1955. 1984. pp. 119-124.

HURSTON, ZORA NEALE - BIBLIOGRAPLHY

"Hurston, Zora Neale" in The Harlem Renaissance. 1982. pp. 100-107.

HYPNOTISTS - BIOGRAPHY - INDEX

"Hypnotists" in In Black and White. 1980. See index, V. 2, p. 1160.

ICONOGRAPHY - MUSIC - BIBLIOGRAPHY

"Iconographies" in Bibliography of Black Music. 1981. V. 1 pp. 61-63.

IDAHO - EDUCATION - BIBLIOGRAPHY

"Idaho" in The Education of Poor and Minority Children. 1981. p. 257.

ILLINOIS - EDUCATION - BIBLIOGRAPHY

"Illinois" in The Education of Poor and Minority Children. 1981. pp.
     257-273.

ILLINOIS - EDUCATION, HIGHER - BIBLIOGRAPHY

"Higher Education by State: Illinois" in The Education of Poor and
     Minority Children. 1981. pp. 881-884.

ILLINOIS - GENEALOGY - BIBLIOGRAPHY

"Illinois" in Black Genesis. 1978. pp. 195-199.

ILLINOIS - SLAVERY - BIBLIOGRAPHY

"Illinois" in Black Slavery in the Americas. 1982. pp. 806-809.

ILLUSTRATORS - BIOGRAPHY - INDEX

"Artists: Illustrators" in <u>In Black and White</u>. 1980. See index, V. 2,
     pp. 1114-1115.

INCOME

"Income, Poverty and Incidence of Poverty" in <u>The Negro Almanac</u>. 1983.
     pp. 645-678.

INCOME - FAMILIES

"The Black Family: Income" in <u>The Negro Almanac</u>. 1983. pp. 478-479.

INCOME - STATISTICS

"Income and Poverty" in <u>Facts About Blacks</u>. 1986. pp. 10-13.

INDENTURED SERVANTS - BIOGRAPHY - INDEX

"Indentured Servants" in <u>In Black and White</u>. 1980. See index, V. 2, p.
     1161.

INDIA

"Who Were the First Inhabitants of India?" in <u>Sex and Race</u>. 1944. V. 1,
     pp. 62-66.

INDIAN CAMPAIGNS, MILITARY - BIOGRAPHY - INDEX

"Military Service: Indian Campaigns" in <u>In Black and White</u>. 1980. See
     index, V. 2, p. 1176.

INDIANA - EDUCATION - BIBLIOGRAPHY

"Indiana" in <u>The Education of Poor and Minority Children</u>. 1981. pp.
     273-276.

INDIANA - EDUCATION, HIGHER - BIBLIOGRAPHY

"Higher Education by State: Indiana" in <u>The Education of Poor and
     Minority Children</u>. 1981. p. 884.

INDIANA - GENEALOGY - BIBLIOGRAPHY

"Indiana" in <u>Black Genesis</u>. 1978. pp. 200-203.

INDIANA - SLAVERY - BIBLIOGRAPHY

"Indiana" in <u>Black Slavery in the Americas</u>. 1982. pp. 809-811.

INDUSTRY - CARIBBEAN - BIBLIOGRAPHY

"Industry, Business and Investments" in <u>The Complete Caribbeana</u>. V. 3,
     pp. 1509-1528.

INNKEEPERS - BIOGRAPHY - INDEX

"Innkeepers" in <u>In Black and White</u>. 1980. See index, V. 2, p. 1161.

INNOVATORS - BIOGRAPHY - INDEX

"Innovators" in In Black and White. 1980. See index, V. 2, pp. 1161-1162.

INSURANCE COMPANIES - DIRECTORY

"Insurance Companies" in Black Resource Guide. 1986. pp. 92-93.

INSURANCE INDUSTRY - BIBLIOGRAPHY

"Life Insurance" in The Progress of Afro-American Women. 1980. p. 124.

INSURANCE INDUSTRY - BIOGRAPHY - INDEX

"Insurance Pioneers, Leaders" in In Black and White. 1980. See index, V. 2, p. 1162.

INSURRECTIONISTS - BIOGRAPHY - INDEX

"Insurrectionists" in In Black and White. 1980. See index, V. 2, p. 1162.

INSURRECTIONS - SLAVERY

"Runaways and Rebels" in The Slave Community. 1979. pp. 192-222.

INTELLECTUAL HISTORY - BIBLIOGRAPHY

"With A Sense of Pride: Black Cultural and Intellectual History" in Blacks in the Humanities. 1986. pp. 161-168.

INTELLIGENCE - BIBLIOGRAPHY

"The I. Q. Issue" in The Education of Poor and Minority Children. 1981. pp. 49-70.

INTELLIGENCE TESTING - BIBLIOGRAPHY

"Children: Tests and Measurements" in The Education of Poor and Minority Children. 1981. pp. 36-49.

INTERIOR DECORATORS - BIOGRAPHY - INDEX

"Interior Decorators, Designers" in In Black and White. 1980. See index, V. 2, p. 1162.

INTERNATIONAL COUNCIL OF WOMEN - BIBLIOGRAPHY

"International Council of Women" in The Progress of Afro-American Women. 1982. p. 257.

INVENTORS

"Black Firsts: Business and Inventions" in Before the Mayflower. 1982. pp. 641-642.

"Inventors and Scientists" in The Negro Almanac. 1983. pp. 1052-1076.

INVENTORS - BIBLIOGRAPHY

"Scientists and Inventors" in Afro-American Reference. 1985. pp. 18-19.

INVENTORS - BIOGRAPHY - INDEX

"Inventors" in In Black and White. 1980. See index, V. 2, p. 1163.

INVESTIGATORS - BIOGRAPHY - INDEX

"Detectives, Investigators" in In Black and White. 1980. See index, V. 2, p. 1139.

INVESTMENTS - CARIBBEAN - BIBLIOGRAPHY

"Industry, Business and Investments" in The Complete Caribbeana. 1977. V. 3, pp. 1509-1528.

IOWA - EDUCATION - BIBLIOGRAPHY

"Iowa" in The Education of Poor and Minority Children. 1981. pp. 276-277.

IOWA - EDUCATION, HIGHER - BIBLIOGRAPHY

"Higher Education by State: Iowa" in The Education of Poor and Minority Children. 1981. p. 884.

IOWA - GENEALOGY - BIBLIOGRAPHY

"Iowa" in Black Genesis. 1978. pp. 204-206.

IOWA - SLAVERY - BIBLIOGRAPHY

"Iowa" in Black Slavery in the Americas. 1982. p. 811.

IRONWORK

"Negro's Art Lives in His Wrought Iron" in The Other Slaves. 1978. pp. 227-241.

IRONWORK - BIBLIOGRAPHY

"Ironwork" in 250 Years of Afro-American Art. 1981. pp. 386-388.

ISLAM

"Notes and References to the Negro Under Islam" in Sex and Race. 1944. pp. 284-287.

ISLAMIC CULTURAL INFLUENCE - BIBLIOGRAPHY

"Islam, Influence" in Afro-American Folk Culture. 1981. See index, p. 776.

ISRAEL - BIBLIOGRAPHY

"Blacks and the PLO, Arabs and Israel" in Black-Jewish Relations. 1984.
    pp. 81-87.

ISRAEL - ETHNIC GROUPS - BIBLIOGRAPHY

"Israel" in The Education of Poor and Minority Children. 1981. pp.
    1220-1238.

ITALIAN LANGUAGE - DIALECT - BIBLIOGRAPHY

"Italian Based Pidgins and Lingua Franca" in A Bibliography of Pidgin
    and Creole Languages. 1975. pp. 70-72.

ITALY

"Miscegenation in Spain, Portugal and Italy" in Sex and Race. 1944. V.
    1, pp. 151-168.

ITALY - ETHNIC GROUPS - BIBLIOGRAPHY

"Italy" in The Education of Poor and Minority Children. 1981. pp. 1239-
    1240.

ITALY - SLAVERY - BIBLIOGRAPHY

"Italy and Colonies" in Slavery: A Worldwide Bibliography. 1985. pp.
    312-315.

IVORY COAST - MUSIC - BIBLIOGRAPHY

"Ivory Coast" in Bibliography of Black Music. 1981. V. 3, p. 82.

JACKSON, ANGELA

"Angela Jackson," D. L. Smith in Afro-American Poets Since 1955. 1985.
    pp. 176-183.

JACKSON, JESSE

"The Phenomenon of the Jesse Jackson Candidacy and the 1984 Presidential
    Election," Charles V. Hamilton in The State of Black America, 1985.
    pp. 21-35.

JACKSON, MAHALIA - BIBLIOGRAPHY

"Jackson, Mahalia" in Black Music in America. 1981. pp. 350-357.

JACKSON FIVE - BIBLIOGRAPHY

"Jackson Five" in Black Music in America. 1981. pp. 357-362.

JAMAICA

"Blacks in the Western Hemisphere: Jamaica" in The Negro Almanac. 1983.
    pp. 1477-1479.

"Introduction" in <u>Jamaica</u>. 1984. pp. xvii-xxii.

JAMAICA - BIBLIOGRAPHY

<u>Jamaica</u>. 1984. 369 p.

"Jamaica" in <u>The Complete Caribbeana</u>. 1977. See index, V. 4, pp. 2173-2177.

"Jamaica" in <u>Race and Ethnic Relations</u>. 1980. pp. 175-180.

JAMAICA - LINGUISTICS - BIBLIOGRAPHY

"Jamaica" in <u>A Bibliography of Pidgin and Creole Languages</u>. 1975. pp. 383-395.

JAMAICA - MUSIC - BIBLIOGRAPHY

"Jamaica" in <u>Bibliography of Black Music</u>. 1981. V. 3, pp. 150-153.

JAMAICAN ALPHABET - BIBLIOGRAPHY

"Jamaican Alphabet" in <u>Afro-American Folk Culture</u>. 1978. See index, p. 777.

JAMES, C. L. R.

"C. L. R. James," Eugenia Collier in <u>50 Caribbean Writers</u>. 1986. pp. 229-238.

JAPAN - ETHNIC GROUPS - BIBLIOGRAPHY

"Japan" in <u>The Education of Poor and Minority Children</u>. 1981. pp. 1240-1242.

JAPANESE AMERICANS - EDUCATION - BIBLIOGRAPHY

"Japanese Americans" in <u>The Education of Poor and Minority Children</u>. 1981. pp. 590-599.

JARRETT, KEITH - BIBLIOGRAPHY

"Jarrett, Keith" in <u>Black Music in America</u>. 1981. pp. 362-368.

JAZZ

"Jazz" in <u>Roots of Black Music</u>. 1982. pp. 149-155.

"The Jazz Scene" in <u>The Negro Almanac</u>. 1983. pp. 1149-1183.

JAZZ - BIBLIOGRAPHIES - BIBLIOGRAPHY

"Bibliographies" in <u>Jazz Bibliography</u>. 1981. pp. 27-34.

JAZZ - BIBLIOGRAPHY

"Jazz" in <u>Afro-American Folk Culture</u>. 1978. See index, p. 777.

"Jazz" in Bibliography of Black Music. 1981. V. 2, pp. 142-220.

Jazz Bibliography. 1981. 368 p.

"Jazz Music" in A Bibliography of the Negro. 1928. pp. 442-443.

Jazz Reference and Research Materials: A Bibliography. 1981. 300 p.

JAZZ - DISCOGRAPHY - BIBLIOGRAPHY

"Discographies" in Jazz Bibliography. 1981. pp. 35-42.

"Jazz Discographies" in Bibliography of Black Music. 1981. V. 1, pp.
    47-52.

JAZZ - EDUCATION - BIBLIOGRAPHY

"Didactics of Jazz" in Jazz Bibliography. 1981. pp. 190-197.

JAZZ - PICTORIAL WORKS - BIBLIOGRAPHY

"Jazz in Pictures" in Jazz Bibliography. 1981. pp. 324-325.

JAZZ CLUBS - BIBLIOGRAPHY

"Jazz Clubs" in Jazz Bibliography. 1981. p. 306.

JAZZ MUSICIANS

"The Jazz Scene" in The Negro Almanac. 1983. pp. 1149-1183.

JAZZ MUSICIANS - BIBLIOGRAPHY

"Jazz People" in Jazz Bibliography. 1981. pp. 198-303.

JEFFERS, LANCE

"Lance Jeffers," David F. Dorsey in Afro-American Poets Since 1955.
    1985. pp. 183-190.

JEWELRY DESIGNERS - BIOGRAPHY - INDEX

"Jewelry Craftsmen, Designers" in In Black and White. 1980. See index,
    V. 2, p. 1163.

JEWISH DEFENSE LEAGUE - BIBLIOGRAPHY

"Blacks and the Jewish Defense League" in Black-Jewish Relations. 1984.
    p. 80.

JEWS - BIBLIOGRAPHY

Black-Jewish Relations. 1984. 130 p.

JEWS - CIVIL RIGHTS MOVEMENT - BIBLIOGRAPHY

"The Church, Synagogue and Integration: Judaism" in Howard University

Bibliography of African and Afro-American Religious Studies. 1977.
pp. 316-317.

JEWS, BLACK

"Were the Jews Originally Negroes?" in Sex and Race, 1944. V. 1, pp.
91-94.

JEWS, BLACK - BIBLIOGRAPHY

"Black Jews" in Howard University Bibliography of African and Afro-
American Religious Studies. 1977. p. 209.

"Blacks as Jews or Black Jews" in Black-Jewish Relations. 1984. p. 88.

JOANS, TED

"Ted Joans," Jon Woodson in Afro-American Poets Since 1955. 1985. pp.
190-196.

JOHNSON, CHARLES R.

"Charles R. Johnson," Maryemma Graham in Afro-American Fiction Writers
After 1955. 1984. pp. 124-127.

JOHNSON, FENTON

"Fenton Johnson," Hammett Worthington-Smith in Afro-American Writers
Before the Harlem Renaissance. 1986. pp. 202-205.

JOHNSON, JAMES WELDON - BIBLIOGRAPHY

"Black Poetry - James Weldon Johnson" in Blacks in America;
Bibliographical Essays. 1971. p. 248.

"Johnson, James Weldon" in The Harlem Renaissance. 1982. pp. 108-116.

JOHNSON, LYNDON B. - BIBLIOGRAPHY

"The Johnson Administration" in Blacks in America; Bibliographical
Essays. 1971. pp. 308-310.

JOINT CENTER FOR POLITICAL STUDIES

"The Joint Center for Political Studies" in The Negro Almanac. 1983. p.
364.

JOKES AND JOKING - BIBLIOGRAPHY

"Joking" in Afro-American Folk Culture. 1978. See index, pp. 777-778.

JONES, GAYL

"Gayl Jones," Keith Byerman in Afro-American Fiction Writers After 1955.
1984. pp. 128-135.

JONES, MARION PATRICK

"Marion Patrick Jones," Harold Barratt in 50 Caribbean Writers. 1986.
    pp. 239-245.

JONES, QUINCY - BIBLIOGRAPHY

"Jones, Quincy Delight" in Black Music in America. 1981. pp.   369-374.

JOPLIN, SCOTT - BIBLIOGRAPHY

"Joplin, Scott" in Black Music in America. 1981. pp. 374-382.

JORDAN, JUNE

"June Jordan," Peter B. Erickson in Afro-American Writers After 1955:
    Dramatists and Prose Writers. 1985. pp. 146-162.

JOURNALISM - BIBLIOGRAPHY

"Journalism" in Afro-American Reference. 1986. pp. 160-161.

"Journalism" in Black Media in America. 1984. pp. 75-84.

"To Plead Our Own Cause: Blacks in Journalism" in Blacks in the
    Humanities. 1986. pp. 47-62.

JOURNALISTS

"Black Newspapers and Journalists" in The Negro Almanac. 1983. pp.
    1211-1218.

JOURNALISTS - BIOGRAPHY - INDEX

"Journalists" in In Black and White. 1980. See index, V. 2, pp. 1163-
    1165.

JOURNALS

Black Journals of the United States. 1982. 432 p.

JUBA - BIBLIOGRAPHY

"Juba" in Afro-American Folk Culture. 1978. See index, p. 778.

JUDGES

"Blacks in the Judiciary" in The Negro Almanac. 1983. pp. 324-346.

JUDGES - BIBLIOGRAPHY

"Black Judges" in The Study and Analysis of Black Politics. 1973. pp.
    130-131.

"Judges and Lawyers" in The Progress of Afro-American Women. 1980. pp.
    196-200.

JUDGES - BIOGRAPHY - INDEX

"Judges" in In Black and White. 1980. See index, V. 2, pp. 1165-1166.

JUDGES - DIRECTORY

"Judiciary" in Black Resource Guide. 1986. pp. 94-97.

JUDICIARY

"Black Firsts-Judiciary" in Before the Mayflower. 1982. p. 631.

JUNETEENTH - BIBLIOGRAPHY

"July 4th and Juneteenth" in Afro-American Folk Culture. 1978. See
    index, p. 778.
JURIES

"Important Cases: Jury Service" in The Negro Almanac. 1983. pp. 313-314.

JUVENILE DELINQUENCY - BIBLIOGRAPHY

"Criminology and Juvenile Delinquency" in Afro-American Reference. 1985.
    pp. 66-67.

"Negro Juvenile Delinquency" in A Bibliography of the Negro. 1928. pp.
    547-549.

KANSAS - EDUCATION - BIBLIOGRAPHY

"Kansas" in The Education of Poor and Minority Children. 1981. pp. 277-
    278.

KANSAS - EDUCATION, HIGHER - BIBLIOGRAPHY

"Higher Education by State: Kansas" in The Education of Poor and
    Minority Children. 1981. pp. 885.

KANSAS - GENEALOGY - BIBLIOGRAPHY

"Kansas" in Black Genesis. 1978. pp. 247-250.

KANSAS - SLAVERY - BIBLIOGRAPHY

"Kansas" in Black Slavery in the Americas. 1982. pp. 812-813.

KAUFMAN, BOB

"Bob Kaufman," Jon Woodson in Afro-American Poets Since 1955. 1985. pp.
    196-202.

KELLEY, WILLIAM MELVIN

"William Melvin Kelley," Valerie Babb in Afro-American Fiction Writers
    After 1955. 1984. pp. 135-143.

KENNEDY, ADRIENNE

"Adrienne Kennedy," Margaret B. Wilkerson. Afro-American Writers After

1955: Dramatists and Prose Writers. 1985. pp. 162-169.

KENNEDY, JOHN F. - BIBLIOGRAPHY

"The Kennedy Administration" in Blacks in America; Bibliographical Essays. 1971. p. 307.

KENTUCKY - EDUCATION - BIBLIOGRAPHY

"Kentucky" in The Education of Poor and Minority Children. 1981. pp. 278-281.

KENTUCKY - EDUCATION, HIGHER - BIBLIOGRAPHY

"Higher Education by State: Kentucky" in The Education of Poor and Minority Children. 1981. p. 885.

KENTUCKY - GENEALOGY - BIBLIOGRAPHY

"Kentucky" in Black Genesis. 1978. pp. 133-137.

KENTUCKY - LIBRARIANS

"Black Librarians in Kentucky," Mary Mace Spradling in The Black Librarian in the Southeast. 1976. pp. 37-52.

KENTUCKY - SLAVERY - BIBLIOGRAPHY

"Kentucky" in Black Slavery in the Americas. 1982. pp. 837-846.

KENYA - MUSIC - BIBLIOGRAPHY

"Kenya" in Bibliography of Black Music. 1981. V. 3, pp. 83-84.

KHAN, ISMITH

"Ismith Khan," Arthur Drayton in 50 Caribbean Writers. 1986. pp. 246-254.

KILLENS, JOHN OLIVER

"John Oliver Killens," William H. Wiggins in Afro-American Fiction Writers After 1955. pp. 144-152.

KINCAID, JAMAICA

"Jamaica Kincaid," Bryant Mangum in 50 Caribbean Writers. 1986. pp. 255-263.

KING, B. B. - BIBLIOGRAPHY

"King, B. B." in Black Music in America. 1981. pp. 382-391.

KING, MARTIN LUTHER - BIBLIOGRAPHY

Free at Last: A Bibliography of Martin Luther King, Jr. 1977. 169. p.

Martin Luther King, Jr.: An Annotated Bibliography. 1986. 154 p.

"Martin Luther King, Jr.'s Opinion of Jews" in Black-Jewish Relations. 1984. pp. 34 and 93.

"Montgomery: Non-Violent Direct Action and the Emergence of Martin Luther King" in Blacks in America; Bibliographical Essays. 1971. pp. 316-318.

"Southern Christian Leadership Conference and Martin Luther King, Jr." in Howard University Bibliography of African and Afro-American Religious Studies. 1977. pp. 330-339.

KING, WOODIE

"Woodie King, Jr.," Stephen M. Vallillo in Afro-American Writers After 1955: Dramatists and Prose Writers. 1985. pp. 170-174.

KITT, EARTHA - BIBLIOGRAPHY

"Kitt, Eartha" in Black Music in America. 1981. pp. 391-396.

KNIGHT, ETHERIDGE

"Etheridge Knight," Shirley Lumpkin in Afro-American Poets Since 1955. 1985. pp. 202-211.

KOREAN AMERICANS - EDUCATION - BIBLIOGRAPHY

"Korean Americans" in The Education of Poor and Minority Children. 1981. pp. 599-600.

KOREAN WAR - BIOGRAPHY - INDEX

"Military Service: Korea" in In Black and White. 1980. See index, V. 2, p. 1176.

KRIO - BIBLIOGRAPHY

"Krio" in A Bibliography of Pidgin and Creole Languages. 1975. pp. 365-372.

KU KLUX KLAN - HISTORY - BIBLIOGRAPHY

"The Ku Klux Klan of the Reconstruction Period" in A Bibliography of the Negro. 1928. pp. 376-379.

LABELLE - BIBLIOGRAPHY

"Labelle" in Black Music in America. 1981. pp. 396-399.

LABOR

"The Black American Worker," Dorothy K. Newman in The Black American Reference Book. 1976. pp. 251-283.

"The Black Worker in the Labor Movement" in The Negro Almanac. 1983. pp.

527-549.

"The Crisis of the Black Working Class" in How Capitalism Underdeveloped
Black America. 1983. pp. 23-51.

"Employment and Labor" in The Ebony Handbook. 1974. pp. 263-329.

LABOR - AFRICA - BIBLIOGRAPHY

"The Labor Question in Africa" in A Bibliography of the Negro. 1928. pp.
184-189.

LABOR - BELIZE - BIBLIOGRAPHY

"Labor" in Belize. 1980. pp. 162-164.

LABOR - BIBLIOGRAPHY

"Afro-Americans and the Labor Movement" in Black Rhetoric. 1976. pp.
94-95.

"Blacks and the Labor Movement" in The Economics of Minorities. 1976.
pp. 133-142.

"Blacks and the Manpower Policies of the Business Community" in The
Economics of Minorities. 1976. pp. 111-130.

"The Negro and Peonage" in A Bibliography of the Negro. 1928. pp. 541-
542.

"Organized Labor and Blacks" in Blacks in America; Bibliographical
Essays. 1971. pp. 228-230.

LABOR - CARIBBEAN - BIBLIOGRAPHY

"Employment and Labor Issues" in The Complete Caribbeana. V. 3, pp.
1529-1559.

LABOR - COAL MINING - HISTORY

"Black Labor in the Eastern Virginia Coal Field, 1765-1865," Ronald L.
Lewis in The Other Slaves. 1978. pp. 87-108.

LABOR - HAITI - BIBLIOGRAPHY

"Employment and Labor Issues" in The Complete Haitiana. 1982. V. 2, pp.
1341-1353.

LABOR - HISTORY

"The Antebellum Negro Artisan," W.E.B. DuBois in The Other Slaves. 1978.
pp. 175-182.

"Negro Craftsmanship in Early America," Leonard P. Stavisky in The Other
Slaves. 1978. pp. 193-203.

"The Origins of Negro Craftsmanship in Colonial America," Leonard

Stavisky in The Other Slaves. 1978. pp. 183-191.

"Race Relations in Old South Industries," Robert Starobin in The Other Slaves. 1978. pp. 51-60.

"The Slave Regime: Competition Between Negro and White Labor," Sterling D. Spero and Abram L. Harris in The Other Slaves. 1978. pp. 41-50.

LABOR - HISTORY - BIBLIOGRAPHY

"Black Workers and the Labor Movement Before World War I" in Blacks in America; Bibliographical Essays. 1971. pp. 167-170.

"Social and Economic Dimensions" in Afro-American History, 2. 1981. pp. 143-149.

"The Social and Economic Situation (Reconstruction and the Aftermath)" in Afro-American History, 1. 1974. pp. 407-420.

LABOR - INDUSTRY - BIBLIOGRAPHY

"A General View of the Negro in Industry" in A Bibliography of the Negro. 1928. pp. 497-501.

LABOR MOVEMENT

"Blacks in the U.S. Labor Movement: Working or Not?" Lenneal J. Henderson in The State of Black America, 1985. pp. 105-126.

LABOR MOVEMENT - HISTORY

"Organized Labor: From Underdog to Overseer" in Reluctant Reformers. 1975. pp. 173-216.

LABOR UNIONS - BIBLIOGRAPHY

"The Negro and Organized Labor" in A Bibliography of the Negro. 1928. pp. 501-503.

LAMMING, GEORGE

"George Lamming," Ian H. Munro in 50 Caribbean Writers. 1986. pp. 264-275.

LAND - CARIBBEAN - BIBLIOGRAPHY

"Land Tenure" in The Complete Caribbeana. 1977. V. 3, pp. 1497-1508.

LAND - HAITI - BIBLIOGRAPHY

"Land Tenure" in The Complete Haitiana. 1982. V. 2, pp. 1315-1318.

LAND - HISTORY - BIBLIOGRAPHY

"40 Acres and a Mule, the Failure of Land Reform" in Blacks in America; Bibliographical Essays. 1971. pp. 121-123.

LANDMARKS

"Historic Landmarks of Black America" in The Negro Almanac. 1983. pp. 171-222.

"Where to See the Black Maritime Heritage" in Black Men of the Sea. 1978. pp. 125-131.

LANE, PINKIE GORDON

"Pinkie Gordon Lane," Marilyn B. Craig in Afro-American Poets Since 1955. 1985. pp. 212-216.

LARSEN, NELLA - BIBLIOGRAPHY

"Larsen, Nella" in The Harlem Renaissance. 1982. pp. 116-118.

LATIN AMERICA

"Present Racial Composition of Latin America" in Sex and Race. 1942. V. 2, pp. 145-152.

LATIN AMERICA - ABOLITION MOVEMENT

"Latin America's Bondmen: The Abolition of Slavery" in From Slavery to Freedom. 1980. pp. 75-80.

LATIN AMERICA - BIBLIOGRAPHIES - BIBLIOGRAPHY

"A Bibliography of Bibliographies on Latin America" in A Bibliography of the Negro. 1928. pp. 659-660.

LATIN AMERICA - BIBLIOGRAPHY

"Bibliographical Notes: Latin America's Bondmen" in From Slavery to Freedom. 1980. pp. 516-517.

"General Bibliography" in Race and Ethnic Relations. 1980. pp. 152-162.

"Latin America and the Caribbean" in Afro-American Reference. 1985. pp. 200-214.

"Latin America" in The Education of Poor and Minority Children. 1981. pp. 1342-1346.

LATIN AMERICA - DICTIONARY

Dictionary of Afro-Latin American Civilization. 1980. 525 p.

Race and Ethnic Relations. 1980. 252 p.

LATIN AMERICA - HISTORY

"The Black Latin American Impact on Western Culture," Franck Bayard in The Negro Impact on Western Civilization. 1970. pp. 287-336.

LATIN AMERICA - SLAVERY

"The Implementation of Slave Legislation in Eighteenth Century New Granada," Norman A. Meiklejohn in <u>Slavery and Race Relations in Latin America</u>. 1974. pp. 176-203.

"Latin America's Bondmen" in <u>From Slavery to Freedom</u>. 1980. pp. 65-80.

LATIN AMERICA - SLAVERY - BIBLIOGRAPHY

"Slavery in the United States and Latin America: Comparative Analyses" in <u>Blacks in America; Bibliographical Essays</u>. 1971. pp. 64-66.

LATIN AMERICAN LITERATURE - BIBLIOGRAPHY

<u>The Afro-Spanish American Author: An Annotated Bibliography of Criticism</u>. 1980. 129 p.

LAW

"The Legal Status of Black Americans" in <u>The Negro Almanac</u>. 1983. pp. 300-351.

LAW - BIBLIOGRAPHY

"Civil Rights and Legal Status" in <u>Afro-American Reference</u>. 1985. pp. 63-66.

LAW - HAITI - BIBLIOGRAPHY

"The Legal Process" in <u>The Complete Haitiana</u>. 1982. V. 2, pp. 1119-1151.

LAW ENFORCEMENT BIBLIOGRAPHY

"Law Enforcement" in <u>The Progress of Afro-American Women</u>. 1980. pp. 200-201.

LAW SCHOOL INSTRUCTORS - BIOGRAPHY - INDEX

"Law, Medical School Instructors" in <u>In Black and White</u>. 1980. See index, V. 2, p. 1166.

LAWS, AFRICAN - BIBLIOGRAPHY

"African Laws and Customs" in <u>A Bibliography of the Negro</u>. 1928. pp. 51-65.

LAWYERS - BIBLIOGRAPHY

"Judges and Lawyers" in <u>The Progress of Afro-American Women</u>. 1980. pp. 196-200.

LAWYERS - BIOGRAPHY - INDEX

"Lawyers, Barristers" in <u>In Black and White</u>. 1980. See index, V. 2, pp. 1166-1169.

LEADERS, AFRICAN - BIOGRAPHY - INDEX

"African Leaders, Rulers" in In Black and White. 1980. See index, V. 2, p. 1110.

LEADERSHIP

"Black Brahmins: The Underdevelopment of Black Political Leadership" in How Capitalism Underdeveloped Black America. 1983. pp. 169-194.

LEADERSHIP CONFERENCE ON CIVIL RIGHTS

"The Leadership Conference on Civil Rights" in The Negro Almanac. 1983. pp. 256-257.

LEAGUE FOR COMMUNITY SERVICE - BIBLIOGRAPHY

"League for Community Service" in The Progress of Afro-American Women. 1980. p. 257.

LEDBETTER, HUDDIE WILLIAM (LEADBELLY) - BIBLIOGRAPHY

"Ledbetter, Huddie William (Leadbelly)" in Black Music in America. 1981. pp. 399-402.

LEE, JARENA

"Three Women in the Black Church: An Introduction" in Black Women and Religion. 1980. pp. xv-xxiV.

LEEWARD ISLANDS

"Blacks in the Western Hemisphere (Antigua, Barbado, Redonda, St. Kitts-Nevis-Anguilla, Montserrat)" in The Negro Almanac. 1983. pp. 1483-1484.

LEEWARD ISLANDS - BIBLIOGRAPHY

"Leward Islands" in The Complete Caribbeana. See index, V. 4, pp. 2177-2178.

LEEWARD ISLANDS - MUSIC - BIBLIOGRAPHY

"Leeward Islands" in Bibliography of Black Music. 1981. V. 3, p. 154.

LEGAL CASES

"Important Cases" in The Negro Almanac. 1983. pp. 304-323.

LEGAL HISTORY

"The Legal Status of Black Americans" in The Negro Almanac. 1983. pp. 300-351.

LEGAL HISTORY - BIBLIOGRAPHY

"Applications of Provisions of 13th and 14th Amendments to Property and Other Rights of Individuals and Corporations in General" in A Bibliography of the Negro. 1928. pp. 536-538.

"Slave Law" in Black Slavery in the Americas. 1982. pp. 649-694.

LEGAL STATUS OF AFRO-AMERICANS

"The Legal Status of Black Americans" in The Negro Almanac. 1983. pp. 300-351.

"The Legal Status of the Black American," Constance Baker Motley in The Black American Reference Book. 1976. pp. 90-127.

LEGAL STATUS OF AFRO-AMERICANS - BIBLIOGRAPHY

"Afro-Americans and the Law, 1619-1861" in Blacks in America; Bibliographical Essays. 1971. pp. 73-76.

"State and Local Legislation" in Blacks in America; Bibliographical Essays. 1971. p. 310.

"The Supreme Court and Civil Rights" in Blacks in America; Bibliographical Essays. 1971. pp. 310-313.

"The Supreme Court and Negro Rights, 1873-1915" in Blacks in America; Bibliographical Essays. 1971. pp. 144-145.

LEGAL STATUS OF AFRO-AMERICANS - ECONOMIC ASPECTS

"Blacks and Governmental Law and Policy" in The Economics of Minorities. 1976. pp. 145-163.

LEGENDS - BIBLIOGRAPHY

"Legends" in Afro-American Folk Culture. 1978. See index, p. 778.

LEGISLATION - BIBLIOGRAPHY

"Legislation" in The Progress of Afro-American Women. 1980. p. 201.

LEGISLATION, FEDERAL

"Federal Legislation Affecting Blacks" in The Negro Almanac. 1983. pp. 303-304.

LEMMON CASE - BIBLIOGRAPHY

"Noted Law Suits Relating to the Status of Slaves: Lemmon Case" in A Bibliography of the Negro. 1928. p. 346.

LIBERATION GROUPS - DIRECTORY

"Liberation Movements" in Black Resource Guide. 1986. pp. 78-79.

LIBERIA - EDUCATION - BIBLIOGRAPHY

"Liberia" in The Education of Poor and Minority Children. 1981. p. 1245.

LIBERIA - MUSIC - BIBLIOGRAPHY

"Liberia" in Bibliography of Black Music. 1981. V. 3, p. 85.

LIBRARIANS

The Black Librarian in the Southeast. 1980. p. 286.

LIBRARIANS - BIBLIOGRAPHY

"Library Science" in The Progress of Afro-American Women. 1980. pp. 123-124.

LIBRARIANS - BIOGRAPHY - INDEX

"Librarians" in In Black and White. 1980. See index, V. 2, pp. 1169-1170.

LIBRARIANSHIP - BIBLIOGRAPHY

"Afro-American Librarianship" in Afro-American Reference. 1985. p. 23.

"Thomas Blue's Dream: Blacks in Libraries and Librarianship" in Blacks in the Humanities. 1986. pp. 63-73.

LIBRARIES

"Libraries" in The Ebony Handbook. 1976. pp. 179-193.

LIBRARIES - BELIZE - BIBLIOGRAPHY

"Libraries and Archives" in Belize. 1980. pp. 177-178.

LIBRARIES - BIBLIOGRAPHY

"Libraries" in The Education of Poor and Minority Children. 1981. pp. 984-986.

"Libraries for Negroes" in A Bibliography of the Negro. 1928. p. 429.

LIBRARIES, MUSIC - BIBLIOGRAPHY

"Jazz in Archives, Libraries, Museums" in Jazz Bibliography. 1971. p. 307.

LIBRARIES, PRESIDENTIAL

"Presidential Libraries as Sources for Research on Afro-Americans," J. C. James in Afro-American History; Sources for Research. 1981. pp. 101-112.

LIBRARY COLLECTIONS

Ethnic Collections. 1983. p. 361.

LIBRARY COLLECTIONS - CATALOGS

Catalog of the Azalia B. Hackley Collection of Negro Music, Dance, and Drama (Detroit Public Library). 1979. p. 510.

Catalog of the Old Slave Mart Museum and Library (Charleston, South
      Carolina). 1978. 2 V.

Chicago Afro-American Union Analytic Catalog. 1972. 6 V.

Dictionary Catalog of the Arthur B. Spingarn Collection of Negro Authors
      (Howard University). 1970. 2 V.

Dictionary Catalog of the Jesse E. Moorland Collection of Negro Authors
      (Howard University). 1970-.

Dictionary Catalog of the Negro Collection (Fisk University). 1974. 6
      V.

Dictionary Catalog of the Schomburg Collection of Negro Literature and
      History (New York Public Library). 1962-1974. Updated by the annual
      Bibliographic Guide to Black Studies. 1975-.

Dictionary Catalog of the Vivian G. Harsh Collection of Afro-American
      Life and History (Chicago Public Library). 1978. V. 4.

Guide to the Heartman Manuscripts on Slavery (Xavier University). 1982.
      p. 221.

Rare Afro-Americana: A Reconstruction of the Adger Library
      (Philadelphia). 1981. p. 235.

LIBRARY COLLECTIONS - CATALOGS - BIBLIOGRAPHY

"Catalogs and Guides to Major Collections" in Afro-American Reference.
      1985. pp. 9-13.

"Guides to Collections" in A Comprehensive Bibliography. 1976. p. 42.

LIBRARY COLLECTIONS - HARLEM RENAISSANCE - BIBLIOGRAPHY

"Library and Other Special Collections" in The Harlem Renaissance. 1982.
      pp. 211-232.

LIBRARY COLLECTIONS - MUSIC - BIBLIOGRAPHY

"Libraries, Museums, Collections" in Bibliography of Black Music. 1981.
      V. 1, pp. 3-5.

LIBRARY COLLECTIONS - WOMEN - DIRECTORY

"Special Collections" in The Progress of Afro-American Women. 1980. p.
      325.

LINGUISTICS - AFRICA - BIBLIOGRAPHY

"Pidginized and Other Black African French" in A Bibliography of Pidgin
      and Creole Languages. 1975. pp. 308-310.

"West African Pidgin English" in A Bibliography of Pidgin and Creole
      Languages. 1975. pp. 345-360.

LINGUISTICS - BELIZE - BIBLIOGRAPHY

"Language and Dialects" in Belize. 1980. pp. 92-96.

LINGUISTICS - BIBLIOGRAPHY

A Bibliography of Pidgin and Creole Languages. 1975. 804 p.

"Jist Sayin' It: Blacks in Linguistics" in Blacks in the Humanities.
    1986. pp. 85-96.

"Linguistics" in Afro-American Reference. 1985. pp. 73-75.

"Slave Language" in Black Slavery in the Americas. 1982. pp. 1431-1444.

LINGUISTICS - CARIBBEAN - BIBLIOGRAPHY

"Language and Linguistics" in The Complete Caribbeana. 1977. pp. 799-
    835.

LINGUISTICS - HAITI - BIBLIOGRAPHY

"Creole Studies" in The Complete Haitiana. 1982. V. 2, pp. 779-798.

"Language and Linguistics" in The Complete Haitiana. 1982. V. 1, pp.
    761-777.

LINGUISTICS - MUSIC - BIBLIOGRAPHY

"The Language of Jazz" in Jazz Bibliography. 1981. pp. 171-172.

LINGUISTICS, AFRICAN - BIBLIOGRAPHY

"African Languages" in A Bibliography of the Negro. 1928. pp. 74-92.

LINGUISTS - BIOGRAPHY - INDEX

"Linguists" in In Black and White. 1980. See index, V. 2, pp. 1170-1171.

LINKS - BIBLIOGRAPHY

"Links" in The Progress of Afro-American Women. 1980. p. 258.

LISTON, MELBA - BIBLIOGRAPHY

"Liston, Melba Doretta" in Black Music in America. 1981. pp. 402-403.

LITERARY CRITICS - BIOGRAPHY - INDEX

"Critics: Literary, Art, Music" in In Black and White. 1980. See index,
    V. 2, pp. 1134-1135.

LITERARY HISTORY AND CRITICISM

"The Black American Contribution to Literature," Abraham Chapman in The
    Negro Impact on Western Civilization. 1970. pp. 361-398.

LITERARY HISTORY AND CRITICISM - BIBLIOGRAPHY

"Critiquing Black Bards: Black Literary Criticism" in <u>Blacks in the
    Humanities</u>. 1986. pp. 141-160.

"Literary History and Criticism: General" in <u>A Comprehensive
    Bibliography</u>. 1976. pp. 206-212.

"Literature - General Surveys and Criticism" in <u>Afro-American Reference</u>.
    <u>1985</u>. pp. 137-142.

LITERARY HISTORY AND CRITICISM - BRAZIL - BIBLIOGRAPHY

"Literature - History and Criticism" in <u>Afro-Brasiliana</u>. 1978. pp. 137-
    147.

LITERARY THEMES - WOMEN - BIBLIOGRAPHY

"Literature" in <u>The Progress of Afro-American Women</u>. pp. 206-212.

LITERATURE

"The Black Contribution to American Letters," Arna Bontemps in <u>The Black
    American Reference Book</u>. 1976. pp. 741-766.

"The Black Contribution to American Letters: part II; the Writer as
    Activist - 1960 and After," Larry Neal in <u>The Black American
    Reference Book</u>. 1976. pp. 767-790.

"Introduction" in <u>Interviews with Black Writers</u>. 1973. pp. vii-xiii.

LITERATURE - ANTHOLOGIES - BIBLIOGRAPHY

"Anthologies of Literature" in <u>A Comprehensive Bibliography</u>. 1976. pp.
    220-222.

LITERATURE - BIBLIOGRAPHY

"After Protest: Black Writers in the 1950's and 1960's" in <u>Blacks in
    America; Bibliographical Essays</u>. 1981. pp. 256-265.

"Literature" in <u>Afro-American Reference</u>. 1985. pp. 131-150.

"A Selected Bibliography: Literature" in <u>The Negro Almanac</u>. 1983. pp.
    1507-1514.

LITERATURE - FIRST FACTS

"Black Firsts: The Arts" in <u>Before the Mayflower</u>. 1982. p. 639.

LITERATURE - HISTORY AND CRITICISM (BLACK) - BIBLIOGRAPHY

"Discussions of Literature by Negroes" in <u>A Bibliography of the Negro</u>.
    1928. pp. 456-457.

LITERATURE - HISTORY AND CRITICISM (WHITE) - BIBLIOGRAPHY

"Discussions by Whites of the Negro in Literature" in A Bibliography of the Negro. 1928. pp. 455-456.

LITERATURE - INDEX

Index to Black American Literary Anthologies. 1979. 219 p.

LITERATURE, AFRICAN - BIBLIOGRAPHY

"Pidgin, English in West African Writing" in A Bibliography of Pidgin and Creole Languages. 1975. pp. 361-364.

LITERATURE, ANTEBELLUM - BIBLIOGRAPHY

"Black Literature Before the Civil War" in Blacks in America; Bibliographical Essays. 1971. pp. 103-107.

LITERATURE, BELIZEAN - BIBLIOGRAPHY

"Literature" in Belize. 1980. pp. 171-172.

LITERATURE, BRAZILIAN - BIBLIOGRAPHY

"Literature" in Afro-Braziliana. 1978. pp. 135-170.

"Writings of Selected Authors, with Critical and Biographical References" in Afro-Braziliana. 1978. pp. 173-276.

LITERATURE, CARIBBEAN

"Introduction" in 50 Caribbean Writers. 1986. pp. 1-8.

LITERATURE, CARIBBEAN - BIBLIOGRAPHY

"Short Stories, Novels and Essays" in A Bibliography of the Negro. 1928. pp. 652-654.

LITERATURE, FOLK - BIBLIOGRAPHY

"Literature (Novels, Drama, Poetry) With Folkloric Content" in Afro-American Folk Culture. 1978. See index, pp. 778-779.

LITERATURE, PROTEST

"White Proscriptions and Black Protests" in Long Memory. 1982. pp. 342-387.

LITERATURE, PROTEST - BIBLIOGRAPHY

"Bibliography: White Proscriptions and Black Protests" in Long Memory. 1982. pp.

LITERATURE, SOUTH AMERICAN - BIBLIOGRAPHY

"Short Stories, Novels and Essays" in A Bibliography of the Negro. 1928. pp. 652-654.

LOBBYISTS - BIBLIOGRAPHY

"Black Pressure Groups: State and Local Levels" in The Study and
     Analysis of Black Politics. 1973. pp. 44-53.

LORDE, AUDRE

"Audre Lorde," Irma McClaurin-Allen in Afro-American Poets Since 1955.
     1985. pp. 217-222.

LOS ANGELES - BIBLIOGRAPHY

"Los Angeles and California" in Afro-American Reference. 1985. pp. 215-
     220.

LOUISIANA - EDUCATION - BIBLIOGRAPHY

"Louisiana" in The Education of Poor and Minority Children. 1981. pp.
     281-286.

LOUISIANA - EDUCATION, HIGHER - BIBLIOGRAPHY

"Higher Education by State: Louisiana" in The Education of Poor and
     Minority Children. 1981. pp. 885-886.

LOUISIANA - GENEALOGY - BIBLIOGRAPHY

"Louisiana" in Black Genesis. 1978. pp. 68-76.

LOUISIANA - LINGUISTICS - BIBLIOGRAPHY

"Louisiana" in A Bibliography of Pidgin and Creole Languages. 1975. pp.
     278-290.

LOUISIANA - SLAVERY - BIBLIOGRAPHY

"Louisiana" in Black Slavery in the Americas. 1982. pp. 905-928.

"Louisiana" in Slavery: A Worldwide Bibliography. 1985. pp. 110-112.

LOVELACE, EARL

"Earl Lovelace," Daryl Cumber Dance in 50 Caribbean Writers. 1986. pp.
     276-283.

LULLABIES - BIBLIOGRAPHY

"Lullabies" in Afro-American Folk Culture. 1978. See index, p. 779.

LUTHERAN CHURCH - CIVIL RIGHTS MOVEMENT - BIBLIOGRAPHY

"The Church, Synagogue and Integration: Lutheran" in Howard University
     Bibliography of African and Afro-American Religious Studies. 1977.
     p. 317.

LUTHERAN CHURCH - RACE RELATIONS - BIBLIOGRAPHY

"Lutheran" in Howard University Bibliography of African and Afro-American Religious Studies. 1977. pp. 273-274.

LUTHERAN CHURCH - SLAVERY - BIBLIOGRAPHY

"Slavery, Negroes and the Church: Lutheran" in Howard University Bibliography of African and Afro-American Religious Studies. 1977. p. 136.

LYNCHING

"Lynching" in The Negro Almanac. 1983. p. 324.

LYNCHING - BIBLIOGRAPHY

"The Negro and Lynching" in A Bibliography of the Negro. 1928. pp. 550-559.

"Racial Violence: Lynching and Riots" in Blacks in America; Bibliographical Essays. 1971. pp. 140-142.

LYNCHING - STATISTICS

"Lynching Tables" in The Negro Almanac. 1983. pp. 347-350.

MCADOO, BILL - BIBLIOGRAPHY

"McAdoo, Bill" in Bibliography of Black Music. 1981. p. 403.

MCCLELLAN, GEORGE MARION

"George Marion McClellan," Dickson D. Bruce in Afro-American Writers Before the Harlem Renaissance. 1986. pp. 206-212.

MCCLUSKEY, JOHN A.

"John A. McCluskey, Jr.," Frank E. Moorer in Afro-American Fiction Writers After 1955. 1984. pp. 179-181.

MCGIRT, JAMES E.

"James E. McGirt," Walter C. Daniel in Afro-American Writers Before the Harlem Renaissance. 1986. pp. 212-217.

MCKAY, CLAUDE

"Claude McKay," Eugenia Collier in 50 Caribbean Writers. 1986. pp. 284-293.

MCKAY, CLAUDE - BIBLIOGRAPHY

"Fiction of the Renaissance: Jean Toomer and Claude McKay" in Blacks in America; Bibliographical Essays. 1971. pp. 251-253.

"McKay, Claude" in The Harlem Renaissance. 1982. pp. 118-130.

MACKEY, WILLIAM WELLINGTON

"William Wellington Mackey," Linda E. Scott in Afro-American Writers After 1955: Dramatists and Prose Writers. 1985. pp. 175-177.

MCNEILL, ANTHONY

"Anthony McNeill," Wilfred D. Samuels in 50 Caribbean Writers. 1986. pp. 294-302.

MCPHATTER, CLYDE - BIBLIOGRAPHY

"McPhatter, Clyde L." in Black Music in America. 1981. pp. 403-404.

MCPHERSON, JAMES ALAN

"James Alan McPherson," Patsy B. Perry in Afro-American Writers After 1955: Dramatists and Prose Writers. pp. 185-194.

MCRAE, CARMEN - BIBLIOGRAPHY

"McRae, Carmen" in Black Music in America. 1981. pp. 404-409.

MADHUBUTI, HAKI R.

"Haki R. Madhubuti (Don L. Lee)," Catherine Daniels Hurst in Afro-American Poets Since 1955. 1985. pp. 222-232.

MADONNAS, BLACK - HISTORY

"History of the Black Madonnas" in Sex and Race. 1944. V. 1, pp. 273-283.

MAGAZINES - BIBLIOGRAPHY

"Magazines and Books" in Black Media in America. 1984. pp. 123-134.

MAGAZINES - DIRECTORY

"Magazines" in Black Resource Guide. pp. 99-101.

MAGICIANS - BIOGRAPHY - INDEX

"Magicians" in In Black and White. 1980. See index, V. 2, p. 1171.

MAINE - EDUCATION - BIBLIOGRAPHY

"Maine" in The Education of Poor and Minority Children. 1981. p. 286.

MAINE - GENEALOGY - BIBLIOGRAPHY

"Maine and New Hampshire" in Black Genesis. 1978. pp. 191-193.

MAINE - SLAVERY - BIBLIOGRAPHY

"Maine" in Black Slavery in the Americas. 1982. p. 774.

MAIS, ROGER

"Roger Mais," Daphne Morris in 50 Caribbean Writers. 1986. pp. 303-317.

MAJOR, CLARENCE

"Clarence Major" in Interviews with Black Writers. 1973. pp. 124-139.

"Clarence Major," Joe Weixlmann in Afro-American Fiction Writers After 1955. 1984. pp. 153-161.

MARIE GALANTE - BIBLIOGRAPHY

"Marie Galante" in The Complete Caribbeana. 1977. See index, V. 4, p. 2178.

MARINES - BIOGRAPHY - INDEX

"Military Service: Marines" in In Black and White. 1980. See index, V. 2, p. 1176.

MARITIME HISTORY

Black Men of the Sea. 1978. 158 p.

MARKETING - BIBLIOGRAPHY

"Marketing/Consumerism" in Black Media in America. 1984. pp. 135-161.

MARKETING - CARIBBEAN - BIBLIOGRAPHY

"External Trade and Internal Marketing" in The Complete Caribbeana. V. 3, pp. 1561-1593.

MARKETING - HAITI - BIBLIOGRAPHY

"External Trade and Internal Marketing" in The Complete Haitiana. 1982. V. 2, pp. 1355-1386.

MAROONS - BIBLIOGRAPHY

"Escaped Slaves" in Afro-American Folk Culture. 1978. See index, p. 772.

MAROONS - CARIBBEAN - BIBLIOGRAPHY

"Population Segments: Maroon" in The Complete Caribbeana. V. 1, pp. 545-558.

MAROONS - HAITI - BIBLIOGRAPHY

"Slavery, Marronage and Emancipation, 1492-1803" in The Complete Haitiana. V. 1, pp. 277-368.

MARRIAGE - BIBLIOGRAPHY

"Black Nuptiality, Family, and Fertility Outside Marriage" in Demography of the Black Population. 1983. pp. 80-108.

"Marriage and Divorce" in The Progress of Afro-American Women. 1980. pp.

150-153.

"Marriage, Courtship and Weddings" in <u>Afro-American Folk Culture</u>. 1978.
    See index, p. 780.

MARRIAGE, INTERRACIAL

<u>Sex and Race</u>. 3 V.

MARRIAGE, INTERRACIAL - BIBLIOGRAPHY

"Black-Jewish Marriage" in <u>Black-Jewish Relations</u>. 1984. p. 76.

MARRIAGE, INTERRACIAL - LEGAL ASPECTS

"Important Cases: Racial Intermarriage" in <u>The Negro Almanac</u>. 1983. p.
    319.

"Mixed Marriages as Seen by the Law - Ancient and Early Historic" in <u>Sex
    and Race</u>. 1944. V. 3, pp. 1-14.

"Mixed Marriages as Seen by the Law - Our Times" in <u>Sex and Race</u>. 1944.
    V. 3, pp. 15-25.

MARRIAGE, SLAVE - BIBLIOGRAPHY

"Slave Marriages" in <u>Black Slavery in the Americas</u>. 1982. pp. 1233-1236.

MARSHALL, PAULE

"Paule Marshall," Barbara Christian in <u>Afro-American Fiction Writers
    After 1955</u>. 1984. pp. 161-170.

MARTELL, LINDA - BIBLIOGRAPHY

"Martell, Linda" in <u>Black Music in America</u>. 1981. p. 409.

MARTINIQUE

"Blacks in the Western Hemisphere: Martinique" in <u>The Negro Almanac</u>.
    1983. p. 1481.

"Haiti, Martinique, Guadeloupe" in <u>Sex and Race</u>. 1942. V. 2, pp. 97-121.

MARTINIQUE - BIBLIOGRAPHY

"Martinique" in <u>The Complete Caribbeana</u>. See index, V. 4, p. 2179.

MARVIN X

"Marvin X," Lorenzo Thomas in <u>Afro-American Writers After 1955:
    Dramatists and Prose Writers</u>. 1985. pp. 177-184.

MARYLAND - EDUCATION - BIBLIOGRAPHY

"Maryland" in <u>The Education of Poor and Minority Children</u>. 1981. pp.
    286-289.

MARYLAND - EDUCATION, HIGHER - BIBLIOGRAPHY

"Higher Education by State: Maryland" in The Education of Poor and
     Minority Children. 1981. pp. 886-888.

MARYLAND - GENEALOGY - BIBLIOGRAPHY

"Maryland" in Black Genesis. 1978. pp. 77-87.

MARYLAND - SLAVERY

"Colonia Slavery: Virginia and Maryland" in From Slavery to Freedom.
     1980. pp. 54-57.

MARYLAND - SLAVERY - BIBLIOGRAPHY

"Maryland" in Black Slavery in the Americas. 1982. pp. 846-856.

MASCARENES - LINGUISTICS - BIBLIOGRAPHY

"Mascarenes" in A Bibliography of Pidgin and Creole Languages. 1975. pp.
     291-295.

MASCULINITY

"Black Manhood in the 1970's: A Critical Look Back" in Black
     Masculinity. 1982. pp. 135-146.

MASONS - DIRECTORY

"Prince Hall Masonry" in Black Resource Guide. 1986. pp. 186-191.

MASSACHUSETTS - EDUCATION - BIBLIOGRAPHY

"Massachusetts" in The Education of Poor and Minority Children. 1981.
     pp. 289-301.

MASSACHUSETTS - EDUCATION, HIGHER - BIBLIOGRAPHY

"Higher Education by State: Massachusetts" in The Education of Poor and
     Minority Children. 1981. pp. 888-890.

MASSACHUSETTS - GENEALOGY - BIBLIOGRAPHY

"Massachusetts" in Black Genesis. 1978. pp. 155-159.

MASSACHUSETTS - SLAVERY - BIBLIOGRAPHY

"Massachusetts" in Black Slavery in the Americas. 1982. pp. 774-781.

MATHEMATICIANS - BIOGRAPHY - INDEX

"Mathematicians" in In Black and White. 1980. See index, V. 2, pp.
     1172-1173.

MATHEMATICS - EDUCATION

"Helping Minority Students to Excel in University-level Mathematics and
    Science Courses: The Professional Development Program at the
    University of California, Berkeley," Katharyn Culler in The State
    of Black America, 1985. pp. 225-231.

MATHIS, JOHNNY - BIBLIOGRAPHY

"Mathis, Johnny" in Black Music in America. 1981. pp. 409-414.

MATHIS, SHARON BELL

"Sharon Bell Mathis," Frances Smith Foster in Afro-American Fiction
    Writers After 1955. 1984. pp. 170-173.

MATRIARCHY - BIBLIOGRAPHY

"Matriarchy" in The Progress of Afro-American Women. 1980. pp. 153-156.

MAURITANIA - MUSIC - BIBLIOGRAPHY

"Mauritania" in Bibliography of Black Music. 1981. V. 3, p. 89.

MAURITIUS - LINGUISTICS - BIBLIOGRAPHY

"Mauritius" in A Bibliography of Pidgin and Creole Languages. 1975. pp.
    300-306.

MAYFIELD, JULIAN

"Julian Mayfield," Estelle W. Taylor in Afro-American Fiction Writers
    After 1955. 1984. pp. 174-178.

"Julian Mayfield" in Interviews with Black Writers. 1973. pp. 140-151.

MAYNOR, DOROTHY - BIBLIOGRAPHY

"Maynor, Dorothy" in Black Music in America. 1981. pp. 414-416.

MAYORS

"Black Mayors" in The Negro Almanac. 1983. pp. 404-417.

MAYORS - DIRECTORY

"Mayors" in Black Resource Guide. 1986. pp. 157-167.

MBUGU - BIBLIOGRAPHY

"Mbugu" in A Bibliography of Pidgin and Creole Languages. 1975. pp. 59-
    60.

MEDIA

"The Black Press and Broadcast Media" in The Negro Almanac. 1983. pp.
    1211-1249.

"Blackening the Media: The State of Blacks in the Press," Samuel L.

Adams in The State of Black America, 1985. pp. 65-103.

"Media Technology and African-American Sociology," Juanita Howard.
Contemporary Black Thought. 1982. pp. 165-180.

"The Popular Media: Part II; the Black Role in Radio and Television,"
George E. Norford. The Black American Reference Book. 1976. pp.
875-888.

"Press" in The Ebony Handbook. 1974. pp. 413-429.

MEDIA - BIBLIOGRAPHY

Black Media in America: A Resource Guide. 1984. 333 p.

"Mass Media" in Afro-American Reference. 1985. pp. 151-161.

MEDIA - BIOGRAPHY - BIBLIOGRAPHY

"Biography" in Black Media in America. 1984. pp. 53-62.

MEDIA - DIRECTORY

Burelle's Black Media Directory. 1984. 154 p.

MEDIA - MUSIC - BIBLIOGRAPHY

"Jazz and TV, Radio and Film" in Jazz Bibliography. 1981. pp. 308-310.

MEDIA EMPLOYEES AND OFFICIALS - BIOGRAPHY - INDEX

"Communication" in In Black and White. 1980. See index, V. 2, p. 1133.

MEDIA ORGANIZATIONS - DIRECTORY

"National Media Organizations" in Black Resource Guide. 1986. p. 101.

MEDICAL INSTITUTIONS - BIBLIOGRAPHY

"Health: Institutions" in A Comprehensive Bibliography. 1976. pp. 188-
189.

MEDICAL RARITIES - BIOGRAPHY - INDEX

"Medical Rarities" in In Black and White. 1980. See index, V. 2, p.
1173.

MEDICAL SCHOOL INSTRUCTORS - BIOGRAPHY - INDEX

"Law, Medical School Instructors" in In Black and White. 1980. See
index, V. 2, p. 1166.

MEDICINE - BIBLIOGRAPHY

"Medicine" in The Progress of Afro-American Women. 1980. pp. 216-219.

"Medicine and Health Care" in Afro-American Reference. 1985. pp. 188-

193.

MEDICINE - SLAVERY - BIBLIOGRAPHY

"Medicine" in Afro-American Folk Culture. 1978. See index, pp. 780-781.

"Slave Medicine" in Black Slavery in the Americas. 1982. pp. 1161-1181.

MEN

Black Masculinity. 1982. 181 p.

Black Men. 1981. 295 p.

"Sex and Racism" in Long Memory. 1982.

MEN - BIBLIOGRAPHY

"Black Male Role in the Family" in The Black Family in the United
     States. 1986. pp. 139-141.

"Black Male's Role in the Family" in The Black Family in the United
     States. 1986. pp. 205-206.

"Men and Women" in Afro-American Reference. 1985. pp. 175-181.

MEN - HAITI - BIBLIOGRAPHY

"Population Categories: Afro-Haitian Men, Women and Children" in The
     Complete Haitiana. 1982. pp. 561-575.

MEN - STATISTICS

"A Social Profile," Laurence E. Gary in Black Men. 1981. pp. 21-45.

MENDES, ALFRED H.

"Alfred H. Mendes," Reinhard W. Sander in 50 Caribbean Writers. 1986.
     pp. 318-326.

MENTAL CHARACTERISTICS

"Race and Mental Characteristics" in A Bibliography of the Negro. 1928.
     pp. 570-576.

MENTAL HEALTH - BIBLIOGRAPHY

"Black Family and Mental Illness" in The Black Family in the United
     States. 1986. pp. 191-192.

"Health: Mental" in A Comprehensive Bibliography. 1976. pp. 186-188.

"Psychology and Mental Health" in Afro-American Reference. 1985. pp.
     184-188.

"Psychology and Mental Health" in The Progress of Afro-American Women.
     1980. pp. 292-303.

MENTAL HEALTH - CARIBBEAN - BIBLIOGRAPHY

"Psychiatry and Mental Health" in The Complete Haitiana. 1982. V. 2, pp.
971-976.

MERCHANT SEAMEN - BIOGRAPHY - INDEX

"Merchant Seamen" in In Black and White. 1980. See index, V. 2, p. 1173.

MERIWETHER, LOUISE

"Louise Meriwether," Rita B. Dandridge in Afro-American Fiction Writers
After 1955. 1984. pp. 182-186.

METEOROLOGISTS - BIOGRAPHY - INDEX

"Meteorologists" in In Black and White. 1980. See index, V. 2, p. 1173.

METHODIST EPISCOPAL CHURCH - CIVIL RIGHTS MOVEMENT - BIBLIOGRAPHY

"The Church, Synagogue and Integration: Methodist Episcopal (United
Methodist)" in Howard University Bibliography of African and Afro-
American Religious Studies. 1977. pp. 317-319.

METHODIST EPISCOPAL CHURCH - RACE RELATIONS - BIBLIOGRAPHY

"Methodist Episcopal (United Methodist)" in Howard University
Bibliography of African and Afro-American Religious Studies. 1977.
pp. 274-280.

METHODIST EPISCOPAL CHURCH - SLAVERY - BIBLIOGRAPHY

"Slavery, Negroes and the Church: Methodist Episcopal (United
Methodist)" in Howard University Bibliography of African and Afro-
American Religious Studies. 1977. pp. 136-139.

MEXICAN-AMERICANS - EDUCATION - BIBLIOGRAPHY

"Mexican-Americans" in The Education of Poor and Minority Children.
1981. pp. 427-475.

MEXICAN-AMERICANS - EDUCATION, HIGHER - BIBLIOGRAPHY

"Mexican-American Students" (Higher Education) in The Education of Poor
and Minority Children. 1981. pp. 932-934.

MEXICO

"Blacks in the Western Hemisphere: Mexico" in The Negro Almanac. 1983.
pp. 1466-1467.

"Mexico" in Sex and Race. 1942. V. 2, pp. 72-79.

MEXICO - BIBLIOGRAPHY

"Mexico" in The Education of Poor and Minority Children. 1981. pp.
1248-1251.

"Mexico" in <u>Race and Ethnic Relations</u>. 1980. pp. 195-203.

MEXICO - SLAVERY - BIBLIOGRAPHY

"Mexico" in <u>Slavery: A Worldwide Bibliography</u>. 1977. pp. 127-130.

MICHEAUX, OSCAR

"Oscar Micheaux," J. Randall Woodland in <u>Afro-American Writers Before the Harlem Renaissance</u>. 1986. pp. 218-225.

MICHIGAN - EDUCATION - BIBLIOGRAPHY

"Michigan" in <u>The Education of Poor and Minority Children</u>. 1981. pp. 301-310.

MICHIGAN - EDUCATION, HIGHER - BIBLIOGRAPHY

"Higher Education by State: Michigan" in <u>The Education of Poor and Minority Children</u>. 1981. pp. 891-893.

MICHIGAN - GENEALOGY - BIBLIOGRAPHY

"Michigan" in <u>Black Genesis</u>. 1978. pp. 207-210.

MICHIGAN - SLAVERY - BIBLIOGRAPHY

"Michigan" in <u>Black Slavery in the Americas</u>. 1982. p. 813.

MICROBIOLOGISTS - BIOGRAPHY - INDEX

"Microbiologists" in <u>In Black and White</u>. 1980. See index, V. 2, p. 1173.

MIDDLE COLONIES - SLAVERY - BIBLIOGRAPHY

"New England and the Middle Colonies" in <u>Slavery: A Worldwide Bibliography</u>. 1977. pp. 76-80.

MIDWEST - SLAVERY - BIBLIOGRAPHY

"Slavery in the Midwest" in <u>Black Slavery in the Americas</u>. 1982. pp. 803-816.

MIGRANT LABORERS - BIBLIOGRAPHY

"Migrant Labor" in <u>The Progress of Afro-American Women</u>. 1980. p. 125.

MIGRATION - BIBLIOGRAPHY

"Bibliographical Notes: The Westward March" in <u>From Slavery to Freedom</u>. 1980. pp. 519-520.

"Black Migration, Urbanization and Ecology" in <u>Black Demography in the United States</u>. 1983. pp. 235-298.

"Black Nationalism and Migration, 1865-1915" in <u>Blacks in America; Bibliographical Essays</u>. 1971. pp. 170-173.

"The Great Migration" in <u>Blacks in America; Bibliographical Essays</u>.
     1971. pp. 185-188.

"Negro Population Movements" in <u>A Bibliography of the Negro</u>. 1928. pp.
     480-486.

"Statistics, Demography and Migration" in <u>Afro-American Reference</u>. 1985.
     pp. 87-92.

MIGRATION - CARIBBEAN - BIBLIOGRAPHY

"Internal and External Migration" in <u>The Complete Caribbeana</u>. 1977. V.
     1, pp. 595-614.

"West Indian and Latin American Peoples in North America" in <u>Afro-</u>
     <u>American Folk Culture</u>. 1978. See index, p. 805.

MIGRATION - ECONOMIC ASPECTS - BIBLIOGRAPHY

"Black Movement to and Within Urban Areas" in <u>The Economics of</u>
     <u>Minorities</u>. 1976. pp. 59-66.

MIGRATION - HAITI - BIBLIOGRAPHY

"Internal and External Migration" in <u>The Complete Haitiana</u>. 1982. V. 1,
     pp. 595-607.

MILITARY

"Armed Forces" in <u>The Ebony Handbook</u>. 1974. pp. 195-224.

"The Black Man as a Soldier," Jack J. Cardoso in <u>The Negro Impact on</u>
     <u>Western Civilization</u>. 1970. pp. 337-360.

"Black Participation in the Armed Forces," Richard J. Stillman II in <u>The</u>
     <u>Black American Reference Book</u>. 1976. pp. 889-926.

"Black Servicemen and the Military Establishment" in <u>The Negro Almanac</u>.
     1983. pp. 827-903.

"Military Service and the Paradox of Loyalty" in <u>Long Memory</u>. 1982. pp.
     295-341.

MILITARY - BIBLIOGRAPHY

"Armed Forces" in <u>Afro-American Reference</u>. 1985. pp. 195-200.

"Armed Forces" in <u>The Education of Poor and Minority Children</u>. 1981. pp.
     978-980.

"Armed Services and Defense Work" in <u>The Progress of Afro-American</u>
     <u>Women</u>. 1980. pp. 3-15.

"Bibliography: Military Service and the Paradox of Loyalty" in <u>Long</u>
     <u>Memory</u>. 1982. pp. 447-449.

"The Negro as a Soldier in the Regular Army" in <u>A Bibliography of the</u>

<u>Negro</u>. 1928. pp. 401-402.

MILITARY - BIOGRAPHY - INDEX

"Military Service" in <u>In Black and White</u>. 1980. See index, V. 2, pp. 1173-1178.

MILITARY - FIRST FACTS

"Black Firsts: Military" in <u>Before the Mayflower</u>. 1982. pp. 634-635.

MILITARY - HAITI - BIBLIOGRAPHY

"Army, Police, Navy, and Air Force" in <u>The Complete Haitiana</u>. 1982. V. 2, pp. 1187-1198.

MILITARY ACADEMICIANS - BIOGRAPHY - INDEX

"Military Service Academies" in <u>In Black and White</u>. 1980. See index, V. 2, p. 1174.

MILITARY FAMILIES - BIBLIOGRAPHY

"Black Family and Military Families" in <u>The Black Family in the United States</u>. 1986. p. 192.

MILITARY HISTORY - CIVIL WAR

"The Jubilee War: Witnesses and Warriors" in <u>Before the Mayflower</u>. 1982. pp. 187-213.

MILITARY HISTORY - CIVIL WAR - BIBLIOGRAPHY

"The Negro as a Soldier in the Civil War" in <u>A Bibliography of the Negro</u>. 1928. pp. 398-401.

"Slavery and the Civil War: Slaves and the Union" in <u>Black Slavery in the Americas</u>. 1982. pp. 1530-1568.

MILITARY HISTORY - REVOLUTIONARY WAR - BIBLIOGRAPHY

"The Negro as a Soldier in the Revolutionary and the War of 1812" in <u>A Bibliography of the Negro</u>. 1928. p. 397.

MILITARY HISTORY - SPANISH-AMERICAN WAR - BIBLIOGRAPHY

"The Negro as a Soldier in the Spanish-American War" in <u>A Bibliography of the Negro</u>. 1928. p. 402.

MILITARY HISTORY - WAR OF 1812 - BIBLIOGRAPHY

"The Negro as a Soldier in the Revolutionary War and the War of 1812" in <u>A Bibliography of the Negro</u>. 1928. p. 397.

MILITARY HISTORY - WORLD WAR I - BIBLIOGRAPHY

"Blacks in World War I" in <u>Blacks in America; Bibliographical Essays</u>.

1971. pp. 192-194.

"The Negro as a Soldier in the World War" in A Bibliography of the Negro. 1928. pp. 403-404.

MILITARY HISTORY - WORLD WAR II

"Negroes in the Service" in From Slavery to Freedom. 1980. pp. 428-437.

MILITARY HISTORY - WORLD WAR II - BIBLIOGRAPHY

"Blacks in World War II" in Blacks in America; Bibliographical Essays. 1971. pp. 234-238.

MILITARY PERSONNEL - STATISTICS

"Blacks in the Armed Forces" in Facts About Blacks. 1986. pp. 42-47.

MILLER, E. ETHELBERT

"E. Ethelbert Miller," Priscilla R. Ramsey in Afro-American Poets Since 1955. 1985. pp. 233-240.

MILLER, MAY

"May Miller," Winifred L. Stoelting in Afro-American Poets Since 1955. 1985. pp. 241-247.

MILLICAN, ARTHENIA J. BATES

"Arthenia J. Bates Millican," Virginia Whatley Smith in Afro-American Writers After 1955: Dramatists and Prose Writers. 1985. pp. 195-201.

MILLINERS - BIOGRAPHY - INDEX

"Milliners" in In Black and White. 1980. See index, V. 2, p. 1178.

MILLS, STEPHANIE - BIBLIOGRAPHY

"Mills, Stephanie" in Black Music in America. 1981. pp. 416-417.

MILNER, RON

"Ron Milner," Beunyce Rayford Cunningham in Afro-American Writers After 1955: Dramatists and Prose Writers. 1985. pp. 201-207.

MINERS - BIOGRAPHY - INDEX

"Miners" in In Black and White. 1980. See index, V. 2, p. 1178.

MINING - CARIBBEAN - BIBLIOGRAPHY

"Mining and Economic Geology" in The Complete Caribbeana. V. 3, pp. 1625-1644.

MINING - HAITI - BIBLIOGRAPHY

"Mining and Economic Geology" in The Complete Haitiana. 1982. V. 2, pp.
    1421-1423.

MINNESOTA - EDUCATION - BIBLIOGRAPHY

"Minnesota" in The Education of Poor and Minority Children. 1981. pp.
    310-311.

MINNESOTA - EDUCATION, HIGHER - BIBLIOGRAPHY

"Higher Education by State: Minnesota" in The Education of Poor and
    Minority Children. 1981. p. 893.

MINNESOTA - GENEALOGY - BIBLIOGRAPHY

"Minnesota" in Black Genesis. 1978. pp. 211-214.

MINNESOTA - SLAVERY - BIBLIOGRAPHY

"Minnesota" in Black Slavery in the Americas. 1982. p. 814.

MINSTRELS - BIBLIOGRAPHY

"Minstrelsy (Black and White)" in Afro-American Folk Culture. 1978. See
    index, p. 781.

"Minstrelsy: Songsters and Music" in Bibliography of Black Music. 1981.
    V. 2, pp. 15-29.

MINSTRELS - INDEX

"Minstrels: Name Index" in Bibliography of Black Music. 1981. V. 2, pp.
    30-33.

MINSTRELS, WHITE - BIBLIOGRAPHY

"Negro Minstrelsy (Representations of the Negro by White Persons)" in A
    Bibliography of the Negro. 1928. pp. 444-445.

MINSTRELSY - HISTORY AND CRITICISM - BIBLIOGRAPHY

"Minstrelsy: Literature" in Bibliography of Black Music. 1981. V. 2, pp.
    10-14.

MISCEGENATION

Sex and Race. 3 V.

"Sex and Racism" in Long Memory. 1982. pp. 114-141.

MISCEGENATION - BIBLIOGRAPHY

"Bibliography: Sex and Racism" in Long Memory. 1982. pp. 432-435.

"Interracial Mating" in Afro-American Reference. pp. 181-183.

"Race and Ethnic Relations - Mulattoes and Miscegenation" in Afro-

American Reference. 1985. pp. 84-85.

"Race Mixture" in A Bibliography of the Negro. 1928. pp. 578-582.

MISSIONARIES - BIOGRAPHY - INDEX

"Missionaries" in In Black and White. 1980. See index, V. 2, p. 1178.

MISSIONS AND MISSIONARIES - AFRICA - BIBLIOGRAPHY

"Christian Missions in Africa" in A Bibliography of the Negro. 1928. pp. 190-226.

MISSISSIPPI - EDUCATION - BIBLIOGRAPHY

"Mississippi" in The Education of Poor and Minority Children. 1981. pp. 311-320.

MISSISSIPPI - EDUCATION, HIGHER - BIBLIOGRAPHY

"Higher Education by State: Mississippi" in The Education of Poor and Minority Children. 1981. pp. 894-895.

MISSISSIPPI - GENEALOGY - BIBLIOGRAPHY

"Mississippi" in Black Genesis. 1978. pp. 138-143.

MISSISSIPPI - HISTORY - RECONSTRUCTION - BIBLIOGRAPHY

"Blacks in Southern Reconstruction: South Carolina and Mississippi" in Blacks in America; Bibliographical Essays. 1971. pp. 125-127.

MISSISSIPPI - LIBRARIANS

"See How They Ran: Black Librarians in Mississippi," Lelia G. Rhodes in Black Librarian in the Southeast. 1976. pp. 53-71.

MISSISSIPPI - SLAVERY - BIBLIOGRAPHY

"Mississippi" in Black Slavery in the Americas. 1982. pp. 928-936.

MISSOURI - EDUCATION - BIBLIOGRAPHY

"Missouri" in The Education of Poor and Minority Children. 1981. pp. 320-325.

MISSOURI - EDUCATION, HIGHER - BIBLIOGRAPHY

"Higher Education by State: Missouri" in The Education of Poor and Minority Children. 1981. p. 895.

MISSOURI - GENEALOGY - BIBLIOGRAPHY

"Missouri" in Black Genesis. 1978. pp. 215-221.

MISSOURI - SLAVERY - BIBLIOGRAPHY

"Missouri" in <u>Black Slavery in the Americas</u>. 1982. pp. 856-865.

MITCHELL, LOFTEN

"Loften Mitchell," Ja A. Jahannes in <u>Afro-American Writers After 1955:
     Dramatists and Prose Writers</u>. 1985. pp. 208-214.

MITTELHOLZER, EDGAR

"Edgar Mittelholzer," Victor L. Chang in <u>50 Caribbean Writers</u>. 1986. pp.
     327-340.

MODELS - BIBLIOGRAPHY

"Modeling" in <u>The Progress of Afro-American Women</u>. 1980. pp. 125-127.

MODELS - BIOGRAPHY - INDEX

"Models" in <u>In Black and White</u>. 1980. See index, V. 2, p. 1179.

MONK, THELONIOUS - BIBLIOGRAPHY

"Monk, Thelonious" in <u>Black Music in America</u>. 1981. pp. 417-424.

MONTANA - EDUCATION - BIBLIOGRAPHY

"Montana" in <u>The Education of Poor and Minority Children</u>. 1981. p. 325.

MONUMENTS, HISTORICAL

"Monuments" in <u>The Ebony Handbook</u>. 1974. pp. 478-480.

MOORE, CARMEN - BIBLIOGRAPHY

"Moore, Carmen" in <u>Black Music in America</u>. 1981. p. 425.

MOORS

"The Moorish Impact on Western Europe" Philip S. Cohen and Francesco
     Cordasco in <u>The Negro Impact on Western Civilization</u>. 1970. pp.
     421-444.

MORGAN STATE UNIVERSITY - MUSIC EDUCATION - BIBLIOGRAPHY

"Colleges and Universities: Morgan State University" in <u>Bibliography of
     Black Music</u>. 1984. V. 4, p. 104.

MORMONS - BIOGRAPHY - INDEX

"Mormons" in <u>In Black and White</u>. 1980. See index, V. 2, p.1180.

MORMONS - RACE RELATIONS - BIBLIOGRAPHY

"Mormons" in <u>Howard University Bibliography of African and Afro-American
     Religious Studies</u>. 1977. p. 292.

MOROCCO - MUSIC - BIBLIOGRAPHY

"Morocco" in <u>Bibliography of Black Music</u>. 1981. V. 3, p. 90.

MORRIS, MERVYN

"Mervyn Morris," Pamela C. Mordecai in <u>50 Caribbean Writers</u>. 1986. pp. 341-356.

MORRISON, TONI

"Toni Morrison," Susan L. Blake in <u>Afro-American Fiction Writers After 1955</u>. 1984. pp. 187-199.

MORTALITY - BIBLIOGRAPHY

"Black Health and Mortality" in <u>Black Demography in the United States</u>. 1983. pp. 203-234.

MORTON, JELLY ROLL - BIBLIOGRAPHY

"Morton, Ferdinand Joseph (Jelly Roll)" in <u>Black Music in America</u>. 1981. pp. 425-433.

MOTHERHOOD - BIBLIOGRAPHY

"Childrearing and Motherhood" in <u>The Progress of Afro-American Women</u>. 1980. pp. 138-144.

MOTHERS - BIOGRAPHY - INDEX

"Mothers" in <u>In Black and White</u>. 1980. See index, V. 2, p. 1180.

MOZAMBIQUE - MUSIC - BIBLIOGRAPHY

"Mozambique" in <u>Bibliography of Black Music</u>. 1981. V. 3, p. 91.

MULATTOES - BIBLIOGRAPHY

"Race and Ethnic Relations - Mulattoes and Miscegenation" in <u>Afro-American Reference</u>. 1985. pp. 84-85.

MULTIMEDIA MATERIALS

"Nonprint Ethnic Resources," Adele S. Dendy in <u>Ethnic Collections</u>. 1983. p. 36-45.

MULTIMEDIA MATERIALS - BIBLIOGRAPHY

"Multimedia Sources" in <u>Afro-American Reference</u>. 1985. pp. 169-170.

MURRAY, ALBERT L.

"Albert L. Murray," Elizabeth Schultz in <u>Afro-American Writers After 1955: Dramatists and Prose Writers</u>. 1985. pp. 214-224.

MURRAY, PAULI

"Pauli Murray," Nellie McKay in <u>Afro-American Poets Since 1955</u>. 1985.

pp. 248-251.

MUSEUMS

"Black Museums and Galleries" in The Negro Almanac. 1983. pp. 1011-1016.

"Where to See Black Maritime Heritage" in Black Men of the Sea. 1978.
    pp. 125-131.

MUSEUMS - BIBLIOGRAPHY

"Art Galleries and Museums" in 250 Years of Afro-American Art. 1981. pp.
    254-322.

MUSEUMS - DIRECTORIES

"Afro-American Art Organizations, Art Museums and Art Galleries" in The
    Complete Annotated Resource Guide to Black American Art. 1978. pp.
    216-239.

MUSEUMS - DIRECTORY

"Museums" in Black Resource Guide. 1986. pp. 140-145.

MUSEUMS - MUSIC - BIBLIOGRAPHY

"Jazz in Archives, Libraries, Museums" in Jazz Bibliography. 1981. p.
    307.

"Libraries, Museums, Collections" in Bibliography of Black Music. 1981.
    V. 1, pp. 3-5.

MUSIC

"Afro-American Music," Wendell Whalum, David Baker, and Richard Long in
    The Black American Reference Book. 1976. pp. 791-826.

"Afro-American Music and Dance" Mohan Lal Sharma in The Negro Impact on
    Western Civilization. 1970. pp. 139-158.

"The Music of Black Americans" in The Roots of Black Music. 1982. pp.
    127-134.

MUSIC - BIBLIOGRAPHIES - BIBLIOGRAPHY

"Bibliographies of the Music" in Bibliography of Black Music. 1981. V.
    1, pp. 11-14.

MUSIC - BIBLIOGRAPHY

Bibliography of Black Music. 1981. V. 1-4.

"Book Citations" in Black Music. 1979. pp. 191-202.

"Jazz and Other Forms of Music" in Jazz Bibliography. 1981. pp. 178-183.

"Jazz, Spirituals, Blues and Gospel: Black Music" in Blacks in the

Humanities. 1986. pp. 109-121.

"Music" in Afro-American Reference. 1985. pp. 105-115.

"Music" in Black Women and Religion. 1980. pp. 73-93.

"Music" in The Progress of Afro-American Women. 1980. pp. 20-22.

"Music and Dance" in A Comprehensive Bibliography. 1976. pp. 256-261.

"Poetry: General Studies - Anthologies: Appendix of Folk Songs, Blues, and Spirituals" in Afro-American Poetry and Drama. 1979. pp. 51-54.

"Songs" in Afro-American Folk Culture. 1978. See index, p. 794.

"Songs, Secular" in Afro-American Folk Culture. 1978. See index, pp. 796-797.

MUSIC - DICTIONARIES - BIBLIOGRAPHY

"Lexicons, Etymologies" in Bibliography of Black Music. 1981. V. 1, pp. 9-10.

MUSIC - DIRECTORIES - BIBLIOGRAPHY

"Directories and Organization News" in Bibliography of Black Music. 1981. V. 1, pp. 65-68.

MUSIC - DISCOGRAPHY

Black Music. 1979. 262 p.

MUSIC - DISCOGRAPHY - BIBLIOGRAPHY

"Discographies" in Bibliography of Black Music. 1981. V. 1, pp. 25-60.

MUSIC - HAITI - BIBLIOGRAPHY

"Music and Dance" in The Complete Haitiana. 1982. V. 1, pp. 799-806.

MUSIC - HISTORY AND CRITICISM - BIBLIORAPHIES - BIBLIOGRAPHY

"Bibliographies of the Literature" in Bibliography of Black Music. 1981. V. 1, pp. 15-23.

MUSIC - HISTORY AND CRITICISM - BIBLIOGRAPHY

"Background" in Jazz Bibliography. 1981. pp. 49-73.

"Discussions of the Negro in Music" in A Bibliography of the Negro. 1928. pp. 441-442.

"General Histories" in Bibliography of Black Music. 1983. V. 2, pp. 209.

MUSIC - PERIODICALS - BIBLIOGRAPHY

"Periodical Citations" in Black Music. 1979. pp. 203-205.

"Periodicals" in Bibliography of Black Music. 1981. V. 1, pp. 99-124.

MUSIC - SLAVERY - BIBLIOGRAPHY

"Slave Culture: Music" in Black Slavery in the Americas. 1982. pp. 1304-1339.

MUSIC - SOCIOLOGY - BIBLIOGRAPHY

"Sociology of Jazz" in Jazz Bibliography. 1981. pp. 141-170.

MUSIC, AFRICAN

"Music and Other Aspects of African Culture" in The Roots of Black Music. 1982. pp. 93-124.

"Music in African Societies: in The Roots of Black Music. 1982. pp. 107-124.

"Third-Stream African Music" in The Roots of Black Music. 1982. pp. 117-124.

MUSIC, AFRICAN - BIBLIOGRAPHY

"African Music" in A Bibliography of the Negro. 1928. pp. 98-100.

MUSIC, AFRICAN - DISCOGRAPHY - BIBLIOGRAPHY

"Discographies: Non-United States Music" in Bibliography of Black Music. 1981. V. 1, pp. 57-59.

MUSIC, AFRICAN - TECHNOLOGY

"Technology and African Music" in The Roots of Black Music. 1982. pp. 109-111.

MUSIC, AFRICAN - WESTERN INFLUENCES

"Euro-American Elements in African Music" in The Roots of Black Music. 1982. pp. 112-116.

MUSIC COLLECTIONS - BIBLIOGRAPHY

"Libraries, Museums, Collections" in Bibliography of Black Music. 1981. V. 1, pp. 3-5.

MUSIC CRITICS - BIOGRAPHY - INDEX

"Critics: Literary, Art, Music" in In Black and White. 1980. See index, V. 2, pp. 1134-1135.

"Musicians: Critics" in In Black and White. 1980. See index, V. 2, p. 1183.

MUSIC EDUCATION - BIBLIOGRAPHY

"Colleges and Universities" in Bibliography of Black Music. 1984. V. 4,

pp. 93-105.

"Primary and Secondary Schools: Jazz, Pop and Blues" in Bibliography of Black Music. 1984. V. 4, p. 92.

MUSIC HISTORIANS - BIOGRAPHY - INDEX

"Musicians: Historians" in In Black and White. 1980. See index, V. 2, p. 1184.

MUSIC ORGANIZATIONS - FOUNDERS AND OFFICIALS - BIOGRAPHY - INDEX

"Music Organizations Founders, Officials" in In Black and White. 1980. See index, V. 2, p. 1191.

MUSIC PUBLISHERS - BIOGRAPHY - INDEX

"Music Publishers" in In Black and White. 1980. See index, V. 2, p. 1191.

MUSIC TEACHERS - BIOGRAPHY - INDEX

"Musicians: Teachers" in In Black and White. 1980. See index, V. 2, p. 1196.

MUSICAL INSTRUMENTS

"African-Derived Instruments in Black American Music" in Roots of Black Music. 1982. pp. 145-148.

"Musical Instruments" in The Roots of Black Music. 1982. pp. 47-89.

MUSICAL INSTRUMENTS - BIBLIOGRAPHY

"Instruments" in Bibliography of Black Music. 1984. V. 4, pp. 3-11.

"Jazz Instruments" in Jazz Bibliography. 1981. pp. 315-318.

"Musical Instruments" in Afro-American Folk Culture. 1978. See index, pp. 782-783.

"Strings" in Bibliography of Black Music. 1984. V. 4, pp. 17-26.

MUSICAL RECORDING COMPANIES - DISCOGRAPHY - BIBLIOGRAPHY

"Label Discographies" in Bibliography of Black Music. 1981. V. 1, pp. 55-57.

MUSICAL RECORDINGS, JAZZ - BIBLIOGRAPHY

"Jazz and Phonorecords" in Jazz Bibliography. 1981. pp. 311-314.

MUSICIANS - BIBLIOGRAPHY

"Music" in The Progress of Afro-American Women. 1980. pp. 20-22.

"Selected Musicians and Singers" in Black Music in America. pp. 1-558.

MUSICIANS - BIOGRAPHY - INDEX

"Musicians" in In Black and White. 1980. See index, V. 2, pp. 1180-1196.

MUSICIANS - DIRECTORIES

Directory of Blacks in the Performing Arts. 1978. 428 p.

MUSICIANS - DISCOGRAPHIES - BIBLIOGRAPHY

"Discographies: Individual Discographies" in Bibliography of Black
     Music. 1981. V. 1, pp. 31-46.

MUSLIMS - BIBLIOGRAPHY

"Black Muslims and Jews" in Black-Jewish Relations. 1984. p. 18.

MUSLIMS - SLAVERY - BIBLIOGRAPHY

"Muslim" in Slavery: A Worldwide Bibliography. 1985. pp. 235-247.

MYERS, WALTER DEAN

"Walter Dean Myers," Carmen Subryan in Afro-American Fiction Writers
     After 1955. 1984. pp. 199-202.

MYSTICS - BIOGRAPHY - INDEX

"Mystics" in In Black and White. 1980. See index, V. 2, p. 1196.

MYTHS - BIBLIOGRAPHY

"Myth" in Afro-American Folk Culture. 1978. See index, p. 783.

NAIPAUL, V.S.

"V.S. Naipaul," Robert D. Hamner in 50 Caribbean Writers. 1986. pp.
     357-367.

NAMES, PERSONAL - INDEX

"Name Index by State" in Index to the American Slave. 1980. pp. 77-143.

"Slave Identification File" in Index to the American Slave. 1980. pp.
     3-76.

NAMIBIA - MUSIC - BIBLIOGRAPHY

"Namibia" in Bibliography of Black Music. 1981. V. 3, p. 92.

NATION OF ISLAM - BIBLIOGRAPHY

"The Black Muslims" in Black Rhetoric. 1976. pp. 131-133.

"Black Muslims" in Howard University Bibliography of African and Afro-
     American Religious Studies. 1977. pp. 210-217.

NATIONAL ARCHIVES

"A Love-Hate Relationship with the National Archives," Mary Frances
Berry in Afro-American History; Sources for Research. 1981. pp.
35-40.

"The National Archives and Records Service: An Evaluation of Afro-
American Resources," John W. Blassingame in Afro-American History;
Sources for Research. 1981. pp. 165-170.

NATIONAL ASSOCIATION FOR THE ADVANCEMENT OF COLORED PEOPLE

"The National Association for the Advancement of Colored People" in The
Negro Almanac. 1983. pp. 247-249.

NATIONAL ASSOCIATION FOR THE ADVANCEMENT OF COLORED PEOPLE -
BIBLIOGRAPHY

"The NAACP" in Blacks in America; Bibliographical Essays. 1971. pp.
198-201.

NATIONAL ASSOCIATION FOR THE ADVANCEMENT OF COLORED PEOPLE - LEGAL
DEFENSE AND EDUCATION FUND

"The NAACP Legal Defense and Education Fund" in The Negro Almanac. 1983.
p. 257.

NATIONAL ASSOCATION FOR THE RELIEF OF DESTITUE COLORED WOMEN AND
CHILDREN - BIBLIOGRAPHY

"National Association for the Relief of Destitute Colored Women and
Children" in The Progress of Afro-American Women. 1980. p. 258.

NATIONAL ASSOCIATION OF BEAUTY CULTURE SCHOOL OWNERS AND TEACHERS -
BIBLIOGRAPHY

"National Association of Beauty Culture School Owners and Teachers" in
The Progress of Afro-American Women. 1980. pp. 258-259.

NATIONAL ASSOCIATION OF BLACK PROFESSIONAL WOMEN IN HIGHER EDUCATION -
BIBLIOGRAPHY

"National Association of Black Professional Women in Higher Education"
in The Progress of Afro-American Women. 1980. p. 259.

NATIONAL ASSOCIATION OF BLACK WOMEN ATTORNEYS - BIBLIOGRAPHY

"National Association of Black Women Attorneys" in The Progress of
Afro-American Women. 1980. p. 259.

NATIONAL ASSOCIATION OF COLLEGE WOMEN - BIBLIOGRAPHY

"National Association of College Women" in The Progress of Afro-American
Women. 1980. pp. 259-262.

NATIONAL ASSOCIATION OF COLORED GRADUATE NURSES - BIBLIOGRAPHY

"National Association of Colored Graduate Nurses" in The Progress of
    Afro-American Women. 1980. pp. 262-263.

NATIONAL ASSOCIATION OF BUSINESS AND PROFESSIONAL WOMEN - BIBLIOGRAPHY

"National Association of Negro Business and Professional Women" in The
    Progress of Afro-American Women. 1980. p. 267.

NATIONAL ASSOCIATION OF COLORED WOMEN - BIBLIOGRAPHY

"National Association of Colored Women" in The Progress of Afro-American
    Women. 1980. pp. 263-267.

NATIONAL BAPTIST CHURCH - BIBLIOGRAPHY

"National Baptist" in Howard University Bibliography of African and
    Afro-American Studies. 1977. p. 193.

NATIONAL BAPTIST CONVENTION - BIBLIOGRAPHY

"National Baptist Convention, U.S.A. - Negro Baptist in General" in
    Howard University Bibliography of African and Afro-American
    Religious Studies. 1977. pp. 193-199.

NATIONAL BLACK SISTERS CONFERENCE - BIBLIOGRAPHY

"National Black Sisters Conference" in The Progress of Afro-American
    Women. 1980. pp. 267-268.

NATIONAL COMMITTEE OF BLACK CHURCHMEN - BIBLIOGRAPHY

"National Committee of Black Churchmen - Local Groups" in Howard
    University Bibliography of African and Afro-American Religious
    Studies. 1977. pp. 366-367.

NATIONAL CONVENTION OF AMERICA - BIBLIOGRAPHY

"National Convention of America" in Howard University Bibliography of
    African and Afro-American Religious Studies. 1972. p. 199.

NATIONAL COUNCIL OF CHURCHES OF CHRIST - BIBLIOGRAPHY

"National Council of Churches of Christ in the U.S.A." in Howard
    University Bibliography of African and Afro-American Religious
    Studies. 1977. pp. 295-296.

NATIONAL COUNCIL OF NEGRO WOMEN - BIBLIOGRAPHY

"National Council of Negro Women" in The Progress of Afro-American
    Women. 1980. pp. 268-272.

NATIONAL FEDERATION OF AFRO-AMERICAN WOMEN - BIBLIOGRAPHY

"National Federation of Afro-American Women" in The Progress of Afro-
    American Women. 1980. p. 272.

NATIONAL GUARD - BIOGRAPHY - INDEX

"Military Service: National Guard" in In Black and White. 1980. See
     index, V. 2, p. 1176.

NATIONAL URBAN LEAGUE

"The National Urban League" in The Negro Almanac. 1983. pp. 249-251.

NATIONAL URBAN LEAGUE - BIBLIOGRAPHY

"The National Urban League" in Blacks in America; Bibliographical
     Essays. 1971. pp. 201-203.

NATIONAL WELFARE RIGHTS ORGANIZATION

"The National Welfare Rights Organization" in The Negro Almanac. 1983.
     pp. 260-261.

NATIONALISM

"Africa in the Development of Black-American Nationalism," Emmanuel
     Akpan in Contemporary Black Thought. 1980. pp. 225-231.

"Black Nationalism" in Long Memory. 1982. pp. 388-423.

NATIONALISM - BIBLIOGRAPHY

"Bibliography: Black Nationalism: in Long Memory. 1982. pp. 454-456.

"Black Nationalism" in Afro-American Reference. 1985. pp. 61-62.

"Black Nationalism" in A Comprehensive Bibliography. 1976. pp. 83-90.

"Black Nationalism: Marcus Garvey" in Blacks in America; Bibliographical
     Essays. 1971. pp. 203-205.

"Black Nationalism Since World War II" in Blacks in America;
     Bibliographical Essays. 1971. pp. 379-383.

"Nationalism and Pan-Africanism" in Black Rhetoric. 1976. pp. 135-138.

"The Twenty Years Since Brown" in Black Separatism: A Bibliography.
     1976. pp. 17-40.

NATIONALISM - CARIBBEAN - BIBLIOGRAPHY

"Ethnic and National Identity" in The Complete Caribbeana. 1977. V. 2,
     pp. 693-711.

NATIONALISM - HISTORY - BIBLIOGRAPHY

"Black Nationalism and Migration, 1865-1915" in Blacks in America;
     Bibliographical Essays. 1971. pp. 170-173.

"Black Nationalism Before the Civil War" in Blacks in America;
     Bibliographical Essays. 1971. pp. 107-108.

"Historical Perspectives" in Black Separatism: a Bibliography. 1976. pp.

3-16.

NATIVE AMERICAN STUDIES - LIBRARY COLLECTIONS

"Library Resources on Native Americans," G. Edward Evans in Ethnic
    Collections. 1983. pp. 150-179.

NATIVE AMERICANS - CARIBBEAN - BIBLIOGRAPHY

"Population Segments: Amerindian and Black Carib" in The Complete
    Caribbeana. 1977. V. 1, pp. 509-543.

NATIVE AMERICANS - EDUCATION - BIBLIOGRAPHY

"American Indians" in The Education of Poor and Minority Children. 1981.
    pp. 503-578.

NATIVE AMERICANS - EDUCATION, HIGHER - BIBLIOGRAPHY

"Higher Education: American Indian Students" in The Education of Poor
    and Minority Children. 1981. pp. 930-932.

NATIVE AMERICANS AND SLAVERY - BIBLIOGRAPHY

"Amerindian" in Slavery: A Worldwide Bibliography. 1985. pp. 329-332.

"Black Slavery Among the Indians" in Black Slavery in the Americas.
    1982. pp. 1031-1042.

NAVY

"Navy Men" in Black Men of the Sea. 1978. pp. 114-124.

NAVY - BIOGRAPHY - INDEX

"Military Service: Navy" in In Black and White. 1980. See index, V. 2,
    pp. 1176-1177.

NAZISM - BIBLIOGRAPHY

"Black American Support of Jews Against Hitler and Nazism" in Black-
    Jewish Relations. 1984. pp. 48-56.

NEALE, LARRY

"Larry Neale," Norman Harris in Afro-American Writers After 1955:
    Dramatists and Prose Writers. 1985. pp. 225-230.

NEBRASKA - EDUCATION - BIBLIOGRAPHY

"Nebraska" in The Education of Poor and Minority Children. 1981. p. 325.

NEBRASKA - EDUCATION, HIGHER - BIBLIOGRAPHY

"Higher Education by State: Nebraska" in The Education of Poor and
    Minority Children. 1981. p. 896.

NELSON, ALICE DUNBAR

"Alice Moore Dunbar Nelson," Ora Williams in Afro-American Writers
    Before the Harlem Renaissance. 1986. pp. 225-233.

NELSON, OLIVER EDWARD - BIBLIOGRAPHY

"Nelson, Oliver Edward" in Black Music in America. 1981. pp. 433-436.

NETHERLANDS

"Miscegenation in Holland, Belgium, Austria, Poland, Russia" in Sex and
    Race. 1944. V. 1, pp. 169-175.

NETHERLANDS - BIBLIOGRAPHY

"Netherlands" in The Complete Caribbeana. 1977. See index, V. 4, p.
    2179.

NETHERLANDS - SLAVE TRADE - BIBLIOGRAPHY

"Atlantic - Dutch" in Slavery: A Worldwide Bibliography. 1985. pp. 369-
    370.

NETWORKS - DIRECTORY

"Networks" in Black Resource Guide. 1986. pp. 101-102.

NEVADA - EDUCATION - BIBLIOGRAPHY

"Nevada" in The Education of Poor and Minority Children. 1981. p. 325.

NEVADA - SLAVERY - BIBLIOGRAPHY

"Nevada" in Black Slavery in the Americas. 1982. p. 824.

NEVIS - BIBLIOGRAPHY

"Nevis" in The Complete Caribbeana. 1977. See index, V. 4, p. 2181.

NEW DEAL - BIBLIOGRAPHY

"Blacks and the New Deal" in Blacks in America: Bibliographical Essays.
    1971. pp. 221-225.

"The New Deal" in Blacks in America; Bibliographical Essays. 1971. pp.
    221-225.

"The New Deal, 1933-1941" in Black Rhetoric. 1976. pp. 99-100.

NEW ENGLAND - AUTHORS - BIBLIOGRAPHY

Black Writers in New England. 1985. 76 p.

NEW ENGLAND - SLAVERY

"Colonial Slavery: Negroes in Colonial New England" in From Slavery to

<u>Freedom</u>. 1980. pp. 63-64.

NEW ENGLAND - SLAVERY - BIBLIOGRAPHY

"New England and the Middle Colonies" in <u>Slavery: A Worldwide
    Bibliography</u>. 1977. pp. 76-80.

NEW GRANADA - SLAVERY - BIBLIOGRAPHY

"New Granada and Gran Colombia" in <u>Slavery: A Worldwide Bibliography</u>.
    1985. pp. 132-133.

NEW GUINEA - EDUCATION - BIBLIOGRAPHY

"Papua - New Guinea" in <u>The Education of Poor and Minority Children</u>.
    1981. pp. 1263-1265.

NEW HAMPSHIRE - EDUCATION, HIGHER - BIBLIOGRAPHY

"Higher Education by State: New Hampshire" in <u>The Education of Poor and
    Minority Children</u>. 1981. p. 896.

NEW HAMPSHIRE - GENEALOGY - BIBLIOGRAPHY

"Maine and New Hampshire" in <u>Black Genesis</u>. 1978. pp. 191-193.

NEW HAMPSHIRE - SLAVERY - BIBLIOGRAPHY

"New Hampshire" in <u>Black Slavery in the Americas</u>. 1982. p. 781.

NEW JERSEY - EDUCATION - BIBLIOGRAPHY

"New Jersey" in <u>The Education of Poor and Minority Children</u>. 1981. pp.
    325-330.

NEW JERSEY - EDUCATION, HIGHER - BIBLIOGRAPHY

"Higher Education by State: New Jersey" in <u>The Education of Poor and
    Minority Children</u>. 1981. pp. 896-897.

NEW JERSEY - GENEALOGY - BIBLIOGRAPHY

"New Jersey" in <u>Black Genesis</u>. 1978. pp. 160-163.

NEW JERSEY - SLAVERY - BIBLIOGRAPHY

"New Jersey" in <u>Black Slavery in the Americas</u>. 1982. pp. 781-788.

NEW MEXICO - EDUCATION - BIBLIOGRAPHY

"New Mexico" in <u>The Education of Poor and Minority Children</u>. 1981. p.
    330.

NEW MEXICO - EDUCATION, HIGHER - BIBLIOGRAPHY

"Higher Education by State: New Mexico" in <u>The Education of Poor and
    Minority Children</u>. 1981. p. 897.

NEW MEXICO - SLAVERY - BIBLIOGRAPHY

"New Mexico" in Black Slavery in the Americas. 1982. pp. 824-825.

NEW YORK (CITY) - EDUCATION - BIBLIOGRAPHY

"New York City" in The Education of Poor and Minority Children. 1981.
    pp. 338-368.

NEW YORK (CITY) - JEWS - BIBLIOGRAPHY

"Jews in New York City and Harlem" in Black-Jewish Relations. 1984. pp.
    23-25.

NEW YORK (STATE) - EDUCATION - BIBLIOGRAPHY

"New York" in The Education of Poor and Minority Children. 1981. pp.
    330-368.

NEW YORK (STATE) - EDUCATION, HIGHER - BIBLIOGRAPHY

"Higher Education by State: New York" in The Education of Poor and
    Minority Children. 1981. pp. 897-905.

NEW YORK (STATE) - GENEALOGY - BIBLIOGRAPHY

"New York" in Black Genesis. 1978. pp. 164-175.

NEW YORK (STATE) - POPULATION - HISTORY

Free Black Heads of Household. 1981. 301 p.

NEW YORK (STATE) - SLAVERY - BIBLIOGRAPHY

"New York" in Black Slavery in the Americas. 1983. pp. 728-795.

NEW ZEALAND - EDUCATION - BIBLIOGRAPHY

"New Zealand" in The Education of Poor and Minority Children. 1981. pp.
    1254-1259.

NEWSPAPER ASSOCIATIONS - DIRECTORY

"Newspaper Associations" in Black Resource Guide. 1986. p. 102.

NEWSPAPERS

"Black Newspapers and Journalists" in The Negro Almanac. 1983. pp.
    1211-1218.

NEWSPAPERS - BIBLIOGRAPHY

"Newspapers" in Black Media in America. 1984. pp. 170-217.

NEWSPAPERS - DIRECTORY

"Newspapers" in Black Resource Guide. pp. 102-111.

NIAGARA MOVEMENT

"The Niagara Movement" in The Negro Almanac. 1983. pp. 258-259.

NICARAGUA - MUSIC - BIBLIOGRAPHY

"Nicaragua" in Bibliography of Black Music. 1981. V. 3, p. 186.

NIGER - MUSIC - BIBLIOGRAPHY

"Niger" in Bibliography of Black Music. 1971. V. 3, p. 93.

NIGERIA - HISTORY

"Afro States" in The African Background Outlined. 1936. pp. 82-88.

NIGERIA - MUSIC - BIBLIOGRAPHY

"Nigeria" in Bibliography of Black Music. 1981. V. 3, pp. 94-101.

NORTH - SLAVERY - BIBLIOGRAPHY

"Slavery in the North - General" in Black Slavery in the Americas. 1982.
    pp. 768-772.

NORTH AMERICA - SLAVE TRADE - BIBLIOGRAPHY

"Atlantic - English North American Colonies, United States" in Slavery:
    A Worldwide Bibliography. 1985. pp. 376-379.

NORTH AMERICA - SLAVERY - BIBLIOGRAPHY

"North America" in Slavery: A Worldwide Bibliography. 1985. pp. 33-119.

NORTH AMERICA - SLAVERY - BIBLIOGRAPHY

"Origins of Slavery in British North America" in Black Slavery in the
    Americas. 1982. pp. 607-612.

NORTH CAROLINA - EDUCATION - BIBLIOGRAPHY

"North Carolina" in The Education of Poor and Minority Children. 1981.
    pp. 368-374.

NORTH CAROLINA - EDUCATION, HIGHER - BIBLIOGRAPHY

"Higher Education by State: North Carolina" in The Education of Poor and
    Minority Children. 1981. pp. 905-907.

NORTH CAROLINA - GENEALOGY - BIBLIOGRAPHY

"North Carolina" in Black Genesis. 1978. pp. 88-95.

NORTH CAROLINA - LIBRARIANS

"Profiles of Pioneers: Selected North Carolina Black Librarians,"
    Benjamin F. Speller, Jr. and James R. Jarrell in The Black

Librarian in the Southeast. 1976. pp. 72-86.

NORTH CAROLINA - RECONSTRUCTION - BIBLIOGRAPHY

"Blacks in Southern Reconstruction: Virginia, Tennessee, and North Carolina" in Blacks in America; Bibliographical Essays. 1971. pp. 127-128.

NORTH CAROLINA - SLAVERY

"Colonial Slavery: The Carolinas and Georgia" in From Slavery to Freedom. 1980. pp. 58-60.

NORTH CAROLINA - SLAVERY - BIBLIOGRAPHY

"North Carolina" in Black Slavery in the Americas. 1982. pp. 936-950.

NORTH CAROLINA CENTRAL SCHOOL OF LIBRARY SCIENCE

"The School of Library Science of North Carolina Central University," Karen Crumpton in The Black Librarian in the Southeast. 1980. pp. 276-281.

NORTH DAKOTA - EDUCATION, HIGHER - BIBLIOGRAPHY

"Higher Education by State: North Dakota" in The Education of Poor and Minority Children. 1981. p. 907.

NOVELISTS - BIOGRAPHY - INDEX

"Novelists" in In Black and White. 1980. See index, V. 2, pp. 1196-1197.

NURSES - BIOGRAPHY - INDEX

"Nurses" in In Black and White. 1980. See index, V. 2, pp. 1197-1198.

NURSING - BIBLIOGRAPHY

"Nursing" in The Progress of Afro-American Women. 1980. pp. 219-235.

NUTRITION - CARIBBEAN - BIBLIOGRAPHY

"Food and Nutrition" in The Complete Caribbeana. V. 2, pp. 1001-1024.

NUTRITION - HAITI - BIBLIOGRAPHY

"Food and Nutrition" in The Complete Haitiana. V. 2, pp. 957-970.

NUTRITION - SLAVERY - BIBLIOGRAPHY

"Slave Diet" in Black Slavery in the Americas. 1982. pp. 1146-1152.

NUTRITIONISTS - BIOGRAPHY - INDEX

"Dieticians, Home Economists, Nutritionists" in In Black and White. 1980. See index, V. 2, p. 1139.

OBEAH - BIBLIOGRAPHY

"Obeah" in Afro-American Folk Culture. 1978. See index, p. 784.

OBOE PLAYERS - BIOGRAPHY - INDEX

"Oboe Players" in In Black and White. 1980. See index, V. 2, p. 1187.

OBSTETRICIANS - BIOGRAPHY - INDEX

"Obstetricians, Gynecologists" in In Black and White. 1980. See index,
      V. 2, p. 1198.

OCEANOGRAPHERS - BIOGRAPHY - INDEX

"Oceanographers" in In Black and White. 1980. See index, V. 2, p. 1198.

OCEANOGRAPHY - CARIBBEAN - BIBLIOGRAPHY

"Weather and Oceanography" in The Complete Caribbeana. 1977. V. 3, pp.
      1841-1869.

OCEANOGRAPHY - HAITI - BIBLIOGRAPHY

"Weather and Oceanography" in The Complete Haitiana. 1982. V. 1, pp.
      113-117.

OHIO - EDUCATION - BIBLIOGRAPHY

"Ohio" in The Education of Poor and Minority Children. 1981. pp. 375-
      381.

OHIO - EDUCATION, HIGHER - BIBLIOGRAPHY

"Higher Education by State: Ohio" in The Education of Poor and Minority
      Children. 1981. pp. 907-909.

OHIO - GENEALOGY - BIBLIOGRAPHY

"Ohio" in Black Genesis. 1978. pp. 222-228.

OHIO - SLAVERY - BIBLIOGRAPHY

"Ohio" in Black Slavery in the Americas. 1982. pp. 815-816.

OKLAHOMA - EDUCATION - BIBLIOGRAPHY

"Oklahoma" in The Education of Poor and Minority Children. 1981. pp.
      381-383.

OKLAHOMA - EDUCATION, HIGHER - BIBLIOGRAPHY

"Higher Education by State: Oklahoma" in The Education of Poor and
      Minority Children. 1981. p. 909.

OKLAHOMA - GENEALOGY - BIBLIOGRAPHY

"Oklahoma" in Black Genesis. 1978. pp. 251-252.

OKLAHOMA - SLAVERY - BIBLIOGRAPHY

"Oklahoma" in Black Slavery in the Americas. 1982. pp. 825-826.

OLIVER, JOE - BIBLIOGRAPHY

"Oliver, Joe" in Black Music in America. 1981. pp. 436-439.

OMENS - BIBLIOGRAPHY

"Signs" in Afro-American Folk Culture. 1978. See index, p. 791.

OPERA - DISCOGRAPHIES - BIBLIOGRAPHY

"Discographies: Concert Music and Opera" in Bibliography of Black
    Music. 1981. V. 1. p. 29.

OPERATION PUSH

"Operation PUSH (People United to Save Humanity) in The Negro Almanac.
    1983. pp. 253-255.

OPTHAMOLOGISTS - BIOGRAPHY - INDEX

"Optometrists, Opthamologists" in In Black and White. 1980. See index,
    V. 2, p. 1202.

OPTOMETRISTS - BIOGRAPHY - INDEX

"Optometrists, Opthamologists" in In Black and White. 1980. See index,
    V. 2, p. 1202.

ORAL HISTORY

"Oral History" in Black Genesis. 1978. pp. 22-23.

ORATORS - BIOGRAPHY - INDEX

"Orators" in In Black and White. 1980. See index, V. 2, pp. 1202-1203.

ORATORY - BIBLIOGRAPHY

"Public Address" in Black Rhetoric. 1976. pp. 115-127.

"Speeches and Essays" in Black Rhetoric. 1976. pp. 139-347.

ORCHESTRA LEADERS - BIOGRAPHY - INDEX

"Musicians: Band, Orchestra Leaders" in In Black and White. 1980. See
    index, V. 2, pp. 1180-1181.

ORDER OF THE EASTERN STAR - BIBLIOGRAPHY

"Order of the Eastern Star" in The Progress of Afro-American Women.
    1980. pp. 272-273.

OREGON - EDUCATION - BIBLIOGRAPHY

"Oregon" in <u>The Education of Poor and Minority Children</u>. 1981. pp. 383-384.

OREGON - EDUCATION, HIGHER - BIBLIOGRAPHY

"Higher Education by State: Oregon" in <u>The Education of Poor and Minority Children</u>. 1981. pp. 909-910.

OREGON - SLAVERY - BIBLIOGRAPHY

"Oregon" in <u>Black Slavery in the Americas</u>. 1982. pp. 826-828.

ORGAN - BIBLIOGRAPHY

"Piano and Organ" in <u>Bibliography of Black Music</u>. 1984. V. 4, pp. 14-16.

ORGANISTS - BIOGRAPHY - INDEX

"Organists" in <u>In Black and White</u>. 1980. See index, V. 2, p. 1187.

ORGANIZATION FOUNDERS - BIOGRAPHY - INDEX

"Organization Founders" in <u>In Black and White</u>. 1980. See index, V. 2, pp. 1203-1207.

ORGANIZATION OFFICIALS - BIOGRAPHY - INDEX

"Organization Officials" in <u>In Black and White</u>. 1980. See index, V. 2, pp. 1207-1216.

ORGANIZATIONS

"Civil Rights Organizations" in <u>The Negro Almanac</u>. 1983. pp. 247-261.

"Forging a Partnership with Professional Ethnic Associations," John C. Tyson in <u>Ethnic Collections</u>. 1983. pp. 310-317.

"National Black Organizations" in <u>The Negro Almanac</u>. 1983. pp. 1287-1308.

"Organizations" in <u>The Ebony Handbook</u>. 1974. pp. 492-498.

ORGANIZATIONS - BIBLIOGRAPHY

"Jazz Organizations" in <u>Jazz Bibliography</u>. 1981. pp. 304-305.

"Negro Secret Societies" in <u>A Bibliography of the Negro</u>. 1928. pp. 414-415.

"Organizations" in <u>Afro-American Reference</u>. 1985. pp. 21-22.

"Organizations" in <u>250 Years of Afro-American Art</u>. 1981. pp. 299-395.

"Organizations and Institutions" in <u>The Progress of Afro-American Women</u>. 1980. pp. 239-279.

"The Origins of Modern Protest and Reform: The NAACP and the National Urban League" in Blacks in America; Bibliographical Essays. 1971. pp. 197-203.

"Social Welfare Organizations and Fraternal Societies" in Blacks in America; Bibliographical Essays. 1971. pp. 157-159.

ORGANIZATIONS - DIRECTORIES

"Afro-American Art Organizations, Art Museums and Art Galleries" in The Complete Annotated Resource Guide to Black American Art. 1978. pp. 216-239.

The Black Resource Guide. 1984. 176 p.

"Cultural and Historical Organizations or Museums" in The Complete Annotated Resource Guide to Black American Art. 1978. pp. 241-249.

"National Associations" in Black Resource Guide. 1986. pp. 147-154.

The National Civil Rights Directory. 1979. 183 p.

"National Private Organizations with Civil Rights Programs" in The Negro Almanac. 1983. pp. 295-298.

"Organizations - Addresses" in The Progress of Afro-American Women. 1980. pp. 280-282.

"Resource Organizations" in Black Resource Guide. 1986. pp. 192-202.

OUTLAWS - BIOGRAPHY - INDEX

"Outlaws" in In Black and White. 1980. See index, V. 2, p. 1216.

PACIFIC ISLANDS - LIBRARY COLLECTIONS

"Library Resources on Pacific Island Peoples," Miles M. Jackson in Ethnic Collections. 1983. pp. 230-245.

PAINTERS - BIOGRAPHY - INDEX

"Artists: Painting" in In Black and White. 1980. See index, V. 2, pp. 1115-1116.

PALESTINE

"The Mixing of Black and White in Syria, Palestine, Arabia, Persia" in Sex and Race. 1944. V. 1, pp. 37-57.

PALESTINE - BIBLIOGRAPHY

"Blacks and the PLO, Arabs and Israel" in Black-Jewish Relations. 1984. pp. 81-87.

PAN-AFRICANISM

"Africa in the Development of Black American Nationalism," Emmanuel

Akpan in <u>Contemporary Black Thought</u>. 1980. pp. 225-231.

"Black Americans and Africa," Inez Smith Reid in <u>The Black American Reference Book</u>. 1976. p. 648-683.

"Pan-Africanism in World History," Sulayman S. Nyang and Abdulai S. Vandi in <u>Contemporary Black Thought</u>. 1980. pp. 243-256.

PAN-AFRICANISM - BIBLIOGRAPHY

"The Pan-African Impulse and Other Cultural Perspectives" in <u>Afro-American History, 1</u>. 1974. pp. 490-495.

"The Pan-African Impulse and Other Cultural Perspectives" in <u>Afro-American History, 2</u>. 1981. pp. 168-172.

PANAMA - BIBLIOGRAPHY

"Panama" in <u>The Complete Caribbeana</u>. 1977. See index, V. 4, p. 2181.

PANAMA - EDUCATION - BIBLIOGRAPHY

"Panama" in <u>The Education of Poor and Minority Children</u>. 1981. pp. 1262-1263.

PANAMA CANAL ZONE

"Blacks in the Western Hemisphere: Panama Canal Zone" in <u>The Negro Almanac</u>. 1983. pp. 1485-1486.

PARADES - BIBLIOGRAPHY

"Parades" in <u>Afro-American Folk Culture</u>. 1978. See index, p. 785.

PARAGUAY

"Uruguay, Argentina, Paraguay, Chile" in <u>Sex and Race</u>. 1942. V. 2, pp. 57-65.

PARAGUAY - BIBLIOGRAPHY

"Paraguay" in <u>Race and Ethnic Relations</u>. 1980. pp. 216-217.

PARAGUAY - EDUCATION - BIBLIOGRAPHY

"Paraguay" in <u>The Education of Poor and Minority Children</u>. 1981. p. 1265.

PARAGUAY - LINGUISTICS - BIBLIOGRAPHY

"Paraguay: Spanish - Guanari Bilingualism" in <u>A Bibliography of Pidgin and Creole Languages</u>. 1975. pp. 61-62.

PARAGUAY - SLAVERY - BIBLIOGRAPHY

"Paraguay" in <u>Slavery: A Worldwide Bibliography</u>. 1985. p. 142.

PARKER, CHARLIE - BIBLIOGRAPHY

"Parker, Charles Christopher (Charlie)" in <u>Black Music in America</u>. 1981.
    pp. 439-456.

PARKS, GORDON

"Gordon Parks," Jane Ball in <u>Afro-American Fiction Writers After 1955</u>.
    1984. pp. 203-208.

PATTERSON, ORLANDO

"Orlando Patterson," Bridget Jones in <u>50 Caribbean Writers</u>. 1986. pp.
    368-376.

PEACE CORPS - BIOGRAPHY - INDEX

"Peace Corps" in <u>In Black and White</u>. 1980. See index, V. 2, p. 1216.

PEASANTS - CARIBBEAN - BIBLIOGRAPHY

"Population Categories: Classes, Peasants, Women" in <u>The Complete
    Caribbeana</u>. 1977. V. 1, pp. 443-460.

PEDIATRICIANS - BIOGRAPHY - INDEX

"Pediatricians" in <u>In Black and White</u>. 1980. See index, V. 2, pp. 1216-
    1217.

PENDERGRASS, TEDDY - BIBLIOGRAPHY

"Pendergrass, Teddy" in <u>Black Music in America</u>. 1981. pp. 456-457.

PENNSYLVANIA - EDUCATION - BIBLIOGRAPHY

"Pennsylvania" in <u>The Education of Poor and Minority Children</u>. 1981. pp.
    384-392.

PENNSYLVANIA - EDUCATION, HIGHER - BIBLIOGRAPHY

"Higher Education by State: Pennsylvania" in <u>The Education of Poor and
    Minority Children</u>. 1981. pp. 910-911.

PENNSYLVANIA - GENEALOGY - BIBLIOGRAPHY

"Pennsylvania" in <u>Black Genesis</u>. 1978. pp. 176-183.

PENNSYLVANIA - SLAVERY - BIBLIOGRAPHY

"Pennsylvania" in <u>Black Slavery in the Americas</u>. 1982. pp. 795-800.

PENTACOSTAL CHURCH - BIBLIOGRAPHY

"Holiness and Pentacostal Churches" in <u>Howard University Bibliography of
    African and Afro-American Religious Studies</u>. 1977. pp. 204-205.

PERCUSSIONISTS - BIOGRAPHY - INDEX

"Musicians: Instrumental: Drums, Percussion" in In Black and White. 1980. See index, V. 2, pp. 1185-1186.

PERFORMERS - BIBLIOGRAPHY

"Black Performers and Black Theatre" in Blacks in America; Bibliographical Essays. 1971. pp. 277-280.

"Minstrels, Vaudeville, and Popular Entertainment" in Blacks in America; Bibliographical Essays. 1971. pp. 274-275.

PERFORMERS - DIRECTORIES

Directory of Blacks in the Performing Arts. 1978. 428 p.

PERFORMING ARTISTS

"Arts and Letters" in The Ebony Handbook. 1974. pp. 431-462.

"The Black Entertainer in the Performing Arts" in The Negro Almanac. 1983. pp. 1077-1126.

PERFORMING ARTS - BELIZE - BIBLIOGRAPHY

"Performing Arts" in Belize. 1980. pp. 174-175.

PERFORMING ARTS - BIBLIOGRAPHY

"Shadows in the Wings: Blacks in the Performing Arts in Blacks in the Humanities. 1986. pp. 123-139.

PERIODICALS

Black Journals of the United States. 1982. 432 p.

"The Journal of Negro History and the National Archives," W. Augustus Low in Afro-American History; Sources for Research. 1981. pp. 3-5.

PERIODICALS - BIBLIOGRAPHY

"The Black Press Since Booker T. Washington" in Blacks in America; Bibliographical Essays. 1971. pp. 293-297.

"Discographical Journals" in Bibliography of Black Music. 1983. V. 1, pp. 53-54.

"Periodicals" in Bibliography of Black Music. 1981. V. 1, pp. 99-124.

"Periodicals" in A Comprehensive Bibliography. 1976. pp. 43-47.

PERKINS, EUGENE

"Eugene Perkins," Michael Greene in Afro-American Poets Since 1955. 1985. pp. 251-257.

PERSONALITY - BIBLIOGRAPHY

"Slave Personality" in <u>Black Slavery in the Americas</u>. 1982. pp. 1392-1396.

PERSONNEL OFFICERS - BIOGRAPHY - INDEX

"Personnel Officers" in <u>In Black and White</u>. 1980. See index, V. 2, p.

PERU

"Peru, Ecuador, Colombia, Panama" in <u>Sex and Race</u>. 1942. V. 2, pp. 66-71.

PERU - BIBLIOGRAPHY

"Peru" in <u>Race and Ethnic Relations</u>. 1980. pp. 217-220.

PERU - EDUCATION - BIBLIOGRAPHY

"Peru" in <u>The Education of Poor and Minority Children</u>. 1981. pp. 1265-1267.

PERU - SLAVERY - BIBLIOGRAPHY

"Peru" in <u>Slavery: A Worldwide Bibliography</u>. 1985. pp. 138-139.

PETRY, ANN

"Ann Petry" in <u>Interviews with Black Writers</u>. 1973. pp. 152-163.

PETRY, ANN - BIBLIOGRAPHY

"Black Social Fiction; the Protest School - Ann Petry" in <u>Blacks in America; Bibliographical Essays</u>. 1981. p. 256.

PHARMACISTS - BIOGRAPHY - INDEX

"Pharmacists, Pharmacologists" in <u>In Black and White</u>. 1980. See index, V. 2, p. 1217.

PHARMACOLOGISTS - BIBLIOGRAPHY

"Pharmacy" in <u>The Progress of Afro-American Women</u>. 1980. p. 235.

PHARR, ROBERT DEANE

"Robert Deane Pharr," Richard Yarborough in <u>Afro-American Fiction Writers After 1955</u>. 1984. pp. 208-214.

PHI BETA KAPPA - BIOGRAPHY - INDEX

"Phi Beta Kappa" in <u>In Black and White</u>. 1980. See index, V. 2, p. 1217.

PHI DELTA KAPPA SORORITY - BIBLIOGRAPHY

"Phi Delta Kappa Sorority" in <u>The Progress of Afro-American Women</u>. 1980. p. 273.

PHILADELPHIA - HISTORY

"Introduction: Race Men, Bibliophiles, and Historians, the World of
     Roger M. Adger and the Negro Historical Society of Philadelphia" in
     Rare Afro-Americana. 1982. pp. 1-55.

PHILADELPHIA - LIBRARY COLLECTIONS - CATALOGS

Rare Afro-Americana. 1982. 235 p.

PHILANTHROPISTS - BIOGRAPHY - INDEX

"Philanthropists" in In Black and White. 1980. See index, V. 2, p. 1217.

PHILANTHROPISTS, JEWISH - BIBLIOGRAPHY

"Jews as Philanthropists" in Black-Jewish Relations. 1984. p. 20.

PHILANTHROPY

"Blacks and American Foundations: Two Views," Vernon Jordan and Ernest
     Kaiser in The Black American Reference Book. 1976. pp. 480-491.

PHILLIS WHEATLEY ASSOCIATION - BIBLIOGRAPHY

"Phillis Wheatley Association" in The Progress of Afro-American Women.
     1980. pp. 273-274.

PHILOSOPHERS

"Black American Contributions to Western Civilization in Philosophy and
     Social Science," Frank T. Cherry in The Negro Impact on Western
     Civilization. 1970. pp. 399-420.

PHILOSOPHERS - BIOGRAPHY - INDEX

"Philosophers" in In Black and White. 1980. See index, V. 2, p. 1217.

PHILOSOPHY

"European Mythology: The Ideology of 'Progress'," Dona Richards in
     Contemporary Black Thought. 1980. pp. 59-79.

Philosophy Born of Struggle. 1983.

PHILOSOPHY - BIBLIOGRAPHY

"Homage to Alain Locke: Blacks in Philosophy" in Blacks in the
     Humanities. 1986. pp. 11-23.

"Philosophy" in Afro-American Reference. 1985. pp. 115-116.

"Select Bibliography of Afro-American Works in Philosophy," Leonard
     Harris in Philosophy Born of Struggle. 1983, pp. 289-316.

PHOTOGRAPHERS - BIBLIOGRAPHY

"Daguerreans and Photographers" (1840-1940) in <u>Black Photographers</u>.
    1985. pp. 1-22.

PHOTOGRAPHERS - BIOGRAPHY - INDEX

"Photographers" in <u>In Black and White</u>. 1980. See index, V. 2, pp. 1217-
    1218.

PHOTOGRAPHERS - DIRECTORY

"Daguerreans and Photographers" in <u>Black Photographers</u>. 1985. pp. 1-22.

PHOTOGRAPHY - BIBLIOGRAPHY

"Bibliography" in <u>Black Photographers</u>. 1985. pp. 23-24.

PHOTOGRAPHY - COLLECTIONS

"The Photographers" in <u>Black Photographers</u>. 1985. pp. 25-136.

PHYSICAL CHARACTERISTICS - BIBLIOGRAPHY

"Race Characteristics" in <u>A Bibliography of the Negro</u>. 1928. pp. 563-
    570.

PHYSICIANS - BIBLIOGRAPHY

"Medicine" in <u>The Progress of Afro-American Women</u>. 1980. pp. 216-219.

PHYSICIANS - BIOGRAPHY - INDEX

"Physicians, Surgeons" in <u>In Black and White</u>. 1980. See index, V. 2, pp.
    1218-1220.

PHYSICISTS - BIOGRAPHY - INDEX

"Physicists" in <u>In Black and White</u>. 1980. See index, V. 2, p. 1220.

PIANISTS - BIOGRAPHY - INDEX

"Musicians: Instrumental: Piano" in <u>In Black and White</u>. 1980. See index,
    V. 2, pp. 1187-1189.

PIANO - BIBLIOGRAPHY

"Piano and Organ" in <u>Bibliography of Black Music</u>. 1984. V. 4, pp. 14-16.

PICKETT, WILSON

"Pickett, Wilson" in <u>Black Music in America</u>. 1981. pp. 457-459.

PIRATES

"Pirates and Privateers" in <u>Black Men of the Sea</u>. 1978. pp. 28-38.

PLANTATIONS - SOCIAL CONDITIONS

"Plantation Realities" in The Slave Community. 1979. pp. 249-283.

PLANTS - CARIBBEAN - BIBLIOGRAPHY

"Plant and Animal Life" in The Complete Caribbeana. V. 3, pp. 1735-1839.

PLANTS - HAITI - BIBLIOGRAPHY

"Plant and Animal Life" in The Complete Haitiana. 1982. V. 1, pp. 127-157.

PLAYWRIGHTS - BIBLIOGRAPHY

Black American Playwrights. 1976. 295 p.

More Black American Playwrights. 1978. 328 p.

PLAYWRIGHTS - BIOGRAPHY - INDEX

"Dramatists" in In Black and White. 1980. See index, V. 2, pp. 1139-1140.

PLEASANT, MARY ("MAMMY")

"Mammy Pleasant" in Sex and Race. 1944. V. 3, pp. 309-315.

PLUMPP, STERLING D.

"Sterling D. Plumpp," James Cunningham in Afro-American Poets Since 1955. 1985. pp. 257-265.

POETRY - ANTHOLOGIES - BIBLIOGRAPHY
"Poetry: General Studies - Anthologies" in Afro-American Poetry and Drama. 1979. pp. 30-51.

POETRY - BIBLIOGRAPHY

"Afro-American Poetry, 1760-1975," William P. French, Michel J. Fabre, and Amritjit Singh in Afro-American Poetry and Drama: A Guide to Information Sources. 1979. pp. 1-247.

"Black Poetry" in Blacks in America; Bibliographical Essays. 1971. pp. 243-250.

"Individual Writers: Original Works and Criticism: Poetry" in A Comprehensive Bibliography. 1976. pp. 245-250.

"Negro Poets and Their Poetry" in A Bibliography of the Negro. 1928. pp. 457-461.

POETRY - HISTORY AND CRITICISM - BIBLIOGRAPHY

"Poetry: General Studies: Critical Studies" in Afro-American Poetry and Drama. 1979. pp. 13-30.

"Individual Writers: Original Works and Criticism: Poetry" in A

Comprehensive Bibliography. 1976. pp. 245-250.

"Literary History and Criticism: Poetry" in A Comprehensive Bibliography. 1976. pp. 214-215.

"Literature - Poetry" in Afro-American Reference. 1985. pp. 146-148.

POETRY - INDEX

Index to Black American Literary Anthologies. 1979. 219 p.

Index to Black Poetry. 1974. 541 p.

POETRY - REFERENCE WORKS - BIBLIOGRAPHY

"Poetry: General Studies, Bibliographies and Reference" in Afro-American Poetry and Drama, 1760-1975: A Guide to Information Sources. 1979. pp. 7-13.

POETRY, CARIBBEAN - BIBLIOGRAPHY

"Negro Poetry in the West Indies and South America" A Bibliography of the Negro. 1928. pp. 650-652.

POETRY, SOUTH AMERICAN - BIBLIOGRAPHY

"Negro Poetry in the West Indies and South America" in A Bibliography of the Negro. 1928. pp. 650-652.

POETS

Afro-American Poets Since 1955. 1985. 401 p.

"Foreword," Trudier Harris and Thadious M. Davis in Afro-American Poets Since 1955. 1985. pp. xi-xV.

POETS - BIBLIOGRAPHY

"Poetry: Individual Authors" in Afro-American Poetry and Drama. 1979. pp. 55-247.

POETS - BIOGRAPHY - INDEX

"Poets" in In Black and White. 1980. See index, V. 2, pp. 1220-1222.

POISONS - BIBLIOGRAPHY

"Poison and Poisoning" in Afro-American Folk Culture. 1978. See index, p. 785.

POLAND

"Misegenation in Holland, Belgium, Austria, Poland, Russia" in Sex and Race. 1944, V. 1, pp. 169-175.

POLICE

"Blacks and Police" in The Negro Almanac. 1983. p. 303.

POLICE - BIBLIOGRAPHY

"Police Women" in The Progress of Afro-American Women. 1980. pp. 201-
203.

POLICE - BIOGRAPHY - INDEX

"Protective Services: Police, Security Guards, Prison Officials" in In
Black and White. 1980. See index, V. 2, pp. 1224-1225.

POLICE - HAITI - BIBLIOGRAPHY

"Army, Police, Navy, and Air Force" in The Complete Haitiana. 1982. V.
2, pp. 1187-1198.

POLITE, CARLENE HATCHER

"Carlene Hatcher Polite," Hammett Worthington-Smith in Afro-American
Fiction Writers After 1955. 1984. pp. 215-218.

POLITICAL ACTIVITY - BIBLIOGRAPHY

"Politics and Nationalism" in Afro-American Folk Culture. 1978. See
index, p. 785.

POLITICAL CONDITIONS - BIBLIOGRAPHY

"Social, Political and Economic Conditions" in Afro-American History,2.
1981. pp. 217-259.

"Social, Political and Economic Dimensions" in Afro-American History, 2.
1981. pp. 159-168.

"The Social Political and Economic Situation" in Afro-American History,
1. 1974. pp. 460-490 and 628-748.

POLITICAL CONDITIONS - CARIBBEAN - BIBLIOGRAPHY

"Post-Colonial Issues" in The Complete Caribbeana. V. 2, pp. 1335-1351.

POLITICAL OFFICIALS, STATE

"Black Elected Officeholders at the State Level" in The Negro Almanac.
1983. pp. 394-404.

POLITICAL ORGANIZATIONS - DIRECTORY

"Political Organizations" in Black Resource Guide. 1986. pp. 171-172.

POLITICAL PARTIES - BIBLIOGRAPHY

"Major Political Parties" in The Study and Analysis of Black Politics.
1973. p. 27.

POLITICAL PARTIES, BLACK - BIBLIOGRAPHY

"Black Parties" in <u>The Study and Analysis of Black Politics</u>. 1973. pp. 30-33.

POLITICAL PARTIES, INDEPENDENT - BIBLIOGRAPHY

"Blacks and Third Parties" in <u>The Study and Analysis of Black Politics</u>. 1973. pp. 33-37.

POLITICAL SCIENCE - EDUCATION

"Political Science Education in the Black College," Hanes Walton, Jr. and Brenda D. Mobley in <u>The Study and Analysis of Black Politics</u>. 1973. pp. 146-152.

POLITICIANS - BIBLIOGRAPHY

"Black Political Power - Officeholders" in <u>Blacks in America</u>; <u>Bibliographical Essays</u>. 1971. pp. 376-379.

"Black Politicians" in <u>Black Rhetoric</u>. 1976. pp. 90-92.

"Politics and Government" in <u>The Progress of Afro-American Women</u>. 1980. pp. 283-291.

POLITICIANS - BIOGRAPHY - INDEX

"Politicians" in <u>In Black and White</u>. 1980. See index, V. 2, p. 1222.

POLITICS

"Black Brahmins: The Underdevelopment of Black Political Leadership" in <u>How Capitalism Underdeveloped Black America</u>. 1983. pp. 169-194.

"The Black Role in American Politics, Part I, the Present," Hugh H. Smythe and Carl B. Stokes in <u>The Black American Reference Book</u>. 1976. pp. 580-621.

"The Black Vote - The Sleeping Giant," Dianne M. Pinderhughes in <u>The State of Black America, 1984</u>. pp. 69-93.

"The Black Voter and Elected Officeholders" in <u>The Negro Almanac</u>. 1983. pp. 353-444.

"Blacks and the Politics of Redemption" in <u>Long Memory</u>. 1982. pp. 142-226.

"The Phenomenon of the Jesse Jackson Candidacy and the 1984 Presidential Election," Charles V. Hamilton in <u>The State of Black America, 1985</u>. pp. 21-35.

"Political Choices: A Realignment in Partisanship Among Black Voters," Dianne M. Pinderhughes in <u>The State of Black America, 1986</u>. pp. 85-113.

"Politics and Government" in <u>The Ebony Handbook</u>. 1974. pp. 377-412.

POLITICS - BIBLIOGRAPHY

"Bibliography: Blacks and the Politics of Redemption" in Long Memory. 1982. pp. 432-435.

"Black Political Power" in Blacks in America; Bibliographical Essays. 1971. pp. 372-379.

"The Political Scene" in Afro-American History, 2. 1981. pp. 240-249.

"Politics" in A Comprehensive Bibliography. 1976. pp. 171-177.

"Politics and Government" in The Progress of Afro-American Women. 1980. pp. 283-291.

"Politics and Politicians" in Afro-American Reference. 1985. pp. 75-78.

"Politics: Coalitions and Alternatives" in Black Separatism; a Bibliography. 1976. pp. 95-108.

"A Selected Bibliography: Political" in The Negro Almanac. 1983. pp. 1522-1524.

The Study and Analysis of Black Politics. 1973. 161 p.

POLITICS - CARIBBEAN - BIBLIOGRAPHY

"Politics and Government" in The Complete Caribbeana. 1977. V. 2, pp. 1187-1280.

POLITICS - FIRST FACTS

"Black Firsts: Politics" in Before the Mayflower. 1982. pp. 615-622.

POLITICS - HAITI - BIBLIOGRAPHY

"Politics and Government" in The Complete Haitiana. 1982. V. 2, pp. 1037-1117.

POLITICS - HISTORY

"Black Power in the Old South" in Before the Mayflower. 1982. pp. 214-254.

"The Black Role in American Politics: Part II, The Past," G. James Fleming in The Black American Reference Book. 1976. pp. 622-637.

POLITICS - HISTORY - BIBLIOGRAPHY

"Black Politics" in Blacks in America; Bibliographical Essays. 1971. pp. 218-221.

"Development of an Afro-American Community (1865-1900)" in Afro-American History, 1. 1974. pp. 398-407.

"Political History" in Afro-American History, 1. 1974. pp. 29-33.

"Political History" in Afro-American History, 2. 1981. pp. 16-19.

"Post-Reconstruction Political Realignments" (1865-1900) in <u>Afro-American History, 2</u>. 1981. pp. 135-137.

"Post-Reconstruction Realignments" in <u>Afro-American History, 1</u>. 1974. pp. 365-373.

POLITICS, AFRICAN - HISTORY

"The African Way of Life: Political Institutions" in <u>From Slavery to Freedom</u>. 1980. pp. 15-17.

POLITICS, INTERNATIONAL

"The Negro in World Politics," Daryl R. Fair in <u>The Negro Impact on Western Civilization</u>. 1970. pp. 251-286

POPULAR MUSIC - BIBLIOGRAPHY

"Rhythm and Blues and Other Popular Music" in <u>Bibliography of Black Music</u>. 1981. V. 2, pp. 117-141.

"Soul Music: Blues, Jazz and Variations" in <u>Blacks in America: Bibliographical Essays</u>. 1971. pp. 286-29

POPULATION

"The Black Population in the United States," Karl E. Taeuber and Alma F. Taeuber in <u>The Black American Reference Book</u>. 1976. pp. 159-206.

"Growth and Distribution of the Black Population" in <u>The Negro Almanac</u>. 1983. pp. 445-474.

"Population" in <u>The Ebony Handbook</u>. 1974. pp. 4-76.

POPULATION - BIBLIOGRAPHY

<u>Demography of the Black Population of the United States</u>. 1983. 354 p.

"Some General Statistics of the Negro Population" in <u>A Bibliography of the Negro</u>. 1928. pp. 479-480.

POPULISM

"Self-Interest and Southern Populism" in <u>Reluctant Reformers</u>. 1975. pp. 51-83.

PORTRAIT ARTISTS - BIOGRAPHY - INDEX

"Artists: Portrait" in <u>In Black and White</u>. 1980. See index, V. 2, pp. 1116-1117.

PORTUGAL

"Miscegenation in Spain, Portugal, and Italy" in <u>Sex and Race</u>. 1944. V. 1, 151-168.

PORTUGAL - EDUCATION - BIBLIOGRAPHY

"Portugal" in The Education of Poor and Minority Children. 1981. p.
    1275.

POSTUGAL - SLAVE TRADE - BIBLIOGRAPHY

"Atlantic - Portuguese and Brazilian" in Slavery: A Worldwide
    Bibliography. 1985. pp. 352-359.

PORTUGAL - SLAVERY - BIBLIOGRAPHY

"Iberia" in Slavery: A Worldwide Bibliography. 1985. pp. 315-319.

POSSESSION, SPIRITUAL - BIBLIOGRAPHY

"Possession, Spiritual" in Afro-American Folk Culture. 1978. See index,
    pp. 785-786.

POSTAL WORKERS - BIBLIOGRAPHY

"Postal Workers" in The Progress of Afro-American Women. 1980. p. 127.

POSTAL WORKERS - BIOGRAPHY - INDEX

"Postal Service" in In Black and White. 1980. See index, V. 2, pp.
    1222-1223.

POTTERY - BIBLIOGRAPHY

"Pottery" in Afro-American Folk Culture. 1978. See index, p. 786.

"Pottery" in 250 Years of Afro-American Art. 1981. pp. 395-396.

POVERTY

"The Black Poor: Highest Stage of Underdevelopment" in How Capitalism
    Underdeveloped Black America. 1983. pp. 53-67.

POVERTY - BIBLIOGRAPHY

"Black Family and Poverty" in The Black Family in the United States.
    1986. pp. 78-80, 123 and 193-194.

"The Poor" in A Comprehensive Bibliography. 1976. pp. 164-165.

PRAYER - BIBLIOGRAPHY

"Prayer" in Afro-American Folk Culture. 1978. See index, p. 786.

PREACHERS - BIBLIOGRAPHY

"Noted Negro Preachers" in A Bibliography of the Negro. 1928. pp. 405-
    406.

PREACHING - BIBLIOGRAPHY

"Old-Time Negro Preaching" in Black Rhetoric. 1976. p. 130.

PREJUDICE

"Prejudice: A Symposium," Gordon W. Allport, Thomas F. Pettigrew and
     Robin M. Williams, Jr. in The Black American Reference Book. 1976.
     pp. 537-579.

PRESBYTERIAN CHURCH - CIVIL RIGHTS MOVEMENT - BIBLIOGRAPHY

"The Church, Synagogue and Integration: Presbyterian" in Howard
     University Bibliography of African and Afro-American Religious
     Studies. 1977. pp. 319-320.

PRESBYTERIAN CHURCH - RACE RELATIONS - BIBLIOGRAPHY

"Presbyterian" in Howard University Bibliography of African and Afro-
     American Religious Studies. 1977. pp. 280-282.

PRESBYTERIAN CHURCH - SLAVERY - BIBLIOGRAPHY

"Slavery, Negroes and the Church: Presbyterian" in Howard University
     Bibliography of African and Afro-American Religious Studies. 1977.
     pp. 139-143.

PRESIDENTIAL CABINETS - BIBLIOGRAPHY

"Black Cabinet Members" in The Study and Analysis of Black Politics.
     1973. p. 67.

PRESIDENTIAL CANDIDATES - BIBLIOGRAPHY

"Black Presidential Candidates" in The Study and Analysis of Black
     Politics. 1973. p. 57.

PRESS

"The Black Press and Broadcast Media" in The Negro Almanac. 1983. pp.
     1211-1249.

"Contributions of the Negro Press to American Culture," W. Spragens in
     The Negro Impact on Western Civilization. 1970. pp. 173-194.

"The Popular Media: Part 1: The Mission of Black Newsmen," Luther P.
     Jackson in The Black American Reference Book. 1976. pp. 846-874.

"Press" in The Ebony Handbook. 1974. pp. 413-429.

PRESS - BIBLIOGRAPHY

"The Press" in The Progress of Afro-American Women. 1980. pp. 191-193.

PRICE, LEONTYNE - BIBLIOGRAPHY

"Price, Leontyne" in Black Music in America. 1981. pp. 459-470.

PRIDE, CHARLEY - BIBLIOGRAPHY

"Pride, Charley" in Black Music in America. 1981. pp. 470-472.

PRINCIPE - LINGUISTICS - BIBLIOGRAPHY

"Sao Tome and Principe" in A Bibliography of Pidgin and Creole
    Languages. 1975. pp. 92-93.

PRINTERS - BIOGRAPHY - INDEX

"Printers" in In Black and White. 1980. See index, V. 2, p. 1223.

PRINTMAKING - BIBLIOGRAPHY

"Printmaking" in 250 Years of Afro-American Art. 1981. pp. 396-397.

PRINTS - BIBLIOGRAPHY

"Large Prints, Slides and Filmstrips" in The Complete Annotated Resource
    Guide to Black American Art. 1978. pp. 175-191.

PRISON OFFICIALS - BIOGRAPHY - INDEX

"Protective Services: Police, Security Guards, Prison Officials" in In
    Black and White. 1980. See index, V. 2, pp. 1224-1225.

PRISONERS

"Black Prisoners and Punishment in a Racist/Capitalist State" in How
    Capitalism Underdeveloped Black America. 1983. pp. 105-130.

"The Incarceration of Black Men," Roi D. Townsey in Black Men. 1981. pp.
    229-256.

PRISONERS - BIOGRAPHY

"Black Family and Prison" in The Black Family in the United States.
    1986. pp. 123-124.

"Black Family and Prison Families" in The Black Family in the United
    States. 1986. p. 194.

PRISONERS - BIOGRAPHY - INDEX

"Prisoners: Criminal, Political" in In Black and White. 1980. See index,
    V. 2, p. 1223.

PRISONERS - EDUCATION

"Higher Education, Black Inmates, and Corrections," Roosevelt Johnson in
    Black Scholars on Higher Education. 1974. pp. 315-321.

PRISONERS, POLITICAL - BIOGRAPHY - INDEX

"Prisoners: Criminal, Political" in In Black and White. 1980. See index,
    V. 2, p.

PRISONERS, REHABILITATED - BIOGRAPHY - INDEX

"Prisoners: Rehabilitated" in In Black and White. 1980. See index, V. 2,

p. 1223.

PRISONERS, UNJUSTLY IMPRISONED - BIOGRAPHY - INDEX

"Prisoners, Unjustly Imprisoned" in In Black and White. 1980. See index,
    V. 2, p.

PRISONERS OF WAR - BIOGRAPHY - INDEX

"Prisoners of War" in In Black and White. 1980. See index, V. 2, p.
    1223.

PRISONS - BIBLIOGRAPHY

"Convict Systems and the Negro" in A Bibliography of the Negro. 1928.
    pp. 546-547.

PRIZE WINNERS

"Awards and Prizes" in Before the Mayflower. 1982. pp. 639-640.

PROFESSIONS

"The Black Professional," Hugh H. Smythe in The Black American Reference
    Book. 1976. pp. 453-479.

"Professions" in Before the Mayflower. 1982. p. 632.

"Professions" in The Ebony Handbook. 1974. pp. 359-375.

PROGRESSIVE MOVEMENT

"Progressivism: Expediency and Accomodation" in Reluctant Reformers.
    1975. pp. 85-126.

PROGRESSIVE NATIONAL BAPTIST CONVENTION - BIBLIOGRAPHY

"Progressive National Baptist Convention" in Howard University
    Bibliography of African and Afro-American Religious Studies. 1977.
    p. 193.

PROMOTERS - BIOGRAPHY - INDEX

"Promoters" in In Black and White. 1980. See index, V. 2, pp. 1223-1224.

PROSLAVERY MOVEMENTS - EIGHTEENTH CENTURY

"The Conservative Reaction" in From Slavery to Freedom. 1980. pp. 94-96.

PROSTITUTION - HISTORY

"Slaveholders and Their Trade With Houses of Prostitution" in Sex and
    Race. 1942. pp. 193-194.

PROTEST

"White Proscriptions and Black Protests" in Long Memory. 1982. pp. 342-

387.

PROTEST - BIBLIOGRAPHY

"Bibliography; White Proscriptions and Black Protests" in Long Memory.
    1982. pp. 449-453.

"Black Protest" in Black Rhetoric. 1976. pp. 104-109.

"Protest, Revolt and Resistance" in Afro-American Folk Culture. 1978.
    See index, p. 786.

"Strategy and Tactics" in Black Rhetoric. 1976. pp. 133-135.

"Student Movements" in The Education of Poor and Minority Children.
    1981. pp. 726-728.

PROTESTANT EPISCOPAL CHURCH - CIVIL RIGHTS MOVEMENT - BIBLIOGRAPHY

"The Church, Synagogue and Integration: Protestant Episcopal" in Howard
    University Bibliography of African and Afro-American Religious
    Studies. 1977. p. 320.

PROTESTANT EPISCOPAL CHURCH - RACE RELATIONS - BIBLIOGRAPHY

"Protestant Episcopal" in Howard University Bibliography of African and
    Afro-American Religious Studies. 1977. pp. 282-285.

PROVERBS - BIBLIOGRAPHY

"Proverbs and Proverbial Expression" in Afro-American Folk Culture.
    1978. See index, p. 787.

PSYCHIATRISTS - BIOGRAPHY - INDEX

"Psychiatrists" in In Black and White. 1980. See index, V. 2, p. 1225.

PSYCHIATRY - CARIBBEAN - BIBLIOGRAPHY

"Psychiatry and Mental Health" in The Complete Caribbeana. 1977. V. 2,
    pp. 1025-1041.

PSYCHIATRY - HAITI - BIBLIOGRAPHY

"Psychiatry and Mental Health" in The Complete Haitiana. 1982. V. 2, pp.
    971-976.

PSYCHICS - BIOGRAPHY - INDEX

"Psychics" in In Black and White. 1980. See index, V. 2, p. 1225.

PSYCHOANALYSTS - BIOGRAPHY - INDEX

"Psychoanalysts" in In Black and White. 1980. See index, V. 2, p. 1225.

PSYCHOLOGISTS - BIOGRAPHY - INDEX

"Psychologists" in In Black and White. 1980. See index, V. 2, p. 1225.

PSYCHOLOGY

"Black Awareness and Authentic Black/Black Relations," David R. Burgest
    in Contemporary Black Thought. 1980. pp. 138-162.

"Black Personality in American Society," Charles A. Pinderhughes in The
    Black American Reference Book. 1976. pp. 128-158.

"Guilt-Provocation: A Strategy in Black Rhetoric," Dorothy Rennington in
    Contemporary Black Thought. 1980. pp. 111-125.

"Psychological Modes of Adaptation," Ronald L. Taylor in Black Men.
    1981. pp. 141-158.

"The Psychology of Oppression," Joseph A. Baldwin in Contemporary Black
    Thought. 1980. pp. 95-110.

"Slave Personality Types" in The Slave Community. 1979. pp. 284-322.

PSYCHOLOGY - BIBLIOGRAPHY

"Psychological Studies" in A Bibliography of the Negro. 1928. pp. 624-
    626.

"Psychological Studies" in A Comprehensive Bibliography. 1976. pp. 177-
    184.

"Psychology and Mental Health" in Afro-American Reference. 1985. pp.
    184-188.

"Psychology and Mental Health" in The Progress of Afro-American Women.
    1980. pp. 292-303.

The Psychology and Mental Health of Afro-American Women. 1984. 102 p.

PSYCHOLOGY - CARIBBEAN - BIBLIOGRAPHY

"Psychiatry and Mental Health" in The Complete Caribbeana. 1977. V. 2,
    pp. 1025-1041.

PSYCHOLOGY - HAITI - BIBLIOGRAPHY

"Psychiatry and Mental Health" in The Complete Haitiana. 1982. V. 2, pp.
    971-976.

PSYCHOLOGY - POLITICAL ASPECTS - BIBLIOGRAPHY

"Black Personality" in The Study and Analysis of Black Politics. 1973.
    p. 25.

PUBLIC ADMINISTRATION - HAITI - BIBLIOGRAPHY

"Public Administration" in The Complete Haitiana. 1982. V. 2, pp. 1199-
    1216.

PUBLIC ASSISTANCE

"Families Receiving Public Assistance" in The Negro Almanac. 1983. pp.
    479-480.

"The Federal Government and Assistance Programs" in The Negro Almanac.
    1983. pp. 679-709.

PUBLIC POLICY

"The Case for Social Policy," Bernard E. Anderson in The State of Black
    America, 1986. pp. 153-162.

PUBLIC POLICY - LIBRARY COLLECTIONS

"Federal Policy and Ethnic Collections: What it is and Other Comments on
    an Endangered Speciies," William F. Cunningham. Ethnic Collections.
    1983. pp. 303-309.

PUBLIC RELATIONS - BIBLIOGRAPHY

"Communications/Public Relations" in Black Media in America. 1984. pp.
    66-68.

"Public Relations" in Black Media in America. 1984. pp. 85-88.

PUBLIC RELATIONS OFFICERS - BIOGRAPHY - INDEX

"Public Relation Officers" in In Black and White. 1980. See index, V. 2,
    pp. 1225-1226.

PUBLIC UTILITIES - CARIBBEAN - BIBLIOGRAPHY

"Public Utilities and Communication" in The Complete Caribbeana. V. 3,
    pp. 1595-1610.

PUBLIC UTILITIES - HAITI - BIBLIOGRAPHY

"Public Utilities and Communication" in The Complete Haitiana. 1982. pp.
    1387-1394.

PUBLISHERS

"Prominent Black Publishers and Broadcast Executives" in The Negro
    Almanac. 1983. pp. 1218-1222.

PUBLISHERS - BIOGRAPHY - INDEX

"Publishers: Magazine, Newspaper, Other" in In Black and White. 1980.
    See index, V. 2, pp. 1226-1227.

PUBLISHERS - HISTORY

"Famous Publishers of the Past" in The Negro Almanac. 1983. p. 1223.

PUBLISHING

Gatekeepers of Black Culture: Black-Owned Book Publishing in the United States. 1983. 249 p.

"Publishing in the Third World: A Trend Report" in Publishing in the Third World. 1980. pp. 1-80.

PUBLISHING - BIBLIOGRAPHY

"Bibliography" in Publishing in the Third World. 1980. pp. 81-186.

PUERTO RICAN STUDIES - LIBRARY COLLECTIONS

"Developing Collections on Puerto Rican Heritages," Bruni Verges in Ethnic Collections. 1983. pp. 65-74.

PUERTO RICANS - EDUCATION - BIBLIOGRAPHY

"Puerto Ricans" in The Education of Poor and Minority Children. 1981. pp. 475-490.

PUERTO RICO

"Blacks in the Western Hemisphere: Puerto Rico," in The Negro Almanac. 1983. pp. 1486-1487.

"Cuba, Puerto Rico, Surinam" in Sex and Race. 1942. V. 2, pp. 80-90.

"The Question of Color in Puerto Rico," Thomas G. Mathews in Slavery and Race Relations in Latin America. 1974. pp. 299-323.

PUERTO RICO - BIBLIOGRAPHY

"Other Caribbean" in Race and Ethnic Relations. 1980. pp. 193-195.

PUERTO RICO - MUSIC - BIBLIOGRAPHY

"Puerto Rico" in Bibliography of Black Music. 1981. V. 3, pp. 155-157.

PULLMAN PORTERS - BIOGRAPHY - INDEX

"Railroads: Pullman Porters, Redcaps" in In Black and White. 1980. See index, V. 2, pp. 1227-1228.

QUAKERS - CIVIL RIGHTS MOVEMENT - BIBLIOGRAPHY

"The Church, Synagogue, and Integration: Friends - Quakers" in Howard University Bibliography of African and Afro-American Studies. 1977. p. 316.

QUAKERS - RACE RELATIONS - BIBLIOGRAPHY

"Friends - Quakers" in Howard University Bibliography of African and Afro-American Religious Studies. 1977. p. 273.

QUAKERS - SLAVERY - BIBLIOGRAPHY

"Slavery, Negroes and the Church: Friends - Quakers" in Howard -

University Bibliography of African and Afro-American Religious Studies. 1977. pp. 132-136.

QUILTMAKING - BIBLIOGRAPHY

"Quiltmaking" in 250 Years of Afro-American Art. 1981. pp. 397-398.

QUOTATIONS

Anthology: Quotations and Sayings of People of Color. 1973. 137 p.

Quotations in Black. 1981. 344 p.

RACE

Sex and Race. 3 V.

RACE - BIBLIOGRAPHY

"Progressivism and Race" in Blacks in America; Bibliographical Essays. 1971. pp. 146-149.

"The Psychology of Race" in The Economics of Minorities. 1976. pp. 33-41.

"Theories of Race in the Late Nineteenth and Early Twentieth Centuries" in Blacks in America; Bibliographical Essays. 1971. pp. 142-143.

RACE RELATIONS - AFRICA - BIBLIOGRAPHY

"Race and Other Problems of Relationship in the African Situation" in A Bibliography of the Negro. 1928. pp. 166-180.

RACE RELATIONS - BIBLIOGRAPHY

"The Betterment of Race Relations" in A Bibliography of the Negro. 1928. pp. 604-611.

"Race and Ethnic Relations" in Afro-American Reference. 1985. pp. 78-84.

"Race Problem and Race Relations Studies" in A Bibliography of the Negro. 1928. pp. 626-628.

"The Race Problem in the United States" in A Bibliography of the Negro. 1928. pp. 588-603.

RACE RELATIONS - CARIBBEAN - BIBLIOGRAPHY

"Race Relations" in The Complete Caribbeana. 1977. V. 1, pp. 573-593.

RACE RIOTS - BIBLIOGRAPHY

"Race Riots, 1917-1943" in Blacks in America; Bibliographical Essays. 1971. pp. 194-197.

"Racial Violence: Lynching and Riots" in Blacks in America; Bibliographical Essays. 1971. pp. 140-142.

"Urban Racial Violence: The 1960s" in <u>Blacks in America;</u>
     <u>Bibliographical Essays</u>. 1971. pp. 389-396.

RACE RIOTS - HISTORY

"The Pattern of Violence" in <u>From Slavery to Freedom</u>. 1980. pp. 313-317.

RACIAL ATTITUDES - BIBLIOGRAPHY

"Racial Attitudes and Policies" in <u>Afro-American History, 1</u>. 1974. pp.
     63-79 and 373-398.

"Racial Attitudes and Policies" in <u>Afro-American History, 2</u>. 1981. pp.
     43-56 and 137-141.

"Racial Attitudes and Segregation" in <u>Afro-American History, 1</u>. 1974.
     pp. 421-460.

"Racial Attitudes and Segregation" in <u>Afro-American History, 2</u>. pp.
     150-159.

"Racial Attitudes and the Pattern of Discrimination" in <u>Afro-American</u>
     <u>History, 1</u>. 1974. pp. 560-628.

"Racial Attitudes and the Pattern of Discrimination" in <u>Afro-American</u>
     <u>History, 2</u>. 1981. pp. 187-217.

RACISM

"The Meaning of Racist Violence in Late Capitalism" in <u>How Capitalism</u>
     <u>Underdeveloped Black America</u>. 1983. pp. 231-253.

"Prejudice: A Symposium," Gordon W. Allport, Thomas F. Pettigrew and
     Robin M. Williams, Jr. in <u>The Black American Reference Book</u>. 1976.
     pp. 515-536.

"White Proscriptions and Black Protests" in <u>Long Memory</u>. 1982. pp. 342-
     387.

RACISM - BIBLIOGRAPHY

"Bibliography: White Proscriptions and Black Protests" in <u>Long Memory</u>.
     1982. pp. 449-453.

"Losing the Peace" in <u>From Slavery to Freedom</u>. 1980. pp. 531-532.

"Racism" in <u>The Education of Poor and Minority Children</u>. 1981. pp. 986-
     1002.

"Racism and Contemporary Church" in <u>Howard University Bibliography of</u>
     <u>African and Afro-American Religious Studies</u>. 1977. pp. 369-374.

"Some Extreme Views on Race" in <u>A Bibliography of the Negro</u>. 1928. pp.
     576-577.

RADIO - BIBLIOGRAPHY

"Broadcasting" in Black Media in America. 1984. pp. 62-66 and 99-123.

"Radio" in Black Media in America. 1984. pp. 217-253.

"Radio and Television" in The Progress of Afro-American Women. 1980. pp. 193-194.

RADIO - MUSIC - INDEX

"Radio Index" in Blues Who's Who. 1979. pp. 617-620.

RADIO STATIONS - DIRECTORY

"Black Radio Station Formats" in Black Resource Guide. 1986. pp. 111-139.

RAGTIME - BIBLIOGRAPHY

"Ragtime" in Afro-American Folk Culture. 1978. See index, p. 787.

"Ragtime" in Bibliography of Black Music. 1981. V. 2, pp. 65-71.

"Ragtime" in Jazz Bibliography. 1981. pp. 137-140.

RAGTIME - DISCOGRAPHIES - BIBLIOGRAPHY

"Discography: Ragtime" in Bibliography of Black Music. 1981. V. 1, p. 59.

RAILROAD SONGS - BIBLIOGRAPHY

"Railroad Songs" in Afro-American Folk Culture. 1978. See index, p. 787.

RAINEY, GERTRUDE "MA" - BIBLIOGRAPHY

"Rainey, Gertrude 'Ma'" in Black Music in America. 1981. pp. 472-473.

RAMCHAND, KENNETH

"Kenneth Ramchand, Wayne Brown" in 50 Caribbean Writers. 1986. pp. 83-95.

RANCHERS - BIOGRAPHY - INDEX

"Farmers, Ranchers" in In Black and White. 1980. See index, V. 3, pp. 1145-1146.

RANDALL, DUDLEY

"Dudley Randall," R. Baxter Miller in Afro-American Poets Since 1955. 1985. pp. 265-273.

RASTAFARIANISM - BIBLIOGRAPHY

"Rastafarianism" in Afro-American Folk Culture. 1978. See index, p. 787.

RAY, HENRIETTA CORDELIA

"Henrietta Cordelia Ray," Leela Kapai in <u>Afro-American Writers Before the Harlem Renaissance</u>. 1986. pp. 233-237.

RAZAF, ANDY - BIBLIOGRAPHY

"Razaf, Andy" in <u>Black Music in America</u>. 1981. pp. 473-475.

REAGAN APPOINTEES - DIRECTORY

"Black Appointees in the Reagan Administration" in <u>Black Resource Guide</u>. 1986. pp. 172-185.

REAL ESTATE AND REALTORS - BIOGRAPHY - INDEX

"Real Estate" in <u>In Black and White</u>. 1980. See index, V. 2, p. 1228.

RECONSTRUCTION

"Black Power in the Old South" in <u>Before the Mayflower</u>. 1982. pp. 214-254.

"Losing the Peace" in <u>From Slavery to Freedom</u>. 1980. pp. 251-267.

RECONSTRUCTION - BIBLIOGRAPHY

"The Abandonment and Aftermath of Reconstruction" in <u>Blacks in America; Bibliographical Essays</u>. 1971. pp. 129-131.

"An Abortive Revolution of Equality: The Civil War and Reconstruction" in <u>Blacks in America; Bibliographical Essays</u>. 1971. pp. 111-113.

"The Effort to Attain Peace" in <u>From Slavery to Freedom</u>. 1980. pp. 528-530.

"General View of the Negro and Reconstruction" in <u>A Bibliography of the Negro</u>. 1928. pp. 370-376.

"Reconstruction" in <u>Black Rhetoric</u>. 1976. pp. 79-89.

"The Reconstruction Period" in <u>Afro-American History, 1</u>. 1974. pp. 326-364.

"The Reconstruction Period" in <u>Afro-American History, 2</u>. 1981. pp. 125-135.

"Studies Relating to the Reconstruction Period" in <u>A Bibliography of the Negro</u>. 1928. pp. 623-624.

RECONSTRUCTION IN LITERATURE - BIBLIOGRAPHY

"Novels by White Authors Treating of the Reconstruction Period" in <u>A Bibliography of the Negro</u>. p. 128. pp. 468-469.

RECORDINGS - BIBLIOGRAPHY

"Recordings" in <u>Afro-American Folk Culture</u>. 1978. See index, p. 878.

RECORDINGS - WOMEN

"Recordings and Videorecordings" in The Progress of Afro-American Women. 1980. pp. 25-28.

RECREATION - BIBLIOGRAPHY

"Recreational Activities and Agencies" in A Bibliography of the Negro. 1928. pp. 531-532.

"Slave Recreation" in Black Slavery in the Americas. 1982. pp. 1181-1184.

REDCAPS - BIOGRAPHY - INDEX

"Railroads: Pullman Porters, Redcaps" in In Black and White. 1980. See index, V. 2, pp. 1227-1228.

REDMOND, EUGENE

"Eugene B. Redmond," Joyce Pettis in Afro-American Poets Since 1955. 1985. pp. 274-281.

REED, ISHMAEL

"Ishmael Reed," Henry Louis Gates in Afro-American Fiction Writers After 1955. 1984. pp. 219-232.

"Ishmael Reed" in Interviews with Black Writers. 1973. pp. 164-183.

REED, ISHMAEL - BIBLIOGRAPHY

Ishmael Reed: A Primary and Secondary Bibliography. 1982. 155 p.

REFERENCE WORKS - BIBLIOGRAPHY

Afro-American Reference. 1985. 288 p.

An Annotated Guide to Basic Reference Books on the Black American Experience. 1974. 98 p.

"Bibliographies, Reference Works, Teaching Tools, Sources" in Black Slavery in the Americas. 1982. pp. 1-49.

Black Access: A Bibliography of Afro-American Bibliographies. 1984. 249 p.

"Encyclopedias and Handbooks" in A Comprehensive Bibliography. 1976. pp. 42-43.

"Reference Materials: Reference Sources" in Black Women and Religion: A Bibliography. 1980. pp. 105-108.

"Reference Works" in Black Music in America. 1981. pp. 679-685.

REFORM MOVEMENTS

Reluctant Reformers. 1975. 347 p.

REGGAE

"Reggae" in Black Music. 1979. pp. 185-188.

REID, VIC

"Vic Reid," Daryl Cumber Dance in 50 Caribbean Writers. 1986. pp. 377-
    389.

RELIGION

"Afro-American Religion," Harry V. Richardson and Nathan Wright, Jr. in
    The Black American Reference Book. 1976. pp. 492-514.

"The American Negro's Contribution to Religious Thought," J. Deotis
    Roberts in The Negro Impact on Western Civilization. 1970. pp. 75-
    108.

"The Black Religious Tradition" in The Negro Almanac. 1983. pp. 1251-
    1286.

"Religion" in The Ebony Handbook. 1974. pp. 354-357.

"The Religious Experience of Black Men," James S. Tinney in Black Men.
    1981. pp. 269-276.

RELIGION - BIBLIOGRAPHY

"Black Family and Religion" in The Black Family in the United States.
    1986. pp. 80-81.

"Black Religion: Faith, Hope and Liberation" in Blacks in the
    Humanities. 1986. pp. 25-45.

Black Women and Religion. 1980. 139 p.

"Church and Religious Studies" in A Bibliography of the Negro. 1928. pp.
    614-615.

"Churches and Preachers" in Black Rhetoric. 1976. pp. 127-129.

"Churches, Sects and Cults" in Afro-American Folk Culture. See index,
    pp. 762-763.

The Howard University Bibliography of African and Afro-American
    Religious Studies. 1977. 525 p.

"Religion" in Afro-American Folk Culture. 1978. See index, p. 788.

"Religion" in Afro-American Reference. 1985. pp. 116-118.

"Religion" in A Comprehensive Bibliography. 1976. pp. 189-193.

"Religion" in The Progress of Afro-American Women. 1980. pp. 304-311.

"Religion and Race: Church Structures and Redressing Inequities" in
    Black Separatism; a Bibliography. 1976. pp. 118-127.

"Religion and the Churches" in Afro-American History, 1. 1974. pp. 49-
    55.

"Religion and the Churches" in Afro-American History, 2. 1981. pp. 36-
    40.

"Religious Life and Training of the Negro" in A Bibliography of the
    Negro. 1928. pp. 407-410.

"Slave Religion" in Black Slavery in the Americas. 1982. pp. 1237-1294.

"White Denominations and the Negro" in A Bibliography of the Negro.
    1928. pp. 410-413.

RELIGION - CARIBBEAN - BIBLIOGRAPHY

"Religion" in The Complete Caribbeana. 1977. V. 2, pp. 747-783.

RELIGION - FIRST FACTS

"Religion" in Before the Mayflower. 1982. pp. 629-663.

RELIGION - HAITI - BIBLIOGRAPHY

"Religion: Catholicism, Protestantism and Voodoo" in The Complete
    Haitiana. 1982. V. 1, pp. 669-721.

RELIGION - MUSIC - BIBLIOGRAPHY

"Jazz in the Church" in Jazz Bibliography. 1981. pp. 184-189.

RELIGION, AFRICAN

"African Contributions to World Religion," James D. Tyms in The Negro
    Impact on Western Civilization. 1970. pp. 109-138.

RELIGION, AFRICAN - BIBLIOGRAPHY

"African Religious Beliefs and Practices" in A Bibliography of the
    Negro. 1928. pp. 66-73.

RELIGION, AFRICAN - HISTORY

"The Way of Life: Religion" in From Slavery to Freedom. 1974. pp. 22-24.

RELIGION, BRAZILIAN - BIBLIOGRAPHY

"Religion" in Afro-Braziliana. 1978. pp. 121-131.

RELIGION IN ART - BIBLIOGRAPHY

"Art" in Black Women and Religion. 1980. pp. 95-106.

RELIGION IN FILM - BIBLIOGRAPHY

"Audio-Visual Materials: Film" in <u>Black Women and Religion: A Bibliography</u>. 1980. pp. 99-102.

RELIGION IN LITERATURE - BIBLIOGRAPHY

"Literature" in <u>Black Women and Religion: A Bibliography</u>. 1980. pp. 49-72.

RELIGIOUS DENOMINATIONS - DIRECTORY

"Church Denominations and Organizations" in <u>Black Resource Guide</u>. 1986. pp. 49-51.

RELIGIOUS EDUCATION - BIBLIOGRAPHY

"Church" in <u>The Education of Poor and Minority Children</u>. 1981. pp. 827-835.

RELIGIOUS MUSIC - BIBLIOGRAPHY

"Songs, Sacred" in <u>Afro-American Folk Culture</u>. 1978. See index, pp. 794-796.

RELIGIOUS MUSIC - DISCOGRAPHY - BIBLIOGRAPHY

"Discographies: Sacred and Gospel Music" in <u>Bibliography of Black Music</u>. 1981. V. 1, p. 60.

RELIGIOUS ORDERS - BIOGRAPHY - INDEX

"Religious Orders" in <u>In Black and White</u>. 1980. See index, V. 2, p. 1228.

RENT PARTIES - BIBLIOGRAPHY

"Rent Parties" in <u>Afro-American Folk Culture</u>. 1978. See index, p. 789.

REPARATIONS - BIBLIOGRAPHY

"Reparations" in <u>Howard University Bibliography of African and Afro-American Religious Studies</u>. 1977. pp. 364-366.

REPUBLICAN PARTY - BIBLIOGRAPHY

"Blacks and the Republican Party" in <u>The Study and Analysis of Black Politics</u>. 1973. pp. 27-29.

REPUBLICANS - DIRECTORY

"National Black Republican Leadership" in <u>Black Resource Guide</u>. 1986. p. 169-171.

RESEARCH

"Research in Black Colleges and Universities: Administrative Perspectives, Prospectives and Challenges," Leander L. Boykin in <u>Black Scholars on Higher Education</u>. 1974. pp. 125-151.

"Research in Traditionally Black Schools," Arthur L. Bacon in <u>Black Scholars on Higher Education</u>. 1974. pp. 153-158.

"Research: To Do or Not To Do, That is the Question," Nathaniel Boggs, Jr. in <u>Black Scholars on Higher Education</u>. 1974. pp. 175-190.

RESEARCH FELLOWS - BIOGRAPHY - INDEX

"Research Fellows, Officers" in <u>In Black and White</u>. 1980. See index, V. 2, pp. 1228-1230.

RESEARCH OFFICERS - BIOGRAPHY - INDEX

"Research Fellows, Officers" in <u>In Black and White</u>. 1980. See index, V. 2, pp. 1228-1230.

REUNION - LINGUISTICS - BIBLIOGRAPHY

"Reunion" in <u>A Bibliography of Pidgin and Creole Languages</u>. 1975. pp. 296-299.

REVOLTS - BIBLIOGRAPHY

"Protest, Revolt and Resistance" in <u>Afro-American Folk Culture</u>. 1978. See index, p. 786.

REVOLUTIONARY WAR

"Blacks in Colonial and Revolutionary America" in <u>The Negro Almanac</u>. 1983. pp. 789-826.

"The Founding of Black America" in <u>Before the Mayflower</u>. 1982. pp. 54-85.

"Negroes Fighting for American Independence" in <u>From Slavery to Freedom</u>. 1980. pp. 85-91.

REVOLUTIONARY WAR - BIBLIOGRAPHY

"Afro-Americans in the Revolutionary Era" in <u>Blacks in America; Bibliographical Essays</u>. 1971. pp. 45-48.

"The American Revolution" in <u>Afro-American History, 1</u>. 1974. pp. 101-102.

"The American Revolution" in <u>Afro-American History, 2</u>. 1981. pp. 66-68.

REVOLUTIONARY WAR - BIOGRAPHY - INDEX

"Military: Revolutionary War" in <u>In Black and White</u>. 1980. See index, V. 2, p. 1177.

RHETORIC - ANTHOLOGIES - BIBLIOGRAPHY

"Anthologies" in <u>Black Rhetoric</u>. 1976. pp. 6-26.

RHETORIC - BIBLIOGRAPHY

"Speeches and Rhetoric" in Afro-American Reference. 1985. pp. 119-120.

RHODE ISLAND - EDUCATION - BIBLIOGRAPHY

"Rhode Island" in The Education of Poor and Minority Children. 1981. pp. 392-393.

RHODE ISLAND - EDUCATION, HIGHER - BIBLIOGRAPHY

"Higher Education by State: Rhode Island" in The Education of Poor and Minority Children. 1981. pp. 911-912.

RHODE ISLAND - GENEALOGY - BIBLIOGRAPHY

"Rhode Island" in Black Genesis. 1978. pp. 184-188.

RHODE ISLAND - SLAVERY - BIBLIOGRAPHY

"Rhode Island" in Black Slavery in the Americas. 1982. pp. 800-801.

RHYS, JEAN

"Jean Rhys," Jean D'Costa in 50 Caribbean Writers. 1986. pp. 390-404.

RHYTHM AND BLUES

"Rhythm 'n' Blues" in Black Music. 1979. pp. 119-144.

RHYTHM AND BLUES - BIBLIOGRAPHY

"Rhythm and Blues and Other Popular Music" in Bibliography of Black Music. 1981. V. 2, pp. 117-141.

RICHARDSON, WILLIS - BIBLIOGRAPHY

"Richardson, Willis" in The Harlem Renaissance. 1982. pp. 130-132.

RIDDLES - BIBLIOGRAPHY

"Riddles" in Afro-American Folk Culture. 1978. See index, p. 790.

RIOTS - BIBLIOGRAPHY

"The Negro and Riots" in A Bibliography of the Negro. 1928. pp. 560-562.

RIPPERTON, MINNIE - BIBLIOGRAPHY

"Ripperton, Minnie" in Black Music in America. 1981. pp. 475-476.

RITUALS, RELIGIOUS - BIBLIOGRAPHY

"Religious Rites and Services" in Afro-American Folk Culture. 1978. See index, pp. 788-789.

RIVERS, CONRAD KENT

"Conrad Kent Rivers," Edwin L. Coleman in Afro-American Poets Since

<u>1955</u>. 1985. pp. 281-286.

ROBESON, PAUL - BIBLIOGRAPHY

<u>A Paul Robeson Research Guide</u>. 1982. 879 p.

RODGERS, CAROLYN

"Carolyn M. Rodgers," Jean Davis in <u>Afro-American Poets Since 1955</u>.
    1985. pp. 287-295.

ROME (ANCIENT) - BLACK HISTORY

"Negroes in Ancient Rome and Carthage" in <u>Sex and Race</u>. 1944. V. 1, pp.
    86-90.

ROSS, DIANA - BIBLIOGRAPHY

"Ross, Diana" in <u>Black Music in America</u>. 1981. pp. 476-484.

ROYALTY, HONORARY - BIOGRAPHY - INDEX

"Royalty, Honorary" in <u>In Black and White</u>. 1980. See index, V. 2, p.
    1230.

RUANDA - MUSIC - BIBLIOGRAPHY

"Ruanda" in <u>Bibliography of Black Music</u>. 1981. V. 3, p. 102.

RULERS, AFRICAN - BIOGRAPHY - INDEX

"African Leaders, Rulers" in <u>In Black and White</u>. 1980. See index, V. 2,
    p. 1110.

RUNAWAYS - SLAVERY

"Runaways and Rebels" in <u>The Slave Community</u>. 1979. pp. 192-222.

RURAL DEVELOPMENT - CARIBBEAN - BIBLIOGRAPHY

"Rural and Urban Development" in <u>The Complete Caribbeana</u>. 1977. V. 2,
    pp. 1169-1183.

RURAL STUDIES - HAITI - BIBLIOGRAPHY

"Rural Studies" in <u>The Complete Haitiana</u>. 1982. V. 2, pp. 843-874.

RUSSIA

"Miscegenation in Holland, Belgium, Austria, Poland, Russia" in <u>Sex and
    Race</u>. 1944. V. 1, pp. 169-175.

RUSTIN, BAYARD - BIBLIOGRAPHY

"Bayard Rustin's Opinion of Jews" in <u>Black-Jewish Relations</u>. 1984. pp.
    47-48.

SABA - BIBLIOGRAPHY

"Saba" in The Complete Caribbeana. 1977. See index, V. 4, p. 2181.

SAILORS

"Deepwater Seamen" in Black Men of the Sea. 1978. pp. 58-67.

SAINT BARTHELEMY - BIBLIOGRAPY

"Saint Barthelemy" in The Complete Caribbeana. 1977. See index, V. 4, p. 2181.

SAINT CROIX - BIBLIOGRAPHY

"Saint Croix" in The Complete Caribbeana. 1977. See index, p. 2182.

SAINT EUSTATIUS - BIBLIOGRAPHY

"Saint Eustatius" in The Complete Caribbeana. 1977. See index, V. 4, p. 2182.

SAINT KITTS - BIBLIOGRAPHY

"Saint Kitts" in The Complete Caribbeana. 1977. See index, V. 4, p. 2182.

SAINT LUCIA - BIBLIOGRAPHY

"Saint Lucia" in The Complete Caribbeana. 1977. See index, V. 4, p. 2183.

SAINT MARTIN - BIBLIOGRAPHY

"Saint Martin/Sint Maarten" in The Complete Caribbeana. V. 4, p. 2183.

ST. OMER, GARTH

"Garth St. Omer," Roland E. Bush in 50 Caribbean Writers. 1986. pp. 405-417.

SAINT THOMAS - BIBLIOGRAPHY

"Saint Thomas" in The Complete Caribbeana. 1977. See index, V. 4, pp. 2183-2184.

SAINT VINCENT - BIBLIOGRAPHY

"Saint Vincent" in The Complete Caribbeana. 1977. p. 2184.

SALAAM, KALAMU YA

"Kalamu ya Salaam," Arthenia J. Bates Millican in Afro-American Writers After 1955: Dramatists and Prose Writers. 1985. pp. 231-239.

SALESPERSONS - BIOGRAPHY - INDEX

"Salespersons" in In Black and White. 1980. See index, V. 2, pp. 1230-1231.

SALESWOMEN - BIBLIOGRAPHY

"Sales Ladies" in The Progress of Afro-American Women. 1980. p. 128.

SALKEY, ANDREW

"Andrew Salkey," Daryl Cumber Dance in 50 Caribbean Writers. 1986. pp. 418-427.

SANCHEZ, SONIA

"Sonia Sanchez," Kalamu ya Salaam in Afro-American Poets Since 1955. 1985. pp. 295-306.

SAO TOME - LINGUISTICS - BIBLIOGRAPHY

"Sao Tome and Principe" in A Bibliography of Pidgin and Creole Languages. 1975. pp. 92-93.

SAVINGS AND LOAN ASSOCIATIONS - DIRECTORY

"Savings and Loan Associations" in Black Resource Guide. 1986. pp. 85-87.

SAXOPHONE PLAYERS - BIOGRAPHY - INDEX

"Musicians: Instrumental: Saxophone" in In Black and White. 1980. See index, V. 2, p. 1189.

SCHOLARS - BIBLIOGRAPHY

"Higher Education and Black Scholarship" in Blacks in America; Bibliographical Essays. 1971. pp. 212-218.

SCHOLARS - BIOGRAPHY - INDEX

"Scholars" in In Black and White. 1980. See index, V. 2, pp. 1231-1232.

SCHOOL BOARDS - BIOGRAPHY - INDEX

"School Board Members, Officials" in In Black and White. 1980. See index, V. 2, p. 1232.

SCHUYLER, GEORGE - BIBLIOGRAPHY

"Schuyler, George" in The Harlem Renaissance. 1982. pp. 132-134.

SCIENCE - BIBLIOGRAPHY

"Science" in The Progress of Afro-American Women. 1980. pp. 312-313.

SCIENCE - EDUCATION

"Helping Minority Students to Excel in University-level Mathematics and

Science Courses: The Professional Development Program at the University of California, Berkeley," Katharyn Culler in The State of Black America, 1985. pp. 225-231.

SCIENCE ORGANIZATIONS - DIRECTORY

"Science, Engineering and Health Organizations" in Black Resource Guide. 1986. pp. 203-206.

SCIENTISTS

"Inventors and Scientists" in The Negro Almanac. 1983. pp. 1053-1076.

"The Negro in Science," Lewis N. Carlson in The Negro Impact on Western Civilization. 1970. pp. 51-74.

SCIENTISTS - BIBLIOGRAPHY

"Scientists and Inventors" in Afro-American Reference. 1985. pp. 18-19.

SCIENTISTS - BIOGRAPHY - INDEX

"Scientists" in In Black and White. 1980. See index, V. 2, p. 1232.

SCOTT, DENNIS

"Dennis Scott," Ian D. Smith in 50 Caribbean Writers. 1986. pp. 428-438.

SCOTT, HAZEL - BIBLIOGRAPHY

"Scott, Hazel" in Black Music in America. 1981. pp. 484-486.

SCOTT-HERON, GIL

"Gil Scott-Heron," Jon Woodson in Afro-American Poets Since 1955. 1985. pp. 307-311.

SCOUTS - BIOGRAPHY - INDEX

"Scouts, Guides, Interpreters" in In Black and White. 1980. See index, V. 2, p. 1232.

SCULPTORS - BIOGRAPHY - INDEX

"Artists: Sculpture" in In Black and White. 1980. See index, V. 2, p. 1117.

SEA CHANTIES - BIBLIOGRAPHY

"Chanties (Sea and Boating Songs)" in Afro-American Folk Culture. 1978. p. 761.

SEA INDUSTRIES - BIBLIOGRAPHY

"Sea Industries" in The Progress of Afro-American Women. 1980. p. 128.

SEAMEN - BIOGRAPHY - INDEX

"Seamen" in <u>In Black and White</u>. 1980. See index, V. 2, p. 1233.

SECRET SERVICE - BIOGRAPHY - INDEX

"Protective Service: FBI, Secret Service" in <u>In Black and White</u>. 1980.
     See index, V. 2, p. 1224.

SECRETARIES - BIBLIOGRAPHY

"Secretaries" in <u>The Progress of Afro-American Women</u>. 1980. pp. 128-129.

SECRETARIES - BIOGRAPHY - INDEX

"Secretaries" in <u>In Black and White</u>. 1980. See index, V. 2, p. 1233.

SECURITY GUARDS - BIOGRAPHY - INDEX

"Protective Services: Police, Security Guards, Prison Officials" in <u>In
     Black and White</u>. 1980. See index, V. 2, pp. 1224-1225.

SEGREGATION - BIBLIOGRAPHY

"Racial Attitudes and Segregation" in <u>Afro-American History, 1</u>. 1974.
     pp. 421-460.

"Racial Attitudes and Segregation" in <u>Afro-American History, 2</u>. 1982.
     pp. 150-159.

"Segregation of the Races in Public Conveyances and Public Places" in <u>A
     Bibliography of the Negro</u>. 1928. pp. 538-539.

"White Flight" in <u>The Education of Poor and Minority Children</u>. 1981. pp.
     1002-1004.

SEGREGATION - HISTORY

"The Life and Times of Jim Crow" in <u>Before the Mayflower</u>. 1982. pp.
     255-296.

SEGREGATION - HISTORY - BIBLIOGRAPHY

"The Origins of Jim Crow" in <u>Blacks in America; Bibliographical Essays</u>.
     1971. pp. 138-140.

SEJOUR, VICTOR

"Victor Sejour (Juan Victor Sejour Marcou et Ferrand)", Thomas Bonner in
     <u>Afro-American Writers Before the Harlem Renaissance</u>. 1986. pp.
     237-241.

SELVON, SAMUEL DICKSON

"Samuel Dickson Selvon," Sandra Pouchet Paquet in <u>50 Caribbean Writers</u>.
     1986. pp. 439-449.

SENEGAL - LINGUISTICS - BIBLIOGRAPHY

"Ziguinchor (Senegal)" in <u>A Bibliography of Pidgin and Creole Languages</u>. 1975. p. 91.

SENEGAL - MUSIC - BIBLIOGRAPHY

"Senegal" in <u>Bibliography of Black Music</u>. 1981. V. 3, p. 103.

SERMONS - BIBLIOGRAPHY

"Sermons and Preaching" in <u>Afro-American Folk Culture</u>. 1978. See index, pp. 790-791.

SETTLERS - BIOGRAPHY - INDEX

"Settlers, Founders of Cities, Colonizers" in <u>In Black and White</u>. 1980. See index, V. 2, p. 1233.

SEVENTH DAY ADVENTISTS - CIVIL RIGHTS MOVEMENT - BIBLIOGRAPHY

"The Church, Synagogue and Integration: Seventh Day Adventist" in <u>Howard University Bibliography of African and Afro-American Religious Studies</u>. 1977. p. 323.

SEVENTH DAY ADVENTISTS - RACE RELATIONS - BIBLIOGRAPHY

"Seventh Day Adventist" in <u>Howard University Bibliography of African and Afro-American Religious Studies</u>. 1977. pp 290-292.

SEX - BIBLIOGRAPHY

"Sex" in <u>Afro-American Folk Culture</u>. 1978. See index, p. 791.

"Sex and Sexual Discrimination" in <u>The Progress of Afro-American Women</u>. 1980. pp. 314-321.

SEX AND RACE

"Red, White and Black: Race and Sex" in <u>Before the Mayflower</u>. 1982. pp. 297-325.

<u>Sex and Race</u>. 3 V.

"Sex and Racism" in <u>Long Memory</u>. 1982. pp. 114-141.

SEX AND RACE - BIBLIOGRAPHY

"Bibliography: Sex and Racism" in <u>Long Memory</u>. 1982. pp. 432-435.

SEX RATIO

"Shortage of Eligible Black Males" in <u>The Negro Almanac</u>. 1983. pp. 476-477.

SEXUAL DISCRIMINATION - BIBLIOGRAPHY

"Sex and Sexual Discrimination" in <u>The Progress of Afro-American Women</u>. 1980. pp. 314-321.

SEXUALITY

"The Myth of Black Sexual Superiority: A Re-Examination" in <u>Black Masculinity</u>. 1982. pp. 75-86.

SEYCHELLES - LINGUISTICS - BIBLIOGRAPHY

"Seychelles" in <u>A Bibliography of Pidgin and Creole Languages</u>. 1975. p. 307.

SEYMOUR, A.J.

"A.J. Seymour," Lloyd W. Brown in <u>50 Caribbean Writers</u>. 1986. pp. 450-456.

SHANGE, NTOZAKE

"Ntozake Shange," Elizabeth Brown in <u>Afro-American Writers After 1955: Dramatists and Prose Writers</u>. 1985. pp. 240-250.

SHINE, TED

"Ted Shine," Winona L. Fletcher in <u>Afro-American Writers After 1955: Dramatists and Prose Writers</u>. 1985. pp. 250-259.

SHIPBUILDERS

"Shipbuilders" in <u>Black Men of the Sea</u>. 1978. pp. 48-57.

SHIRLEY, GEORGE - BIBLIOGRAPHY

"Shirley, George" in <u>Black Music in America</u>. 1981. pp. 486-489.

SHOCKLEY, ANN ALLEN

"Ann Allen Shockley," Helen R. Houston in <u>Afro-American Fiction Writers After 1955</u>. 1984. pp. 232-236.

SIERRA LEONE - LINGUISTICS - BIBLIOGRAPHY

"Krio" in <u>A Bibliography of Pidgin and Creole Languages</u>. 1975. pp. 365-372.

SIERRA LEONE - MUSIC - BIBLIOGRAPHY

"Sierra Leone" in <u>Bibliography of Black Music</u>. 1981. V. 3, p. 104.

SIMMONS, HERBERT A.

"Herbert Alfred Simmons," Australia Henderson in <u>Afro-American Fiction Writers After 1955</u>. 1984. pp. 236-239.

SIMONE, NINA - BIBLIOGRAPHY

"Simone, Nina" in <u>Black Music in America</u>. 1981. pp. 490-493.

SINT MAARTEN - BIBLIOGRAPHY

"Saint Martin/Sint Maarten" in The Complete Caribbeana. V. 4, p. 2183.

SLANG - BIBLIOGRAPHY

"Slang, Jazz" in Afro-American Folk Culture. 1978. See index, p. 792.

SLAVE ART - BIBLIOGRAPHY

"Slave Art" in Black Slavery in the Americas. 1982. pp. 1382-1389.

SLAVE ARTISANS - BIBLIOGRAPHY

"Slave Artisans and Craftsmen" in The Other Slaves. 1978. pp. 169-241.

SLAVE BIOGRAPHY - BIBLIOGRAPHY

"Biographies" in Slavery: A Worldwide Bibliography. 1977. pp. 116-118.

SLAVE CLOTHING - BIBLIOGRAPHY

"Slave Clothing" in Black Slavery in the Americas. 1982. pp. 1159-1161.

SLAVE CULTURE

"Culture" in The Slave Community. 1979. pp. 105-148.

SLAVE CULTURE - BIBLIOGRAPHY

"Slave Culture" in Black Slavery in the Americas. 1982. pp. 1295-1389.

SLAVE DANCING

"Dance" in Black Slavery in the Americas. 1982. pp. 1368-1373.

SLAVE DRIVERS - BIBLIOGRAPHY

"Slave Drivers" in Black Slavery in the Americas. 1982. pp. 1102-1104.

SLAVE FAMILY

"The Slave Family" in The Slave Community. 1979. pp. 149-191.

SLAVE FAMILY - BIBLIOGRAPHY

"Slave Family" in Black Slavery in the Americas. 1982. pp. 1200-1236.

SLAVE FOLKLORE - BIBLIOGRAPHY

"Folklore" in Black Slavery in the Americas. 1982. pp. 1339-1367.

SLAVE HOUSING - BIBLIOGRAPHY

"Slave Housing" in Black Slavery in the Americas. 1982. pp. 1153-1159.

SLAVE IRONWORKERS

"Disciplining Slave Ironworkers in the Antebellum South: Coercion,

Conciliation and Accommodation," Charles B. Dew in <u>The Other Slaves</u>. 1978. pp. 63-85.

SLAVE LANGUAGE - BIBLIOGRAPHY

"Slave Language" in <u>Black Slavery in the Americas</u>. 1982. pp. 1431-1444.

SLAVE MARRIAGE - BIBLIOGRAPHY

"Slave Marriages" in <u>Black Slavery in the Americas</u>. 1982. pp. 1233-1236.

SLAVE MEDICINE - BIBLIOGRAPHY

"Slave Medicine" in <u>Black Slavery in the Americas</u>. 1982. pp. 1161-1181.

SLAVE MUSIC - BIBLIOGRAPHY

"Music" in <u>Black Slavery in the Americas</u>. 1982. pp. 1304-1339.

SLAVE NARRATIVES - BIBLIOGRAPHY

"Autobiographical Writings" in <u>Black Slavery in the Americas</u>. 1982. pp. 1397-1414.

"Slave Narratives" in <u>A Bibliography of the Negro</u>. 1928. pp. 310-313.

"Slave Narratives" in <u>Black Rhetoric</u>. 1976. pp. 113-114.

"Slave Narratives" in <u>A Comprehensive Bibliography</u>. 1976. pp. 203-204.

"Slave Narratives" in <u>The Progress of Afro-American Women</u>. 1980. pp. 222-324.

"Slave Narratives and Related Works" in <u>The Black Family</u>. 1978. pp. 1-5.

SLAVE OVERSEERS - BIBLIOGRAPHY

"Overseers" in <u>Black Slavery in the Americas</u>. 1982. pp. 1104-1107.

SLAVE OWNERS - BIBLIOGRAPHY

"Jews as Slave Owners and Slave Traders" in <u>Black-Jewish Relations</u>. 1984. pp. 20-23.

"Master/Slave Relationships" in <u>Black Slavery in the Americas</u>. 1982. pp. 1192-1199.

SLAVE PERSONALITIES

"Slave Personality Types" in <u>The Slave Community</u>. 1979. pp. 284-322.

SLAVE RECREATION - BIBLIOGRAPHY

"Slave Recreation" in <u>Black Slavery in the Americas</u>. 1982. pp. 1181-1184.

SLAVE RELIGION

"Afro-American Slave Culture," Monica Shuler in <u>Roots and Branches</u>.
     1979. pp. 121-137.

"Afro-American Slave Culture: Commentary Three," Edward Kamau
     Braithwaite in <u>Roots and Branches</u>. 1979. pp. 150-155.

SLAVE RELIGION - BIBLIOGRAPHY

"Slave Religion" in <u>Black Slavery in the Americas</u>. 1982. pp. 1237-1294.

SLAVE RESISTANCE - BIBLIOGRAPHY

"Day-to-Day Resistance" in <u>Black Slavery in the Americas</u>. 1982. pp.
     1499-1506.

SLAVE REVOLTS

<u>American Negro Slave Revolts</u>. 1983. 411 p.

"Blood on the Leaves: Revolts and Conspiracies" in <u>Before the
     Mayflower</u>. 1982. pp. 112-139.

"Slave Conspiracies in the United States" in <u>The Negro Almanac</u>. 1983.
     pp. 1377-1381.

"Slave Trade" in <u>Black Men of the Sea</u>. 1978. pp. 16-27.

SLAVE REVOLTS - BIBLIOGRAPHY

"Bibliography" in <u>American Negro Slave Revolts</u>. 1983. pp. 375-408.

"Revolts/Insurrections" in <u>Black Slavery in the Americas</u>. 1982. pp.
     1473-1499.

SLAVE REVOLTS - COLOMBIA

"Manumission, Libres, and Black Resistance: The Colombian Choco, 1680-
     1810," William F. Sharp in <u>Slavery and Race Relations in Latin
     America</u>. 1974. pp. 89-111.

SLAVE STEREOTYPES

"Plantation Stereotypes and Institutional Roles" in <u>The Slave Community</u>.
     1979. pp. 223-248.

SLAVE TRADE

"Before the Mayflower" in <u>Before the Mayflower</u>. 1982. pp. 28-54.

"The Closing of the Slave Trade" in <u>From Slavery to Freedom</u>. 1980. pp.
     103-105.

"Persistence of the African Trade" in <u>From Slavery to Freedom</u>. 1980. pp.
     129-131.

"The Slave Trade" in <u>From Slavery to Freedom</u>. 1980. pp. 30-44.

y in its Economic Aspects" in A Bibliography of the Negro. 1928.
. 286-290.

- EIGHTEENTH CENTURY

y and Industrial Revolution" in From Slavery to Freedom. 1980.
. 98-100.

- ETHNIC GROUPS

merican Slave Culture," Monica Schuler in Roots and Braches.
79. pp. 121-137.

merican Slave Culture: Commentary Two," Richard Price in Roots
d Branches. 1979. pp. 141-149.

- ETHNICTY

y and Race," Harry Hoetink in Roots and Branches. 1979. pp. 255-
8.

y and Race: Commentary," Arnold Sio in Roots and Branches. 1979.
. 269-274.

- HAITI - BIBLIOGRAPHY

y, Marronage and Emancipation, 1492-1803" in The Complete
itiana. V 1, pp. 277-368.

- HEMP INDUSTRY

y in the Hemp Induscry," James F. Hopkins in The Other Slaves.
78. pp. 145-156.

- HISTORIOGRAPHY

ng Interpretations of Slavery Since World War II," Colin Palmer
Contemporary Black Thought. 1980. pp. 233-242.

- INDEX

t Index" in Index to the American Slave. 1981. pp. 145-274.

- INTERNATIONAL ASPECTS - BIBLIOGRAPHY

y as an International Issue" in Afro-American History, 2. 1981.
. 107-110.

- LEGAL ASPECTS - BIBLIOGRAPHY

Law Suits Relating to the Status of Slaves" in A Bibliography of
e Negro. 1928. p. 344.

- LEGAL HISTORY - BIBLIOGRAPHY

Law" in Black Slavery in the Americas. 1982. pp. 649-759.

SLAVE TRADE - BIBLIOGRAPHY

"African Origins and the Beginnings of Slavery" in Afro-American
History, 2. 1981. pp. 59-62.

"Atlantic Slave Trade" in Black Slavery in the Americas. 1982. pp. 375-
448.

"The Altantic Trade" in Blacks in America; Bibliographical Essays. 1971.
pp. 29-31.

"Bibliographical Notes: The Slave Trade" in From Slavery to Freedom.
1980. pp. 513-514.

"Conditions of Slave Trade" in Black Slavery in the Americas. 1982. pp.
1130-1199.

"Slave Trade" in Slavery: A Worldwide Bibliography. 1985. pp. 335-388.

SLAVE TRADE - BRAZIL

"African Slave Trade and Economic Development in Amazonia," Colin M.
MacLachlan in Slavery and Race Relations in Latin America. 1974.
pp. 112-145.

SLAVE TRADE - BRAZIL - BIBLIOGRAPHY

"The African Slave Trade, Slavery, and Abolition" in Afro-Braziliana.
1978. pp. 21-37.

SLAVE TRADE - CARIBBEAN - BIBLIOGRAPHY

"Slavery in the Caribbean" in Black Slavery in the Americas. 1982. pp.
449-538.

SLAVE TRADE, AFRICAN - BIBLIOGRAPHY

"The African Slave Trade to America" in A Bibliography of the Negro.
1928. pp. 256-266.

SLAVE TRADE, DOMESTIC

"The Domestic Slave Trade" in From Slavery to Freedom. 1980. pp. 123-
129.

SLAVE TRADE, DOMESTIC - BIBLIOGRAPHY

"Domestic Slave Trade" in Black Slavery in the Americas. 1982. pp.
1122-1131.

"The Internal Slave Trade" in Blacks in America; Bibliographical Essays.
1971. pp. 58-59.

SLAVE TRADERS, JEWISH - BIBLIOGRAPHY

"Jews as Slave Owners and Slave Traders" in Black-Jewish Relations.
1984. pp. 20-23.

SLAVERY

"Behind the Cotton Curtain" in Before the Mayflower. 1982. pp. 86-111.

"Colonial Slavery" in From Slavery to Freedom. 1980. pp. 54-64.

Roots and Branches; Current Directions in Slave Studies. 1979. 292 p.

The Slave Community. 1979. 414 p.

"Slavery in the Americas" in The Negro Almanac. 1983. pp. 1367-1382.

SLAVERY - BIBLICAL REFERENCES - BIBLIOGRAPHY

"Slavery and the Bible" in A Bibliography of the Negro. 1928. pp. 317-320.

SLAVERY - BIBLIOGRAPHY

"African Origins and the Beginnings of Slavery" in Afro-American History, 1. 1974. pp. 83-97.

"Bibliographical Notes: Colonial Slavery" in From Slavery to Freedom. 1980. pp. 1512-516.

"Bibliographical Notes: That Peculiar Institution" in From Slavery to Freedom. 1980. pp. 520-523.

"British North America (United States)" in Slavery. 1977. pp. 11-41.

"Christianity and Slavery in the New World" in Howard University Bibliography of African and Afro-American Religious Studies. 1977.

"General and Comparative" in Slavery. 1977. pp. 1-10.

"General Studies" in Black Slavery in the Americas. 1982. pp. 226-336.

"The Introduction of Negro Slavery Into America" in A Bibliography of the Negro. 1928. pp. 254-255.

"None of the Above" in Slavery. 1977. pp. 89-98.

"The Origins of Slavery in the British Colonies of North America" in Blacks in America; Bibliographical Essays. 1971. pp. 39-42.

"Select Bibliography" in The Slave Community. 1979. pp. 383-402.

"A Selected Bibliography: Slavery" in The Negro Almanac. pp. 1502-1503.

"Slavery" in Afro-American Reference. 1985. pp. 46-58.

"Slavery" in The American South. 1986. V. 1, pp. 108-142.

Slavery: A Worldwide Bibliography. 1985. 451 p.

"Slavery and Freedom (1783-1865)" in Afro-American History, 1. 1974. pp. 103-315.

"Slavery Annual Bibliographical Supplement (1981 Slavery and Abolition: A Journal of Compara 146-205.

"Slavery in the Colonies" in A Bibliography of t 281-282.

"Studies Relating to Slavery" in A Bibliography 620-623.

"The System of Slavery" in Afro-American History

"The System of Slavery" in Afro-American History

SLAVERY - CLASS ANALYSIS

"Slavery and the Rise of Peasantries: Commentar in Roots and Branches. 1979. pp. 252-253.

SLAVERY - COLONIAL PERIOD - BIBLIOGRAPHY

"Slavery in Colonial and Revolutionary America' Americas. 1982. pp. 613-648.

SLAVERY - COMPARATIVE STUDIES - BIBLIOGRAPHY

"Slavery in the United States and Latin Americ in Blacks in America; Bibliographical Ess

SLAVERY - CONDITION OF SLAVES - BIBLIOGRAPHY

"History of the Changes in the Status and Cont Bibliography of the Negro. 1928. pp. 342-

SLAVERY - DISCIPLINE

"Disciplining Slave Ironworkers in the Antebe Conciliation and Accomodation," Charles 1978. pp. 63-85.

SLAVERY - DOCUMENTATION

"The Other Side of Slavery," Andrew Billingsl Greene in Afro-American History; Sources 123-138.

"Slavery" in Black Genesis. 1978. pp. 37-46.

SLAVERY - ECONOMIC ASPECTS

"Slavery and Underdevelopment," Walter Rodne 1979. pp. 275-286.

SLAVERY - ECONOMIC ASPECTS - BIBLIOGRAPHY

"Economics of Slavery" in Black Slavery in t 1043-1131.

SLAVERY - MIDDLE COLONIES

"Colonial Slavery: The Middle Colonies" in From Slavery to Freedom.
    1980. pp. 60-63.

SLAVERY - NORTH - BIBLIOGRAPHY

"Slavery in the Northern States" in A Bibliography of the Negro. 1928.
    pp. 284-285.

SLAVERY - POETRY - BIBLIOGRAPHY

"Poems on Slavery" in A Bibliography of the Negro. 1928. pp. 308-310.

SLAVERY - POLITICAL ASPECTS

"Slavery and Intersectional Strife" in From Slavery to Freedom. 1980.
    pp. 180-204.

SLAVERY - POLITICAL ASPECTS - BIBLIOGRAPHY

"Controversy Over Slavery" in A Bibliography of the Negro. 1928. pp.
    324-333.

"Slavery as an Internal Issue" in Afro-American History, 1. 1974. pp.
    249-256.

SLAVERY - PRO-SLAVERY ARGUMENTS - BIBLIOGRAPHY

"Pro-Slavery Discussion" in A Bibliography of the Negro. 1928. pp. 314-
    317.

"The Southern Defense of Slavery" in Blacks in America; Bibliographical
    Essays. 1971. pp. 67-68.

SLAVERY - RACIAL ASPECTS - BIBLIOGRAPHY

"Slavery and Race" in Black Slavery in the Americas. 1982. pp. 155-225.

SLAVERY - RELIGION - BIBLIOGRAPHY

"The Religious Instruction of the Slaves" in A Bibliography of the
    Negro. 1928. pp. 293-295.

SLAVERY - RELIGIOUS ASPECTS

"Slavery and the Protestant Ethic," Roger Anstey in Roots and Branches.
    1979. pp. 157-172.

"Slavery and the Protestant Ethic: Commentary One," Emilia Viotti da
    Costa in Roots and Branches. 1979. pp. 173-177.

"Slavery and the Protestant Ethic: Commentary Two," David Brian Davis in
    Roots and Branches. 1979. pp. 177-181.

SLAVERY - REVOLUTIONARY PERIOD

"Slavery and the Revolutionary Philosophy" in <u>From Slavery to Freedom</u>. 1980. pp. 81-85.

SLAVERY - REVOLUTIONARY PERIOD - BIBLIOGRAPHY

"Slavery in Colonial and Revolutionary America" in <u>Black Slavery in the Americas</u>. 1982. pp. 613-648.

SLAVERY - SALT INDUSTRY

"Slavery and the Western Virginia Salt Industry," John Edmund Stealey in <u>The Other Slaves</u>. 1978. pp. 109-133.

SLAVERY - SOCIAL ASPECTS - BIBLIOGRAPHY

"Slavery in Its Social Aspects" in <u>A Bibliography of the Negro</u>. 1928. pp. 291-292.

SLAVERY - SOCIOLOGY

"Afro-American Slave Culture," Monica Schuler in <u>Roots and Branches</u>. 1979. pp. 121-137.

"Plantation Realities" in <u>The Slave Community</u>. 1979. pp. 249-283.

"That Peculiar Institution" in <u>From Slavery to Freedom</u>. 1980. pp. 132-156.

SLAVERY - SOURCES

"Critical Essays on Sources" in <u>The Slave Community</u>. 1979. pp. 367-382.

SLAVERY - SOUTH - BIBLIOGRAPHY

"Plantation Slavery in the Antebellum South" in <u>Blacks in America; Bibliographical Essays</u>. 1971. pp. 51-56.

"Slavery in the Southern States" in <u>A Bibliography of the Negro</u>. 1928. pp. 283-284.

SLAVERY - STATISTICS

"Statistics on Slaves and Slavery: Observations and Tables in <u>The Slave Community</u>. 1979. pp. 336-366.

SLAVERY - TOBACCO INDUSTRY

"Slavery in Tobacco Factories," Joseph Clarke Robert in <u>The Other Slaves</u>. 1978. pp. 135-144.

SLAVERY, INDUSTRIAL - BIBLIOGRAPHY

"Industrial Slavery" in <u>Black Slavery in the Americas</u>. pp. 1089-1102.

SLAVERY, ISLAMIC - BIBLIOGRAPHY

"The Muslim World" in <u>Slavery</u>. 1977. pp. 69-72.

SLAVERY, URBAN - BIBLIOGRAPHY

"Slavery in Urban and Industrial Environment" in Blacks in America;
    Bibliographical Essays. 1971. pp. 56-58.

"Urban Slavery" in Black Slavery in the Americas. 1982. pp. 1184-1192.

SLAVERY AND INUSTRY

"Slavery and Industrialism," Charles H. Wesley in The Other Slaves.
    1978. pp. 21-40.

"Slavery and the Beginnings of Industrialism in the American Colonies,"
    Marcus W. Jernegan in The Other Slaves. 1978. pp. 3-20.

SLAVERY AND RELIGION - BIBLIOGRAPHY

"American Churches and Slavery" in Blacks in America; Bibliographical
    Essays. 1971. pp. 78-81.

"Slavery and the Church" in A Bibliography of the Negro. 1928. pp. 320-
    324.

SLAVERY IN FICTION

"Fact from Fiction: Another Look at Slavery in Spanish American Novels,"
    Shirley M. Jackson in Blacks in Hispanic Literature. 1977. pp. 83-
    89.

SLAVERY IN FICTION - BIBLIOGRAPHY

"Novels by White Authors Treating Mainly of Slavery and Slavery Days" in
    A Bibliography of the Negro. 1928. pp. 464-468.

SLAVES - ARTISANS

"Slave Artisans and Craftsmen" in The Other Slaves. 1978. pp. 169-241.

SLAVES - CONFEDERACY - BIBLIOGRAPHY

"Slaves and the Confederacy" in Black Slavery in the Americas. 1982. pp.
    1516-1530.

SLAVES - DIRECTORY

"Slave Identification File," in Index to the American Slave. 1981. pp.
    3-76.

SLAVES - HEALTH AND NUTRITION - BIBLIOGRAPHY

"Slave Diet" in Black Slavery in the Americas. 1982. pp. 1146-1152.

SLAVES - INTERVIEWS - BIBLIOGRAPHY

"Interviews" in Black Slavery in the Americas. 1982. pp. 1414-1421.

SLAVES - IRONWORKERS

"Disciplining Slave Ironworkers in the Antebellum South: Coercion, Conciliation and Accomodation," Charles B. Dew in The Other Slaves. 1978. pp. 63-85.

SLAVES - NORTH - BIBLIOGRAPHY

"Slaves and Black Freemen in the Northern Colonies" in Blacks in America; Bibliographical Essays. 1971. pp. 44-45.

SLAVES - RELATIONS WITH SLAVE OWNERS - BIBLIOGRAPHY

"Master/Slave Relationships" in Black Slavery in the Americas. 1982. pp. 1192-1199.

SLAVES - RIVERMEN

"Simon Gray, Riverman: A Slave Who Was Almost Free," John Hebron Moore in The Other Slaves. 1978. pp. 157-167.

SLAVES - SOUTH - BIBLIOGRAPHY

"Slaves and Black Freemen in the Colonial South" in Blacks in America; Bibliographical Essays. 1971. pp. 42-44.

SLAVES - TREATMENT

"Plantation Realities" in The Slave Community. 1979. pp. 249-283.

SLAVES - TREATMENT - BIBLIOGRAPHY

"Slave Treatment" in Black Slavery in the Americas. 1982. pp. 1139-1146.

SLAVES, INDUSTRIAL

"Skilled Slaves: The Industrial Impact" in The Other Slaves. 1978. pp. 1-60.

SLAVES, SKILLED

The Other Slaves; Mechanics, Artisans and Craftsmen. 1978. 245 p.

SLAVES, WHITE

"The Americanization of the Slave and the Africanization of the South" in The Slave Community. 1979. pp. 49-104.

"White People Sold as Negro Slaves" in Sex and Race. 1942. V. 2, pp. 208-213.

SMITH, BESSIE - BIBLIOGRAPHY

"Smith, Bessie" in Black Music in America. 1981. pp. 493-503.

SOCIAL AND POLITICAL THOUGHT - HISTORY - BIBLIOGRAPHY

"Accomodation and Protest in Black Thought" in Blacks in America; Bibliographical Essays. 1971. pp. 149-153.

SOCIAL CLASS

"The Black Middle Class: Past, Present and Future," Robert B. Hill. The State of Black America, 1986. pp. 43-64.

"The Black Poor: Highest Stage of Underdevelopment" in How Capitalism Underdeveloped Black America. 1983. pp. 53-67.

"The Crisis of the Black Working Class" in How Capitalism Underdeveloped Black America. 1983. pp. 23-51.

SOCIAL CLASS - BIBLIOGRAPHY

"The Black Bourgeoisie" in Blacks in America; Bibliographical Essays. 1971. pp. 209-212.

"Black Lower Class Family" in The Black Family in the United States. 1986. pp. 82-83 and 201-205.

"Black Middle Class Family" in The Black Family in the United States. 1986. pp. 83-84, 141-142 and 206-208.

"Black Working Class" in The Black Family in the United States. 1986. pp. 121-213.

SOCIAL CLASS - CARIBBEAN - BIBLIOGRAPHY

"Population Categories: Classes, Peasants, Women" in The Complete Caribbeana. 1977. pp. 443-460. V. 1, pp. 443-460.

SOCIAL CONDITIONS

"A Black Social Science Research Agenda Through the Year 2000," Ernest J. Wilson in Blacks in the Year 2000. 1981. pp. 57-70.

"Conclusions" in The State of Black America, 1985. pp. 185- 189.

"Conclusions and Recommendations" in The State of Black America, 1986. pp. 175-181.

"One World or Two?" in From Slavery to Freedom. 1980. pp. 418-421.

"An Overview of Black America in 1985," John E. Jacob in The State of Black America, 1986. pp. i-xi.

"An Overview of Black America in 1984," John E. Jacob in The State of Black America, 1985. pp. i-vi.

"An Overview of Black Americans in 1983," John E. Jacob in The State of Black America, 1984. pp. i-vii.

"Race and Masculinity: The Dual Dilemma of Black Men" in Black Masculinity. 1982. pp. 7-20.

SOCIAL CONDITIONS - BIBLIOGRAPHY

"General Social Conditions Studies" in A Bibliography of the Negro.

1928. pp. 628-629.

"The Progress of the Negro" in <u>A Bibliography of the Negro</u>. 1928. pp. 583-584.

"A Selected Bibliography: Culture and Society" in <u>The Negro Almanac</u>. 1983. pp. 1519-1522.

"The Social Fabric" in <u>Afro-American History, 2</u>. 1981. pp. 225-240.

"Social, Political and Economic Dimensions" in <u>Afro-American History, 2</u>. 1981. pp. 159-168.

"The Social, Political and Economic Situation" in <u>Afro-American History, 1</u>. 1974. pp. 460-490 and 628-748.

SOCIAL CONDITIONS - BRAZIL - BIBLIOGRAPHY

"Social Conditions and Race Relations" in <u>Afro-Braziliana.</u> 1978. pp. 53-70.

SOCIAL CONDITIONS - CARIBBEAN - BIBLIOGRAPHY

"The Nature of Society" in <u>The Complete Caribbeana</u>. 1977. V. 1, pp. 375-415.

"Social and Legal Issues" in <u>The Complete Caribbeana</u>. V. 2, pp. 1109-1142.

"Values and Norms" in <u>The Complete Caribbeana</u>. 1977. V. 2, pp. 671-692.

SOCIAL CONDITIONS - FUTURE

<u>Blacks in the Year 2000</u>. 1981. 70 p.

SOCIAL CONDITIONS - HAITI - BIBLIOGRAPHY

"Macro-Analysis of Haitian Society" in <u>The Complete Haitiana</u>. 1982. pp. 809-822.

"Micro-Analysis of Haitian Society" in <u>The Complete Haitiana</u>. 1982. V. 2, pp. 823-831.

SOCIAL CONDITIONS - POST WORLD WAR II

"The Postwar Years" in <u>From Slavery to Freedom</u>. 1980. p. 450-462.

SOCIAL CONDITIONS, AFRICAN - HISTORY

"The African Way of Life: Social Organization" in <u>From Slavery to Freedom</u>. 1980. pp. 19-22.

SOCIAL HISTORY - BIBLIOGRAPHY

"Development of an Afro-American Community" (1865-1900) in <u>Afro-American History, 1</u>. 1974. pp. 398-407.

"The Elements of Black Society" (Colonial Period) in <u>Afro-American History, 1</u>. 1974. pp. 97-101.

"The Elements of Black Society" (Colonial Period) in <u>Afro-American History, 2</u>. 1981. pp. 62-66.

"Social and Cultural History" in <u>Afro-American History, 1</u>. 1974. pp. 33-45.

"Social and Cultural History" in <u>Afro-American History, 2</u>. 1981. pp. 19-32.

SOCIAL MOVEMENTS

"The Negro's World" in <u>From Slavery to Freedom</u>. 1980. pp. 412-418.

<u>Reluctant Reformers</u>. 1975. 347 p.

SOCIAL MOVEMENTS - BIBLIOGRAPHY

"Church, Urban Crisis and Social Action" in <u>Howard University Bibliography of African and Afro-American Religious Studies</u>. 1977. pp. 345-352.

SOCIAL SCIENCE RESEARCH

"A Black Social Science Research Agenda Through the Year 2000," Ernest J. Wilson in <u>Blacks in the Year 2000</u>. 1981. pp. 57-70.

SOCIAL SERVICE WORKERS - BIBLIOGRAPHY

"Social Services" in <u>The Progress of Afro-American Women</u>. 1980. p. 129.

SOCIAL SERVICES

"Human Needs and Human Services: A Research Agenda," June Jackson Christmas in <u>Blacks in the Year 2000</u>. 1981. pp. 45-56.

"Social Services and Black Men." Bogart R. Leashore in <u>Black Men</u>. 1981. pp. 257-267.

SOCIAL THOUGHT

<u>Blacks in the Year 2000</u>. 1981. 70 p.

"The Challenge of America in the Year 2000," Robert Theobald in <u>Blacks in the Year 2000</u>. 1981. pp. 31-38.

"European Mythology: The Ideology of Progress," Dona Richards in <u>Contemporary Black Thought</u>. 1980. pp. 59-79.

<u>How Capitalism Underdeveloped Black America</u>. 1983. 343 p.

<u>Reluctant Reformers</u>. 1975. 324 p.

SOCIAL THOUGHT - INTEGRATIONIST

"A Liberal Integrating Prospectus," Mary F. Berry in <u>Blacks in the Year 2000</u>. 1981. pp. 1-7.

SOCIAL THOUGHT - MARXIST

"An Afro-Marxist Perspective," William Eric Perkins in <u>Blacks in the Year 2000</u>. 1981. pp. 9-18.

SOCIAL THOUGHT - PANAFRICANIST

"A Pan-Africanist Prospectus," Locksley Edmonson in <u>Blacks in the Year 2000</u>. 1980. pp. 19-30.

SOCIAL WORK - HISTORY - BIBLIOGRAPHY

"A General View of Welfare Work Among Negroes" in <u>A Bibliography of the Negro</u>. 1928. pp. 528-531.

SOCIALISM

"Conclusion: Toward a Socialist America" in <u>How Capitalism Underdeveloped Black America</u>. 1983. pp. 255-263.

SOCIALIST MOVEMENT

"Socialists, Communists, and Self-Determination" in <u>Reluctant Reformers</u>. 1975. pp. 217-259.

SOCIOLOGY

"Culture, Technology and Afro-American Sociology," Juanita Howard in <u>Contemporary Black Thought</u>. 1980. pp. 165-180.

SOCIOLOGY - BIBLIOGRAPHY

"Social Roles" in <u>Afro-American Folk Culture</u>. 1978. See index, p. 793.

"Sociology" in <u>Afro-American Reference</u>. 1985. pp. 85-87.

"Sociology" in <u>A Comprehensive Bibliography</u>. 1976. pp. 90-111.

SOCIOLOGY - MEN

"Support Systems and Coping Patterns," Leland K. Hall in <u>Black Men</u>. 1981. pp. 159-167.

SOIL - HAITI - BIBLIOGRAPHY

"Soils and Soil Surveys" in <u>The Complete Haitiana</u>. 1982. V. 1, pp. 169-174.

SOMALI REPUBLIC - MUSIC - BIBLIOGRAPHY

"Somali Republic" in <u>Bibliography of Black Music</u>. 1983. V. 3, p. 105.

SOMERSET CASE - BIBLIOGRAPHY

"Noted Law Suits Relating to the Status of Slaves" in A Bibliography of
the Negro. 1928. p. 346.

SONG WRITERS - BIOGRAPHY - INDEX

"Musicians: Composers, Song Writers" in In Black and White. 1980. See
index, V. 2, pp. 1181-1183.

SONGHAY - HISTORY

"The Songhay Empire" in The African Background Outlined. 1976. pp. 62-
73.

SORORITIES - DIRECTORY

"Sororities" in Black Resource Guide. 1986. pp. 88-89.

SOUL - BIBLIOGRAPHY

"Soul" in Afro-American Folk Culture. 1978. See index, p. 797.

SOUL MUSIC

"Soul" in Black Music. 1979. pp. 161-182.

SOUTH - BLACK/JEWISH RELATIONS - BIBLIOGRAPHY

"Black-Jewish Relationships in the South" in Black-Jewish Relations.
1984. p. 17.

"Southern Jews and Blacks" in Black-Jewish Relations. 1984. pp. 94-95.

SOUTH - HISTORY

"The Americanization of the Slave and the Africanization of the South"
in The Slave Community. 1979. pp. 49-104.

"The Emergence of the Cotton Kingdom" in From Slavery to Freedom. 1980.
pp. 120-123.

"Self-Interest and Southern Populism" in Reluctant Reformers. 1975. pp.
51-83.

SOUTH - HISTORY - BIBLIOGRAPHY

"Shadow of the Plantation: Blacks in the Rural South" in Blacks in
America; Bibliographical Essays. 1971. pp. 226-228.

SOUTH - SLAVERY - BIBLIOGRAPHY

"Ante-Bellum South" in Slavery: A Worldwide Bibliography. 1985. pp. 93-
106.

"Antebellum Upper South" in Slavery: A Worldwide Bibliography. 1985. pp.
106-109.

"Colonial South" in Slavery: A Worldwide Bibliography. 1985. pp. 89-93.

"Slavery in the Lower South" in Black Slavery in the Americas. 1982. pp. 866-1030.

SOUTH AMERICA

"Blacks in the Western Hemisphere: South America" in The Negro Almanac. 1983. pp. 1467-1469.

SOUTH AMERICA - BIBLIOGRAPHY

"Guianas - General" in The Complete Caribbeana. 1977. See index, V. 4, pp. 2169-2170.

"Present Conditions of the Negro in South America" in A Bibliography of the Negro. 1928. pp. 643-645.

"South America" in Race and Ethnic Relations. 1980. pp. 206-243.

SOUTH AMERICA - MUSIC - BIBLIOGRAPHY

"The Southern Americas" in Bibliography of Black Music. 1981. V. 3, pp. 164-193.

SOUTH AMERICA - MUSICAL INSTRUMENTS - BIBLIOGRAPHY

"South American Instruments" in Bibliography of Black Music. 1984. V. 4, pp. 9-11.

SOUTH AMERICA - RELIGION - BIBLIOGRAPHY

"Religious Development of the Negro in Central and South America" in Howard University Bibliography of African and Afro-American Religious Studies. 1977. pp. 252-268.

SOUTH AMERICA - SLAVERY

"Health Conditions in the Slave Trade of Colonial New Granada," David L. Chandler in Slavery and Race Relations in Latin America. 1974. pp. 51-88.

"Latin America's Bondmen" in From Slavery to Freedom. 1980. pp. 65-80.

SOUTH AMERICA - SLAVERY - BIBLIOGRAPHY

"Bibliographical Notes: Latin America's Bondmen" in From Slavery to Freedom. 1980. pp. 516-517.

"Nature and Extent of Slavery in South America," in A Bibliography of the Negro. 1928. pp. 275-278.

"Slavery in Central and South America" in Black Slavery in the Americas. 1982. pp. 539-606.

"Slavery in the United States and Latin America: Comparative Analyses" in Blacks in America; Bibliographical Essays. 1971. pp. 64-66.

"Slavery in the West Indies and South America" in Howard University

Bibliography of African and Afro-American Religious Studies. 1977.
    pp. 117-118.

SOUTH AMERICA - SLAVERY - LEGAL ASPECTS

"The Implementation of Slave Legislation in Eighteenth Century New
    Granada," Norman A. Meiklehohn in Slavery and Race Relations in
    Latin America. 1974. pp. 176-203.

SOUTH CAROLINA - EDUCATION - BIBLIOGRAPHY

"South Carolina" in The Education of Poor and Minority Children. 1981.
    pp. 393-398.

SOUTH CAROLINA - GENEALOGY - BIBLIOGRAPHY

"South Carolina" in Black Genesis. 1978. pp. 96-104.

SOUTH CAROLINA - HISTORY - BIBLIOGRAPHY

"Blacks in Southern Reconstruction: South Carolina and Mississippi" in
    Blacks in America; Bibliographical Essays. 1971. pp. 125-127.

SOUTH CAROLINA - LIBRARIANS

"Black Librarians in South Carolina," Lillie S. Walker in The Black
    Librarian in the Southeast. 1976. pp. 87-103.

SOUTH CAROLINA - SLAVERY

"Colonial Slavery: The Carolinas and Georgia" in From Slavery to
    Freedom. 1980. pp. 58-60.

SOUTH CAROLINA - SLAVERY - BIBLIOGRAPHY

"South Carolina" in Black Slavery in the Americas. 1982. pp. 950-977.

SOUTH DAKOTA - EDUCATION - BIBLIOGRAPHY

"South Dakota" in The Education of Poor and Minority Children. 1981. p.
    398.

SOUTHERLAND, ELLEASE

"Ellease Southerland," Mary Hughes Brookhart in Afro-American Fiction
    Writers After 1955. 1984. pp. 239-244.

SOUTHERN CHRISTIAN LEADERSHIP CONFERENCE

"The Southern Christian Leadership Conference" in The Negro Almanac.
    1983. pp. 251-253.

SOUTHERN CHRISTIAN LEADERSHIP CONFERENCE - BIBLIOGRAPHY

"Southern Christian Leadership Conference and Martin Luther King, Jr."
    in Howard University Bibliography of African and Afro-American
    Religious Studies. 1977. pp. 330-339.

SPAIN - EDUCATION - BIBLIOGRAPHY

"Spain" in The Education of Poor and Minority Children. 1981. p. 1289.

SPAIN - SLAVE TRADE - BIBLIOGRAPHY

"Atlantic-Spanish" in Slavery: A Worldwide Bibliography. 1985. pp. 359-
364.

SPAIN - SLAVERY - BIBLIOGRAPHY

"Iberia" in Slavery: A Worldwide Bibliography. 1985. pp. 315-319.

SPANISH AMERICA - SLAVERY - BIBLIOGRAPHY

"Spanish Mainland" in Slavery: A Worldwide Bibliography. 1985. pp. 121-
142.

SPANISH AMERICAN WAR - BIOGRAPHY - INDEX

"Military Service: Spanish-American War" in In Black and White. 1980.
See index, V. 2, p. 1177.

SPANISH LANGUAGE - CREOLE - BIBLIOGRAPHY

"Paraguay: Spanish-Guanari Bilingualism" in A Bibliography of Pidgin and
Creole Languages. 1975. pp. 61-62.

SPEAKERS - DIRECTORIES

"Partial Listing of Professional Speakers and Lecturers" in The Complete
Annotated Resource Guide to Black America Art. 1978. pp. 250-260.

SPEECHES - BIBLIOGRAPHY

"Speeches and Rhetoric" in Afro-American Reference. 1985. pp. 119-120.

SPELLMAN, A. B.

"A. B. Spellman," Carmen Subryan in Afro-American Poets Since 1955.
1985. pp. 311-315.

SPELLS, MAGIC - BIBLIOGRAPHY

"Charms" in Afro-American Folk Culture. 1978. See index, p. 761.

SPELMAN COLLEGE - BIBLIOGRAPHY

"Spelman College" in The Progress of Afro-American Women. 1980. pp.
274-275.

SPENCER, ANNE - BIBLIOGRAPHY

"Spencer, Anne" in The Harlem Renaissance. 1982. pp. 134-135.

SPIES - BIOGRAPHY - INDEX

"Espionage Agents" in In Black and White. 1980. See index, V. 2, p. 1145.

SPINGARN MEDALISTS

"Spingarn Medalists" in The Negro Almanac. 1983. pp. 1526-1528.

SPIRITUALS - BIBLIOGRAPHY

"Spirituals and Earlier Folk Music" in Bibliography of Black Music. 1981. V. 2, pp. 34-64.

"Spirituals and Gospel Music" in Jazz Bibliography. 1981. pp. 84-89.

SPIRITUALS - COLLECTIONS

"Selected Collections of Negro Spirituals" in Choral Music by Afro-American Composers. 1981. pp. 107-130.

SPORTS

"The Black American in Sports," Edwin B. Henderson in The Black American Reference Book. 1976. pp. 927-963.

"The Black American's Prowess on the Playing Field," Mohan Lal Sharma in The Negro Impact on Western Civilization. 1970. pp. 159-172.

"Black Firsts: Sports" in Before the Mayflower. 1982. pp. 625-629.

"Sports" in The Ebony Handbook. 1974. pp. 463-476.

SPORTS - BIBLIOGRAPHY

Black Athletes in the U.S. 1981. 265 p.

"Blacks in Sports" in Blacks in America; Bibliographical Essays. 1971. pp. 297-300.

"Sports" in Afro-American Folk Culture. 1978. See index, p. 798.

"Sports and Athletes" in Afro-American Reference. 1985. pp. 193-195.

"Sports, Physical Education and Recreation" in The Progress of Afro-American Women. 1980. pp. 329-336.

SPORTS - BRAZIL - BIBLIOGRAPHY

"Football-Soccer" in Afro-Braziliana. 1978. pp.   133-134.

SPORTS CAR RACERS - WOMEN - BIBLIOGRAPHY

"Sports Car Racers" in The Progress of Afro-American Women. 1980. p. 130.

STATISTICS

"The Black Family" (Tables) in The Negro Almanac. 1983. pp. 493-524.

"The Black Population in the United States," Kark E. Taeuber and Alma F. Taeuber in The Black American Reference Book. 1976. pp. 159-206.

Facts About Blacks. 1985.

"Growth and Distribution of the Black Population" in The Negro Almanac. 1983. pp. 445-474.

"Statistical Data" in Black Resource Guide. 1986. pp. 211-240.

"Vital Statistics" in The Ebony Handbook. 1976. pp. 77-85.

STATISTICS - BIBLIOGRAPHY

"Statistics, Demography and Migration" in Afro-American Reference. 1985. pp. 87-92.

STEWART, MARIA

"Three Women in the Black Church: An Introduction" in Black Women and Religion. 1980. pp. xv-xxiv.

STICK FIGHTING - BIBLIOGRAPHY

"Stick Fighting" in Afro-American Folk Culture. 1978. See index, p. 799.

STILL, WILLIAM GRANT - BIBLIOGRAPHY

"Still, William Grant" in Black Music in America. 1981. pp. 503-508.

STUDENT NONVIOLENT COORDINATING COMMITTEE

"The Student Non-Violent Coordinating Committee" in The Negro Almanac. 1983. p. 259.

STUDENTS

"Black Students in White Universities Revisited," Elois Scott in Contemporary Black Thought. 1980. pp. 273-294.

"An Endangered Species: Black Students at White Universities," Richard David Ralston in Black Scholars on Higher Education. 1974. pp. 221-239.

"Higher Education and Its Role in the Psychological Genocide of the Black American Student," Roosevelt Johnson in Black Scholars on Higher Education. 1974. pp. 16-19.

"Resocialization of the Black Student Within a New Permissive Education System," Gerald Eugene Thomas in Black Scholars on Higher Education. 1974. pp. 45-63.

"Serving Black Students: For What," Nathan Wright, Jr. in Black Scholars on Higher Education. 1974. pp. 35-44.

STUDENTS - BIBLIOGRAPHY

"Black and Jewish Students' Opinions" in <u>Black-Jewish Relations</u>. 1984.
    pp. 77-80.

"Student Movements" in <u>The Education of Poor and Minority Students</u>.
    1981. pp. 726-728.

SUDAN - MUSIC - BIBLIOGRAPHY

"Sudan" in <u>Bibliography of Black Music</u>. 1981. V. 3, pp. 106-107.

SUICIDE

"A Demographic Analysis of Suicide," Robert Davis in <u>Black Men</u>. 1981.
    pp. 179-195.

SUMMER, DONNA - BIBLIOGRAPHY

"Summer, Donna" in <u>Black Music in America</u>. 1981. pp. 508-510.

SUPERNATURAL - BIBLIOGRAPHY

"Supernatural Beliefs and Practices" in <u>Afro-American Folk Culture</u>.
    1978. See index, pp. 799-800.

SUPREME COURT - BIBLIOGRAPHY

"Blacks and the Supreme Court" in <u>The Study and Analysis of Black
    Politics</u>. 1973. pp. 122-130.

SURGEONS - BIOGRAPHY - INDEX

"Physicians, Surgeons" in <u>In Black and White</u>. 1980. See index, V. 2, pp.
    1218-1220.

SURINAME

"Blacks in the Western Hemisphere: Suriname" in <u>The Negro Almanac</u>. 1983.
    p. 1482.

"Cuba, Puerto Rico, Suriname" in <u>Sex and Race</u>. 1942. V. 2, pp. 80-90.

SURINAME - BIBLIOGRAPHY

"Dutch Antilles (incl. Suriname)" in <u>Race and Ethnic Relations</u>. 1980.
    pp. 187-190.

"Suriname" in <u>The Complete Caribbeana</u>. V. 4, pp. 2184-2187.

SURINAME - EDUCATION - BIBLIOGRAPHY

"Suriname" in <u>The Education of Poor and Minority Children</u>. 1981. pp.
    1291-1292.

SWAN ISLANDS

"Swan Islands" in <u>The Negro Almanac</u>. 1983. p. 1487.

SWEDEN - EDUCATION - BIBLIOGRAPHY

"Sweden" in The Education of Poor and Minority Children. 1981. pp.
    1292-1295.

SYMBOLISM, AFRICAN - MUSIC

"Symbolism in Musical Instruments" in The Roots of Black Music. 1982.
    pp. 96-100.

TANZANIA - MUSIC - BIBLIOGRAPHY

"Tanzania" in Bibliography of Black Music. 1981. V. 3, pp. 108-109.

TATUM, ART - BIBLIOGRAPHY

"Tatum, Art" in Black Music in America. 1981. pp. 510-515.

TEACHER EDUCATION - BIBLIOGRAPHY

"Teachers and Teacher Training Work for Negroes" in A Bibliography of
    the Negro. 1928. pp. 428-429.

TEACHERS - BIBLIOGRAPHY

"Teachers" in The Education of Poor and Minority Children. 1981. pp.
    659-680.

TELEPHONE WORKERS - BIBLIOGRAPHY

"Telephone Service and Repair" in The Progress of Afro-American Women.
    1980. p. 130.

TELEVISION

"Television" in The Negro Almanac. 1983. pp. 1229-1234.

"Television's Impact on Black Children's Language: An Exploration,"
    Molefi Kete Asante in Contemporary Black Thought, 1980. pp. 181-
    194.

TELEVISION - BIBLIOGRAPHY

"Broadcasting" in Black Media in America. 1984. pp. 62-66 and 99-123.

"Radio and Television" in The Progress of Afro-American Women. 1980. pp.
    193-194.

"Television" in Afro-American Reference. 1985. pp. 157-160.

"Television" in Black Media in America. 1984. pp. 253-303.

TELEVISION - MUSIC - INDEX

"Television Index" in Blues Who's Who. 1979. pp. 621-627.

TELEVISION, CABLE - BIBLIOGRAPHY

"Cable Television" in Black Media in America. 1984. pp. 118-123.

TENNESSEE - EDUCATION - BIBLIOGRAPHY

"Tennessee" in The Education of Poor and Minority Children. 1981. pp. 398-402.

TENNESSEE - EDUCATION, HIGHER - BIBLIOGRAPHY

"Higher Education by State: Tennessee" in The Education of Poor and Minority Children. 1981. pp. 912-914.

TENNESSEE - GENEALOGY - BIBLIOGRAPHY

"Tennessee" in Black Genesis. 1978. pp. 144-149.

TENNESSEE - HISTORY - BIBLIOGRAPHY

"Blacks in Southern Reconstruction: Virginia, Tennessee, and North Carolina" in Blacks in America; Bibliographical Essays. 1971. pp. 127-128.

TENNESSEE - LIBRARIANS

"Library Service to Blacks and Black Librarians in Tennessee," Earline H. Hudson in The Black Librarian in the Southeast. 1980. pp. 104-122.

TENNESSEE - SLAVERY - BIBLIOGRAPHY

"Tennessee" in Black Slavery in the Americas. 1982. pp. 977-985.

TENNIS - BIBLIOGRAPHY

"Tennis" in Black Athletes. 1981. pp. 223-229.

TERRELL, TAMMI - BIBLIOGRAPHY

"Terrell, Tammi" in Black Music in America. 1981. p. 515.

TERRY, LUCY

"Three Women in the Black Church: An Introduction" in Black Women and Religion. 1980. pp. xv-xxiV.

TEXAS - EDUCATION - BIBLIOGRAPHY

"Texas" in The Education of Poor and Minority Children. 1981. pp. 402-409.

TEXAS - EDUCATION, HIGHER - BIBLIOGRAPHY

"Higher Education by State: Texas" in The Education of Poor and Minority Children. 1981. pp. 914-915.

TEXAS - GENEALOGY - BIBLIOGRAPHY

"Texas" in Black Genesis. 1978. pp. 253-256.

TEXAS - SLAVERY - BIBLIOGRAPHY

"Texas" in Black Slavery in the Americas. 1982. pp. 985-998.

"Texas" in Slavery: A Worldwide Bibliography. 1985. pp. 112-113.

THEATRE

"Black Influences in the American Theater: Part I," Langston Hughes in
The Black American Reference Book. 1976. pp. 684-704.

"Black Influences in the American Theatre: Part II, 1960 and After,"
Helen Armstead Johnson in The Black American Reference Book. 1976.
pp. 705-740.

"Black Theatre: A Forum" in Afro-American Writers After 1955:
Dramatists and Prose Writers. 1985. pp. 311-318.

"Community and Commentators: Black Theatre and Its Critics," Rhett S.
Jones in Afro-American Writers After 1955: Dramatists and Prose
Writers. 1985. pp. 301-310.

"A Look at the Contemporary Black Theatre Movement," A. Peter Bailey in
Afro-American Writers After 1955: Dramatists and Prose Writers.
1985. pp. 319-322.

"A Slender Thread of Hope: The Kennedy Center Black Theatre Project,"
Winona L. Fletcher in Afro-American Writers After 1955: Dramatists
and Prose Writers. 1985. pp. 323-327.

THEATRE - BIBLIOGRAPHY

"Blacks and the American Theater" in Blacks in America; Bibliographical
Essays. 1971. pp. 273-284.

"Discussions About the Negro on the Stage" in A Bibliography of the
Negro. 1928. pp. 445-446.

"General Bibliography" in More Black American Playwrights. 1978. pp.
213-306.

"Supplementary Reading List" in Afro-American Writers After 1955:   -
Dramatists and Prose Writers. 1985. pp.355-356.

"Theatre and Film Industry" in The Progress of Afro-American Women.
1980. pp. 345-347.

"Theater Arts" in Afro-American Reference. 1985. pp. 121-129.

THEATRE - DIRECTORY

"Black Theaters and Theatre Organizations in America, 1961-1982: A
Research List," Andrezej Ceynowa in Afro-American Writers After
1955: Dramatists and Prose Writers. 1985. pp. 329-353.

THEATRE - HISTORY AND CRITICSM - BIBLIOGRAPHY

"Literary History and Criticism: Theatre and Film" in A Comprehensive
    Bibliography. 1976. pp. 215-218.

THEATRE - MUSIC - INDEX

"Theater Index" in Blues Who's Who. 1979. pp. 629-633.

THEATRE, MUSICAL - BIBLIOGRAPHY

"Musical Theatre" in Bibliography of Black Music. 1981. V. 2, pp. 72-79.

"Negro Musical Comedies" in A Bibliography of the Negro. 1928. pp. 446-
    447.

THELWELL, MICHAEL

"Michael Thelwell," Daryl Cumber Dance in 50 Caribbean Writers. 1986.
    pp. 457-461.

THOMAS, JOYCE CAROL

"Joyce Carol Thomas," Charles Toombs in Afro-American Fiction Writers
    After 1955. 1984. pp. 245-250.

THOMAS, LORENZO

"Lorenzo Thomas," Tom Dent in Afro-American Poets Since 1955. 1985. pp.
    315-326.

THURMAN, WALLACE - BIBLIOGRAPHY

"Thurman, Wallace" in The Harlem Renaissance. 1982. pp. 135-138.

TIME - BIBLIOGRAPHY

"Time, Conceptions Of" in Afro-American Folk Culture. 1978. See index,
    p. 803.

TOASTS - BIBLIOGRAPHY

"Toasts" in Afro-American Folk Culture. 1978. See index, p. 803.

TOBAGO - BIBLIOGRAPHY

"Tobago" in The Complete Caribbeana. V. 4, p. 2187.

TOGO - MUSIC - BIBLIOGRAPHY

"Togo" in Bibliography of Black Music. 1981. V. 3, p. 110.

TOLSON, MELVIN - BIBLIOGRAPHY

"Black Poetry - Melvin B. Tolson" in Blacks in America; Bibliographical
    Essays. 1971. pp. 248-249.

TOOMER, JEAN - BIBLIOGRAPHY

"Fiction of the Renaissance: Jean Toomer and Claude McKay" in <u>Blacks in America; Bibliographical Essays</u>. 1971. pp. 251-253.

"Toomer, Jean" in <u>The Harlem Renaissance</u>. 1982. pp. 138-158.

TORTOLA - BIBLIOGRAPHY

"Tortola" in <u>The Complete Caribbeana</u>. 1977. See index, V. 4, pp. 2188-2190.

TOURE, ASKIA MUHAMMAD

"Askia Muhammad Toure (Rolland Snellings), Joanne V. Gaffin" in <u>Afro-American Poets Since 1955</u>. 1985. pp. 327-333.

TOURISM - CARIBBEAN - BIBLIOGRAPHY

"The Tourist Industry" in <u>The Complete Caribbeana</u>. V. 3, pp. 1645-1654.

TOURISM - HAITI - BIBLIOGRAPHY

"The Tourist Industry" in <u>The Complete Haitiana</u>. 1982. V. 2, pp. 1425-1430.

TOYS - BIBLIOGRAPHY

"Toys" in <u>Afro-American Folk Culture</u>. 1978. See index, p. 803.

TRADE - CARIBBEAN - BIBLIOGRAPHY

"External Trade and Internal Marketing" in <u>The Complete Caribbeana</u>. V. 3, pp. 1561-1593.

TRADE - HAITI - BIBLIOGRAPHY

"External Trade and Internal Marketing" in <u>The Complete Haitiana</u>. 1982. V. 2, pp. 1355-1386.

TRADERS

"Coastal Traders" in <u>Black Men of the Sea</u>. 1978. pp. 68-81.

TRADERS, AFRICAN

"African Fishermen and Traders" in <u>Black Men of the Sea.</u> 1978. pp. 7-15.

TRANSPORTATION WORKERS - BIBLIOGRAPHY

"Transportation" in <u>The Progress of Afro-American Women</u>. 1980. pp. 130-131.

TRAVEL - BRAZIL - BIBLIOGRAPHY

"Travellers' Accounts" in <u>Afro-Braziliana</u>. 1978. pp. 17-20.

TRAVEL - CARIBBEAN - BIBLIOGRAPHY

"Travel and Description" in The Complete Caribbeana. 1977. V. 1, pp.
    83-132.

TRAVEL - HAITI - BIBLIOGRAPHY

"Travel and Description" in The Complete Haitiana. 1982. V. 1, pp. 75-
    93.

TREATMENT OF SLAVES

"Plantation Stereotypes and Institutional Roles" in The Slave Community.
    1979. pp. 223-248.

TRINIDAD AND TOBAGO

"Blacks in the Western Hemisphere: Trinidad and Tobago" in The Negro
    Almanac. 1983. pp. 1479-1480.

TRINIDAD AND TOBAGO - BIBLIOGRAPHY

"Trinidad-Tobago" in Race and Ethnic Relations. 1980. pp. 180-182.

TRINIDAD AND TOBAGO - MUSIC - BIBLIOGRAPHY

"Trinidad-Tobago" in Bibliography of Black Music. 1981. V. 3, pp. 158-
    161.

TROMBONISTS - BIOGRAPHY - INDEX

"Musicians: Instrumental: Trombone" in In Black and White. 1980. See
    index, V. 2, p. 1190.

TROUPE, QUINCY THOMAS

"Quincy Thomas Troupe," Horace Coleman in Afro-American Poets Since
    1955. 1985. pp. 334-338.

TRUMAN, HARRY S. - BIBLIOGRAPHY

"The Truman Administration" in Blacks in America; Bibliographical
    Essays. 1971. pp. 304-305.

TRUMPET PLAYERS - BIOGRAPHY - INDEX

"Musicians: Instrumental: Trumpet" in In Black and White. 1980. See
    index, V. 2, p. 1190.

TUBA PLAYERS - BIOGRAPHY - INDEX

"Musicians: Instrumental: Tuba" in In Black and White. 1980. See index,
    V. 2, p. 1190.

TUNISIA - MUSIC - BIBLIOGRAPHY

"Tunisia" in Bibliography of Black Music. 1981. V. 3, p. 111.

TURKS AND CAICOS ISLANDS

"Blacks in the Western Hemisphere: Turks (Grand Turk, Salt Cay) and
    Caicos (South Caicos, North Caicos) Islands" in The Negro Almanac.
    1983. p. 1484.

TURKS AND CAICOS ISLANDS - BIBLIOGRAPHY

"Turks and Caicos Islands" in The Complete Caribbeana. 1977. See index,
    V. 4, p. 2191.

TURNER, IKE AND TINA

"Turner, Ike and Tina" in Black Music in America. 1981. pp. 515-520.

TUSKEGEE INSTITUTE - MUSIC EDUCATION - BIBLIOGRAPHY

"Tuskegee Institute" in Bibliography of Black Music. 1984. V. 4, p.
    105.

TUSKEGEE WOMAN'S CLUB - BIBLIOGRAPHY

"Tuskegee Woman's Club" in The Progress of Afro-American Women. 1980.
    pp. 275-276.

TYMPANY PLAYERS - BIOGRAPHY - INDEX

"Musicians: Instrumental: Tympany" in In Black and White. 1980. See
    index, V. 2, p. 1190.

UBANGI-SHARI - MUSIC - BIBLIOGRAPHY

"Ubangi-Shari" in Bibliography of Black Music. 1981. v. 3, pp. 112-113.

UGANDA - MUSIC - BIBLIOGRAPHY

"Uganda" in Bibliography of Black Music. 1981. V. 3, pp. 114-116.

UGGAMS, LESLIE - BIBLIOGRAPHY

"Uggams, Leslie" in Black Music in America. 1981. pp. 520-523.

UNDERGROUND RAILROAD - BIBLIOGRAPHY

"Fugitive Slaves and the Underground Railroad" in A Bibliography of the
    Negro. 1928. pp. 336-339.

"Migratory Patterns" in Black Genesis. 1978. pp. 34-36.

"The Underground Railroad" in Blacks in America; Bibliographical Essays.
    1971. pp. 94-96.

UNEMPLOYMENT

"The Black Family: Death and Illness Caused by Unemployment" in The
    Negro Almanac. 1983. pp. 488-490.

"Employment, Unemployment and the Labor Force" in The Negro Almanac.
    1983. pp. 581-644.

UNITARIAN UNIVERSALIST ASSOCIATION - CIVIL RIGHTS MOVEMENT -
BIBLIOGRAPHY

"The Church, Synagogue and Integration: Unitarian Universalist
    Association" in Howard University Bibliography of African and
    Afro-American Religious Studies. 1977. p. 323.

UNITARIAN UNIVERSALIST CHURCH - SLAVERY - BIBLIOGRAPHY

"Slavery, Negroes and the Church: Unitarian Universalist Association" in
    Howard University Bibliography of African and Afro-American
    Religion. 1977. pp. 145-146.

UNITED CHURCH OF CHRIST - CIVIL RIGHTS MOVEMENT - BIBLIOGRAPHY

"The Church, Synagogue and Integration: Congregational (United Church of
    Christ)" in Howard University Bibliography of African and Afro-
    American Religious Studies. 1977. pp. 315-316.

UNITED CHURCH OF CHRIST - RACE RELATIONS - BIBLIOGRAPHY

"Congregational (United Church of Christ)" in Howard University
    Bibliography of African and Afro-American Religious Studies. 1977.
    pp. 271-272.

UNITED FUND ORGANIZATIONS - DIRECTORY

"United Fund Organizations" in Black Resource Guide. 1986. pp. 207-210.

UNITED METHODIST CHURCH - RACE RELATIONS - BIBLIOGRAPHY

"Methodist Episcopal (United Methodist)" in Howard University
    Bibliography of African and Afro-American Religious Studies. 1977.
    pp. 274-280.

UNITED NATIONS - AFRO-AMERICAN SOCIAL CONDITIONS

"The United Nations and Human Welfare" in From Slavery to Freedom. 1980.
    pp. 444-449.

UNITED NATIONS - BIBLIOGRAPHY

"United Nations and Agencies" in Howard University Bibliography of
    African and Afro-American Religious Studies. 1977. p. 297.

UNIVERSITY OF CALIFORNIA, BERKELEY

"Helping Minority Students to Excel in University-level Mathematics and
    Science Courses: The Professional Development Program at the
    University of California, Berkeley," Katharyn Culler in The State
    of Black America, 1985. pp. 225-231.

UPPER VOLTA - MUSIC - BIBLIOGRAPHY

"Upper Volta" in <u>Bibliography of Black Music</u>. 1981. V. 3, p. 117.

URBAN CULTURE - BIBLIOGRAPHY

"City Life" in <u>Afro-American Folk Culture</u>. 1978. See index, p. 763.

URBAN DEVELOPMENT - CARIBBEAN - BIBLIOGRAPHY

"Rural and Urban Development" in <u>The Complete Caribbeana</u>. 1977. V. 2, pp. 1169-1183.

URBAN ECONOMICS - BIBLIOGRAPHY

"Black Movement to and within Urban Areas" in <u>The Economics of Minorities</u>. 1976. pp. 59-66.

URBAN HISTORY

"Urban Problems" in <u>From Slavery to Freedom</u>. 1980. pp. 308-313.

URBAN HISTORY - BIBLIOGRAPHY

"The Development of the Ghetto" in <u>Blacks in America; Bibliographical Essays</u>. 1971. pp. 188-192.

"The Negro in the City" in <u>A Bibliography of the Negro</u>. 1928. pp. 486-488.

URBAN STUDIES - BIBLIOGRAPHY

"Blacks and Urban Politics" in <u>The Study and Analysis of Black Politics</u>. 1973. pp. 114-119.

"Housing and Urban Conditions" in <u>Afro-American Reference</u>. 1985. pp. 71-73.

URBAN STUDIES - HAITI - BIBLIOGRAPHY

"Urban Studies" in <u>The Complete Haitiana</u>. 1982. V. 2, pp. 875-895.

URBANIZATION - BIBLIOGRAPHY

"Black Migration, Urbanization, and Ecology" in <u>Black Demography in the United States</u>. 1983. pp. 235-298.

URUGUAY

"Uruguay, Argentina, Paraguay, Chile" in <u>Sex and Race</u>. 1942. V. 2, pp. 57-65.

URUGUAY - BIBLIOGRAPHY

"Uruguay" in <u>Race and Ethnic Relations</u>. 1980. pp. 220-221.

URUGUAY - EDUCATION - BIBLIOGRAPHY

"Uruguay" in <u>The Education of Poor and Minority Children</u>. 1981. p. 1311.

URUGUAY - SLAVERY - BIBLIOGRAPHY

"Uruguay" in Slavery A Worldwide Bibliography. 1985. pp. 141-142.

UTAH - EDUCATION - BIBLIOGRAPHY

"Utah" in The Education of Poor and Minority Children. 1981. p. 409.

UTAH - SLAVERY - BIBLIOGRAPHY

"Utah" in Black Slavery in the Americas. 1982. pp. 828-829.

VALUES - HAITI - BIBLIOGRAPHY

"Values and Norms" in The Complete Haitiana. 1982. V. 1, pp. 645-656.

VAN DYKE, HENRY

"Henry Van Dyke," Edward McGehee in Afro-American Fiction Writers After
    1955. 1984. pp. 250-255.

VAN JACKSON, WALLACE M.

"Wallace M. Van Jackson, Librarian, Black Man, Citizen," Lillie Daly
    Caster in The Black Librarian in the Southeast. 1980. pp. 259-274.

VAUGHAN, SARAH - BIBLIOGRAPHY

"Vaughan, Sarah" in Black Music in America. 1981. pp. 523-531.

VENEZUELA

"Elitist Attitudes Toward Race in Twentieth-Century Venezuela," Winthrop
    R. Wright in Slavery and Race Relations in Latin America. 1974. pp.
    325-347.

"Venezuela" in Sex and Race. 1942. V. 2, pp. 14-29.

VENEZUELA - BIBLIOGRAPHY

"Venezuela" in Race and Ethnic Relations. 1980. pp. 221-223.

VENEZUELA - EDUCATION - BIBLIOGRAPHY

"Venezuela" in The Education of Poor and Minority Children. 1981. pp.
    1311-1312.

VENEZUELA - MUSIC - BIBLIOGRAPHY

"Venezuela" in Bibliography of Black Music. 1982. V. 3, pp. 191-193.

VENEZUELA - SLAVERY - BIBLIOGRAPHY

"Venezuela" in Slavery: A Worldwide Bibliography. 1985. pp. 136-137.

VERMONT - GENEALOGY - BIBLIOGRAPHY

"Vermont" in Black Genesis. 1978. p. 194.

VERMONT - SLAVERY - BIBLIOGRAPHY

"Vermont" in Black Slavery in the Americas. 1982. pp. 802-803.

VETERANS' AFFAIRS - BIOGRAPHY - INDEX

"Military Service: Veterans' Affairs" in In Black and White. 1980. See
     index, V. 2, p. 1177.

VIBRAHARP PLAYERS - BIOGRAPHY - INDEX

"Musicians: Instrumental: Vibraphone, Vibraharpists: in In Black and
     White. 1980. See index, V. 2, p. 1190.

VIBRAPHONE PLAYERS - BIOGRAPHY - INDEX

"Musicians: Instrumental: Vibraphone, Vibraharp" in In Black and White.
     1980. See index, V. 2, p. 1190.

VIETNAM WAR - BIOGRAPHY - INDEX

"Military Service: Vietnam War" in In Black and White. 1980. See index,
     V. 2, p. 1177.

VIOLA PLAYERS - BIOGRAPHY - INDEX

"Musicians: Instrumental: Viola, Violin" in In Black and White. 1980.
     See index, V. 2, pp. 1190-1191.

VIOLENCE

"The Masculine Way of Violence" in Black Masculinity. 1982. pp. 55-71.

"The Meaning of Racist Violence in Late Capitalism" in How Capitalism
     Underdeveloped Black America. 1983. pp. 231-253.

VIOLINISTS - BIOGRAPHY - INDEX

"Musicians: Instrumental: Viola, Violin" in In Black and White. 1980.
     See index, V. 2, pp. 1190-1191.

VIRGIN ISLANDS

"Blacks in the Western Hemisphere: Virgin Islands" in The Negro Almanac.
     1983. pp. 1487-1488.

VIRGIN ISLANDS - BIBLIOGRAPHY

"Virgin Islands - General" in The Complete Caribbeana. See index, V. 4,
     p. 2192.

VIRGIN ISLANDS - MUSIC - BIBLIOGRAPHY

"Virgin Islands" in Bibliography of Black Music. 1981. V. 3, p. 162.

VIRGIN ISLANDS (BRITISH)

"Blacks in the Western Hemisphere: British Virgin Islands" in The Negro
    Almanac. 1983. p. 1483.

VIRGIN ISLANDS (BRITISH) - BIBLIOGRAPHY

"British Virgin Islands" in The Complete Caribbeana. 1977. See index, V.
    4, p. 2160.

VIRGIN ISLANDS (U.S.) - BIBLIOGRAPHY

"United States Virgin Islands" in The Complete Caribbeana. 1977. See
    index, V. 4, p. 2192.

VIRGINIA - EDUCATION - BIBLIOGRAPHY

"Virginia" in The Education of Poor and Minority Children. 1981. pp.
    410-416.

VIRGINIA - EDUCATION, HIGHER - BIBLIOGRAPHY

"Higher Education by State: Virginia" in The Education of Poor and
    Minority Children. 1981. pp. 915-917.

VIRGINIA - GENEALOGY - BIBLIOGRAPHY

"Virginia and West Virginia" in Black Genesis. 1978. pp. 105-116.

VIRGINIA - HISTORY - BIBLIOGRAPHY

"Blacks in Southern Reconstruction: Virginia, Tennessee, and North
    Carolina" in Blacks in America; Bibliographical Essays. 1971. pp.
    127-128.

VIRGINIA - SLAVERY

"Colonial Slavery: Virginia and Maryland" in From Slavery to Freedom.
    1980. pp. 54-57.

VIRGINIA - SLAVERY - BIBLIOGRAPHY

"Virginia" in Black Slavery in the Americas. 1982. pp. 998-1030.

VISUAL COMMUNICATIONS - BIBLIOGRAPHY

"Visual Communications" in 250 Years of Afro-American Art. 1981. p. 399.

VITAL STATISTICS - BIBLIOGRAPHY

"Black Population Growth, Composition, Spatial Distribution and Vital
    Rates" in Black Demography in the United States. 1983. pp. 299-345.

VOCAL MUSIC - AFRICA

"Vocal Music" in The Roots of Black Music. 1982. pp. 3-46.

VOCAL MUSIC - BIBLIOGRAPHY

"Voice" in Bibliography of Black Music. 1984. V. 3, pp. 12-13.

VOCALISTS - BIBLIOGRAPHY

"Selected Musicians and Singers" in Black Music in America. 1981. pp.
     1-558.

VOCALISTS - BIOGRAPHY - INDEX

"Musicans: Singers, Not Specified" in In Black and White. 1980. See
     index, V. 2, p. 1191.

VOCALISTS - DIRECTORIES

Directory of Blacks in the Performing Arts. 1978. 428 p.

VOCALISTS, BLUES - BIOGRAPHY - INDEX

"Musicians: Singers, Blues" in In Black and White. 1980. See index, V.
     2, p. 1193.

VOCALISTS, BLUES - DIRECTORY

Blues Who's Who. 1979. 775 p.

VOCALISTS, CLASSICAL

"Black Classical Musicians" in The Negro Almanac. 1983. pp. 1127-1147.

VOCALISTS, CONCERT - BIOGRAPHY - INDEX

"Musicians: Singers, Concert" in In Black and White. 1980. See index, V.
     2, pp. 1193-1194.

VOCALISTS, COUNTRY AND WESTERN - BIOGRAPHY - INDEX

"Musicians: Singers, Country, Western" in In Black and White. 1980. See
     index, V, 2, p. 1194.

VOCALISTS, FOLK - BIOGRAPHY - INDEX

"Musicians: Singers, Folk" in In Black and White. 1980. See index, V. 2,
     p. 1194.

VOCALISTS, GOSPEL - BIOGRAPHY - INDEX

"Musicians: Singers, Gospel" in In Black and White. 1980. See index, V.
     2, pp. 1194-1195.

VOCALISTS, JAZZ - BIOGRAPHY - INDEX

"Musicians: Singers, Jazz" in In Black and White. 1980. See index, V. 2,
     p. 1195.

VOCALISTS, OPERA - BIOGRAPHY - INDEX

"Musicians: Singers, Opera" in In Black and White. 1980. See index, V. 2, pp. 1195-1196.

VOCALISTS, ROCK - BIOGRAPHY - INDEX

"Musicians: Singers, Rock" in In Black and White. 1980. See index, V. 2, p. 1196.

VOODOO - BIBLIOGRAPHY

"Religion: Catholicism, Protestantism and Voodoo" in The Complete Haitiana. 1982. V. 1, pp. 669-721.

"Vodu" in Afro-American Folk Culture. 1978. See index, p. 804.

VOTER EDUCATION PROJECT

"Voter Education Project" in The Negro Almanac. 1983. p. 364.

VOTING

"The Black Vote - The Sleeping Giant," Dianne M. Pinderhughes in The State of Black America, 1984. pp. 69-93.

"The Black Voter and Elected Officeholders" in The Negro Almanac. 1983. pp. 353-444.

VOTING - BIBLIOGRAPHY

"Black Political Behavior" in The Study and Analysis of Black Politics. 1973. pp. 69-94.

"National Elections" in The Study and Analysis of Black Politics. 1973. pp. 39-43.

VOTING - LEGAL CASES

"Voting (Registration and Primaries)" in The Negro Almanac. 1983. pp. 316-317.

VOTING RIGHTS - BIBLIOGRAPHY

"Studies Relating to Negro Suffrage" in A Bibliography of the Negro. 1928. p. 624.

"Suffrage" in The Progress of Afro-American Women. 1980. pp. 337-344.

VOTING RIGHTS - HISTORY - BIBLIOGRAPHY

"Negro Suffrage" in A Bibliography of the Negro. 1928. pp 383-396.

VROMAN, MARY ELIZABETH

"Mary Elizabeth Vroman," Edith Blicksilver. Afro-American Fiction Writers After 1955. 1984. pp. 255-258.

WALCOTT, DEREK

"Derek Walcott," Edward Baugh in <u>50 Caribbean Writers</u>. 1986. pp. 462-473.

WALKER, ALICE

"Alice Walker," Barbara Christian in <u>Afro-American Fiction Writers After 1955</u>. 1984. pp. 258-270.

"Alice Walker" in <u>Interviews with Black Writers</u>. 1973. pp. 184-211.

WALKER, JOSEPH A.

"Joseph A. Walker," Grace Cooper in <u>Afro-American Writers After 1955: Dramatists and Prose Writers</u>. 1985. pp. 260-264.

WALLER, FATS - BIBLIOGRAPHY

"Waller, Fats" in <u>Black Music in America</u>. 1981. pp. 531-538.

WALROND, ERIC

"Eric Walrond," Enid E. Bogle in <u>50 Caribbean Writers</u>. 1986. pp. 474-482.

WALROND, ERIC - BIBLIOGRAPHY

"Walrond, Eric" in <u>The Harlem Renaissance</u>. 1982. pp. 158-160.

WAR OF 1812

"The War of 1812" in <u>From Slavery to Freedom</u>. 1980. pp. 117-120.

WAR OF 1812 - BIOGRAPHY - INDEX

"Military Service: War of 1812" in <u>In Black and White</u>. 1980. See index, V. 2, pp. 1177.

WARD, DOUGLAS TURNER

"Douglas Turner Ward," Stephen M. Vallillo in <u>Afro-American Writers After 1955: Dramatists and Prose Writers</u>. 1985. pp. 264-270.

WARD, DOUGLAS TURNER - BIBLIOGRAPHY

"Black Dramatists: Douglas Turner Ward" in <u>Blacks in America; Bibliographical Essays</u>. 1971. p. 284.

WARWICK, DIONNE - BIBLIOGRAPHY

"Warwick, Dionne" in <u>Black Music in America</u>. 1981. pp. 538-542.

WASHINGTON, BOOKER T. - BIBLIOGRAPHY

"Accommodation and Protest in Black Thought - Accommodation: Booker T. Washington" in <u>Blacks in America; Bibliographical Essays</u>. 1971. pp. 150-152.

"Booker T. Washington's Opinion of Jews" in <u>Black-Jewish Relations</u>.
    1984. pp. 18-89.

"The Era of Booker T. Washington" in <u>Black Rhetoric</u>. 1976. pp. 95-97.

WASHINGTON (STATE) - EDUCATION - BIBLIOGRAPHY

"Washington" in <u>The Education of Poor and Minority Children</u>. 1981. pp.
    416-418.

WASHINGTON (STATE) - EDUCATION, HIGHER - BIBLIOGRAPHY

"Higher Education by State: Washington" in <u>The Education of Poor and
    Minority Children</u>. 1981. p. 917.

WASHINGTON (STATE) - SLAVERY - BIBLIOGRAPHY

"Washington" in <u>Black Slavery in the Americas</u>. 1982. p. 829.

WATERS, ETHEL - BIBLIOGRAPHY

"Waters, Ethel" in <u>Black Music in America</u>. 1981. pp. 542-545.

WATTS, ANDRE - BIBLIOGRAPHY

"Watts, Andre" in <u>Black Music in America</u>. 1981. pp. 545-549.

WEATHER - CARIBBEAN - BIBLIOGRAPHY

"Weather and Oceonography" in <u>The Complete Caribbeana</u>. 1977. V. 3, pp.
    1841-1869.

WEATHER - HAITI - BIBLIOGRAPHY

"Weather and Oceanography" in <u>The Complete Haitiana</u>. 1982. V. 1, pp.
    113-117.

WEATHERLY, TOM

"Tom Weatherly," Evelyn Hoard Roberts in <u>Afro-American Poets Since 1955</u>.
    1985. pp. 338-342.

WEATHERS, FELICIA - BIBLIOGRAPHY

"Weathers, Felicia" in <u>Black Music in America</u>. 1981. pp. 549-551.

WEAVING - BIBLIOGRAPHY

"Weaving" in <u>250 Years of Afro-American Art</u>. 1981. pp. 399-400.

WEBB, CHICK - BIBLIOGRAPHY

"Webb, Chick" in <u>Black Music in America</u>. 1981. pp. 522-523.

WEBB, FRANK J.

"Frank J. Webb," Gregory Candela in <u>Afro-American Writers Before the</u>

Harlem Renaissance. 1986. pp. 242-245.

WELDERS - BIBLIOGRAPHY

"Welders" in The Progress of Afro-American Women. 1980. p. 131.

WELFARE

"Families Receiving Public Assistance" in The Negro Almanac. 1983. pp. 479-480.

WELFARE - BIBLIOGRAPHY

"Welfare" in The Study and Analysis of Black Politics. 1973. p. 120.

WESLEY, RICHARD

"Richard Wesley," Steven R. Carter in Afro-American Writers After 1955: Dramatists and Prose Writers. 1985. pp. 271-278.

WEST INDIANS IN THE UNITED STATES - BIBLIOGRAPHY

"United States of America" in The Complete Caribbeana. See index, V. 3, pp. 2191-2192.

WEST VIRGINIA - EDUCATION - BIBLIOGRAPHY

"West Virginia" in The Education of Poor and Minority Children. 1981. pp. 418-419.

WEST VIRGINIA - EDUCATION, HIGHER - BIBLIOGRAPHY

"Higher Education by State: West Virginia" in The Education of Poor and Minority Children. 1981. p. 917.

WEST VIRGINIA - GENEALOGY - BIBLIOGRAPHY

"Virginia and West Virginia" in Black Genesis. 1978. pp. 105-116.

WESTERN STATES - GENEALOGY - BIBLIOGRAPHY

"Western States" in Black Genesis. 1978. pp. 232-242.

WESTERN STATES - HISTORY

"Negro Pioneers in the Westward March" in From Slavery to Freedom. 1980. pp. 116-117.

WESTERN STATES - SLAVERY - BIBLIOGRAPHY

"Slavery in the West" in Black Slavery in the Americas. 1982. pp. 816-829.

WHALERS

"Whalers" in Black Men of the Sea. 1978. pp. 82-90.

WHEATLEY, PHILLIS

"Phyllis Wheatley," Kenny J. Williams in <u>Afro-American Writers Before the Harlem Renaissance</u>. 1986. pp. 245-259.

WHEATLEY, PHILLIS - BIBLIOGRAPHY

<u>Phillis Wheatley; a Bio-Bibliography</u>. Boston: G.K. Hall, 1981. 166 p.

WHITE, EDGAR B.

"Edgar B. White," Steven R. Carter in <u>Afro-American Writers After 1955: Dramatists and Prose Writers</u>. 1985. pp. 278-283.

WHITE, WALTER - BIBLIOGRAPHY

"White, Walter" in <u>The Harlem Renaissance</u>. 1982. pp. 160-162.

WHITE AMERICANS - BLACK ANCESTRY

"Noted White Americans of Negro Ancestry" in <u>Sex and Race</u>. 1942. V. 2, pp. 249-259.

WHITE FLIGHT - BIBLIOGRAPHY

"White Flight" in <u>The Education of Poor and Minority Children</u>. 1981. pp. 1002-1004.

WHITES AS SLAVES

"The Americanization of the Slave and the Africanization of the South" in <u>The Slave Community</u>. 1979. pp. 49-104.

WHITFIELD, JAMES MONROE

"James Monroe Whitfield," Doris Lucas Laryea in <u>Afro-American Writers Before the Harlem Renaissance</u>. 1986. pp. 260-263.

WHITMAN, ALBERY ALLSON

"Albery Allson Whitman," Blyden Jackson in <u>Afro-American Writers Before the Harlem Renaissance</u>. 1986. pp. 263-267.

WIDEMAN, JOHN EDGAR

"John Edgar Wideman," Wilfred D. Samuels in <u>Afro-American Fiction Writers After 1955</u>. 1984. pp. 271-278.

"John Wideman" in <u>Interviews with Black Writers</u>. 1973. pp. 212-223.

WILLIAMS, DENIS

"Denis Williams," Victor J. Ramraj in <u>50 Caribbean Writers</u>. 1986. pp. 483-492.

WILLIAMS, FRANCIS

"Francis Williams," Arthur Drayton in 50 Caribbean Writers. 1986. pp. 493-497.

WILLIAMS, JOHN A.

"John A. Williams," James L. de Jongh. Afro-American Fiction Writers After 1955. 1984. pp. 279-288.

"John Williams" in Interviews with Black Writers. 1973. pp. 224-243.

WILLIAMS, JOHN A. - BIBLIOGRAPHY

"After Protest: Black Writers in the 1950s and 1960s - John A. Williams" in Blacks in America; Bibliographical Essays. 1971. pp. 262-263.

WILLIAMS, SAMM-ART

"Samm-Art Williams," Trudier Harris in Afro-American Writers After 1955: Dramatists and Prose Writers. 1985. pp. 283-290.

WILLIAMS, SHERLEY ANN

"Sherley Ann Williams," Lillie P. Howard in Afro-American Poets Since 1955. 1985. pp. 343-350.

WILSON, HARRIET E.

"Harriet E. Adams Wilson," Henry Louis Gates in Afro-American Writers Before the Harlem Renaissance. 1986. pp. 268-271.

WINDWARD ISLANDS

"Blacks in the Western Hemisphere: Windward Islands (Dominica, Grenada, Saint Lucia, Saint Vincent)" in The Negro Almanac. 1983. pp. 1484-1485.

WINDWARD ISLANDS - BIBLIOGRAPHY

"Windward Islands" in The Complete Caribbeana. 1977. See index, V. 4, p. 2193.

WINDWARD ISLANDS - MUSIC - BIBLIOGRAPHY

"Windward Islands" in Bibliography of Black Music. 1981. V. 3, p. 163.

WISCONSIN - EDUCATION - BIBLIOGRAPHY

"Wisconsin" in The Education of Poor and Minority Children. 1981. pp. 419-422.

WISCONSIN - EDUCATION, HIGHER - BIBLIOGRAPHY

"Higher Education by State: Wisconsin" in The Education of Poor and Minority Children. 1981. pp. 917-918.

WISCONSIN - GENEALOGY - BIBLIOGRAPHY

"Wisconsin" in <u>Black Genesis</u>. 1978. pp. 229-231.

WISCONSIN - SLAVERY - BIBLIOGRAPHY

"Wisconsin" in <u>Black Slavery in the Americas</u>. 1982. p. 816.

WITCHCRAFT - BIBLIOGRAPHY

"Witchcraft and Magic" in <u>Afro-American Folk Culture</u>. 1978. See index,
    p. 805.

WOMEN

"The Black Woman" in <u>The Negro Almanac</u>. 1983. pp. 1309-1332.

"The Black Woman," Ernestein Walker in <u>The Black American Reference
    Book</u>. 1976. pp. 341-377.

<u>Contributions of Black Women to America</u>. 1982. 2 V.

"Groundings With My Sisters: Patriarchy and the Exploitation of Black
    Women" in <u>How Capitalism Underdeveloped Black America</u>. 1983. pp.
    69-103.

"Sex and Racism" in <u>Long Memory</u>. 1978. pp. 114-141.

WOMEN - AUDIO-VISUAL MATERIALS - BIBLIOGRAPHY

"Bibliographies" in <u>The Progress of Afro-American Women</u>. 1980. pp. 29-
    31.

WOMEN - BIBLIOGRAPHY

"The Black Woman" in <u>The Education of Poor and Minority Children</u>. 1981.
    pp. 175-193.

"General Works" in <u>The Progress of Afro-American Women</u>. 1980. pp. 163-
    167.

"Men and Women" in <u>Afro-American Reference</u>. 1985. pp. 175-181.

"The Status, Progress, and Problems of Negro Women" in <u>A Bibliography of
    the Negro</u>. 1928. pp. 505-507.

WOMEN - BIOGRAPHICAL NOVELS - BIBLIOGRAPHY

"Biographies-Fiction" in <u>The Progress of Afro-American Women</u>. 1980. p.
    32.

WOMEN - BIOGRAPHY - BIBLIOGRAPHY

"Autobiographies and Biographies" in <u>Black Women and Religion: A
    Bibliography</u>. 1980. pp. 113-120.

"Biographies and Autobiographies" in <u>The Progress of Afro-American
    Women</u>. 1980. pp. 3-51.

WOMEN - BIOGRAPHY, COLLECTED - BIBLIOGRAPHY

"Collected Biography" in The Progress of Afro-American Women. 1980. pp.
     52-54.

WOMEN - DISCOGRPHY

"Recordings" in Black Women and Religion: A Bibliography. 1980. pp.
     103-104.

WOMEN - DRAMA - BIBLIOGRAPHY

"Literature: Drama" in Black Women and Religion: A Bibliography. 1980.
     pp. 56-59.

WOMEN - EDUCATION - BIBLIOGRAPHY

"Education" in The Progress of Afro-American Women. 1980. pp. 58-75.

WOMEN - EMPLOYMENT - BIBLIOGRAPHY

"Employment" in The Progress of Afro-American Women. 1980. pp. 58-75.

"Occupations of Negro Women" in A Bibliography of the Negro. 1928. pp.
     504-505.

WOMEN - FAMILY - BIBLIOGRAPHY

"Family Life" in The Progress of Afro-American Women. 1980. pp. 132-162.

WOMEN - FICTION - BIBLIOGRAPHY

"Literature: Fiction" in Black Women and Religion: A Bibliography.
     1980. pp. 49-56.

WOMEN - FILM - BIBLIOGRAPHY

"Motion Pictures and Film Strips" in The Progress of Afro-American
     Women. 1980. pp. 23-25.

"Theater and Film Industry" in The Progress of Afro-American Women.
     1980. pp. 345-347.

WOMEN - FIRST FACTS - BIBLIOGRAPHY

"Black Firsts: Women" in Before the Mayflower. 1982. pp. 636-638.

WOMEN - HISTORY

Beautiful Also Are the Souls of My Black Sisters. 1978. 353 p.

Black Women in Antiquity. 1984. 159 p.

We Are Your Sisters: Black Women in the 19th Century. 1984. 535 p.

WOMEN - HISTORY - BIBLIOGRAPHY

"History" in <u>The Progress of Afro-American Women</u>. 1980. pp. 183-190.

WOMEN - LEGISLATION - BIBLIOGRAPHY

"Legislation" in <u>The Progress of Afro-American Women</u>. 1980. p. 201.

WOMEN - LIBRARY COLLECTIONS - DIRECTORY

"Special Collections" in <u>The Progress of Afro-American Women</u>. 1980. p. 325.

WOMEN - LITERATURE - BIBLIOGRAPHY

"Literature" in <u>Black Women and Religion: A Bibliography</u>. 1980. pp. 49-72.

"Literature" in <u>The Progress of Afro-American Women</u>. 1980. pp. 206-212.

WOMEN - MEDIA - BIBLIOGRAPHY

"Radio and Television" in <u>The Progress of Afro-American Women</u>. 1980. pp. 193-194.

WOMEN - ORGANIZATIONS - BIBLIOGRAPHY

"Organizations and Institutions" in <u>The Progress of Afro-American Women</u>. 1980. pp. 239-279.

WOMEN - PERIODICALS - DIRECTORY

"Magazines" in <u>The Progress of Afro-American Women</u>. 1980. pp. 212-214.

WOMEN - POETRY - BIBLIOGRAPHY

"Literature: Poetry" in <u>Black Women and Religion: A Bibliography</u>. 1980. pp. 68-72.

WOMEN - PSYCHOLOGY - BIBLIOGRAPHY

"Psychology and Mental Health" in <u>The Progress of Afro-American Women</u>. 1980. pp. 292-303.

<u>The Psychology and Mental Health of Afro-American Women</u>. 1984. 102 p.

WOMEN - RELIGION - BIBLIOGRAPHY

<u>Black Women and Religion: A Bibliography</u>. 1980. 139 p.

"Religion" in <u>The Progress of Afro-American Women</u>. 1980. pp. 304-311.

WOMEN - SEX - BIBLIOGRAPHY

"Sex and Sexual Discrimination" in <u>The Progress of Afro-American Women</u>. 1980. pp. 314-321.

WOMEN - SLAVERY - BIBLIOGRAPHY

"Slave Women" in <u>Black Slavery in the Americas</u>. 1982. pp. 1219-1233.

WOMEN - VOTING RIGHTS - BIBLIOGRAPHY

"Suffrage" in <u>The Progress of Afro-American Women</u>. 1980. pp. 337-344.

WOMEN, WHITE - RELATIONSHIPS WITH BLACK MEN

"Black Men/White Women" in <u>Black Masculinity</u>. 1982. pp. 117-131.

WOMEN'S MOVEMENT - BIBLIOGRAPHY

"Women's Rights and Feminist Movement" in <u>The Progress of Afro-American Women</u>. 1980. pp. 348-356.

WOMEN'S MOVEMENT - HISTORY

"Woman Suffrage: Feminism and White Supremacy" in <u>Reluctant Reformers</u>. 1975. pp. 127-172.

WONDER, STEVIE - BIBLIOGRAPHY

"Wonder, Stevie" in <u>Black Music in America</u>. 1981. pp. 553-558.

WORK PRACTICES - BIBLIOGRAPHY

"Work Practices" in <u>Afro-American Folk Culture</u>. 1978. See index, p. 805.

WORK SONGS - BIBLIOGRAPHY

"Work Songs" in <u>Afro-American Folk Culture</u>. 1978. See index, p. 805.

WORLD WAR I - BIOGRAPHY - INDEX

"Military Service: World War I" in <u>In Black and White</u>. 1980. See index, V. 2, pp. 1177-1178.

WORLD WAR II

"Fighting for the Four Freedoms" in <u>From Slavery to Freedom</u>. 1980. pp. 422-449.

WORLD WAR II - BIBLIOGRAPHY

"World War II, 1941-1945" in <u>Black Rhetoric</u>. 1976. pp. 100-101.

WORLD WAR II - BIOGRAPHY - INDEX

"Military Service: World War II" in <u>In Black and White</u>. 1980. See index, V. 2, p. 1178.

WORLD WAR II - CIVILIAN SOCIAL CONDITIONS

"Arsenal of Democracy" in <u>From Slavery to Freedom</u>. 1980. pp. 422-428.

"The Home Fires" in <u>From Slavery to Freedom</u>. 1980. pp. 437-444.

WRIGHT, CHARLES

"Charles Wright" in <u>Interviews with Black Writers</u>. 1973. pp. 244-257.

WRIGHT, RICHARD - BIBLIOGRAPHY

"Black Social Fiction the Protest School - Richard Wright" in <u>Blacks in America; Bibliographical Essays</u>. 1971. pp. 254-255.

<u>Richard Wright; a Primary Bibliography</u>. 1982. 232 p.

WRITERS

"Black Writers, Scholars and Poets" in <u>The Negro Almanac</u>. 1983. pp. 965-1006.

<u>Interviews with Black Writers</u>. 1973. 274 p.

XYLOPHONE PLAYERS - BIOGRAPHY - INDEX

"Musicians: Instrumental: Xylophone" in <u>In Black and White</u>. 1980. See index, V. 2, p. 1191.

Y.M.C.A. - BIBLIOGRAPHY

"The Y.M.C.A. and Y.W.C.A. Among Negroes" in <u>A Bibliography of the Negro</u>. 1928. p. 413.

Y.W.C.A. - BIBLIOGRAPHY

"Young Women's Christian Association" in <u>The Progress of Afro-American Women</u>. 1980. pp. 276-279.

YOUNG, AL

"Al Young" in <u>Interviews With Black Writers</u>. 1973. pp. 258-269.

YOUTH

"To Be Young, Black and Male" in <u>Black Masculinity</u>. 1982. pp. 21-35.

"Young Black Americans," Christine Philpot Clark in <u>The Black American Reference Book</u>. 1976. pp. 378-409.

Author Index

Title Index

About the Compiler

ROSEMARY M. STEVENSON is Afro-American Bibliographer and Assistant Professor of Library Administration at the University of Illinois, Urbana-Champaign.